CU00674099

COVENANT & CONVERSATION:
A WEEKLY READING OF THE JEWISH BIBLE
EXODUS: THE BOOK OF REDEMPTION

Other works by the author

A Letter in the Scroll
Arguments for the Sake of Heaven
Celebrating Life
Ceremonia y Celebración
Ceremony and Celebration
Community of Faith
Crisis and Covenant
The Dignity of Difference
Faith in the Future
From Optimism to Hope
Future Tense
The Home We Build Together
The Jonathan Sacks Haggada
Judaism's Life-Changing Ideas
The Koren Sacks Siddur
The Koren Sacks Maḥzorim
Lessons in Leadership
Morals and Markets
Not in God's Name
One People?
The Persistence of Faith
The Politics of Hope
Radical Then, Radical Now
To Heal a Fractured World
Tradition in an Untraditional Age
Will We Have Jewish Grandchildren?

Rabbi Jonathan Sacks

COVENANT & CONVERSATION

A Weekly Reading of the Jewish Bible

EXODUS: THE BOOK OF REDEMPTION

Maggid Books & The Orthodox Union

Covenant & Conversation
Exodus: The Book of Redemption

First Edition, 2010
Seventh Printing, 2020

Maggid Books
An Imprint of Koren Publishers Jerusalem Ltd.

POB 8531, New Milford, CT 06776-8531, USA
& POB 4044, Jerusalem 9104001, Israel
www.korenpub.com

ISBN 978 159264 021 8, *hardcover*

Cover credit: *Moses Smashing the Tablets of the Law*, 1659 (oil
on canvas) by Rembrandt Harmensz. van Rijn (1606–69)
Gemaldegalerie, Berlin, Germany / The Bridgeman Art Library
Nationality / copyright status: Dutch / out of copyright

A CIP catalogue record for this title is
available from the British Library

Printed and bound in The United States

For Marc Weinberg
A courageous fighter and a natural leader

– J.S.

This publication was made possible with the kind support of the
Raphael and Linda Benaroya Foundation

לעילוי נשמת

בננו יקירנו מחמד לבנו
דוד ז״ל בן רפאל ולינדה (יפה) הי״ו
נלב״ע י״ג כסלו תשס״ח

מו״ר אבינו
יעקב בן רפאל וז׳ולי ז״ל
נלב״ע י״ז אב תשס״ה

מרת אמנו
רחל בת יום טוב ורוזה ז״ל
נלב״ע כ״ו אדר תשס״ז

In loving memory of

Our beloved Son
David ben Raphael and Linda

Our beloved Father
Yaakov ben Raphael and Julie

Our beloved Mother
Rachel bat Yom Tov and Rosa

This publication was made possible with the kind support of the
Frederick and Arlene Horowitz

In loving memory of my father

Paul Sumner Horowitz, *z"l*

*May this book inspire us and our future generations
to continue telling the story of the Exodus*

Frederick and Arlene Horowitz

Contents

Exodus: The Birth of a Nation

T he book of Exodus is the West's meta-narrative of hope. It tells an astonishing story of how a group of slaves were liberated from the mightiest empire of the ancient world. Theologically, its message is even more revolutionary: the supreme power intervenes in history in defence of the powerless. Never before and never since has the message of monotheism been more world-transforming, and the exodus narrative has inspired many of those who, in later times, fought oppression in the name of freedom and began the long journey across the wilderness in search of the promised land.

In the seventeenth century it inspired the English Puritans and parliamentarians in their battle against an overbearing king. It was engraved on the hearts of the Pilgrim Fathers as they set sail across the Atlantic in search of a new world. Thomas Jefferson and Benjamin Franklin used it as their image when, in 1776, they drew their designs for the Great Seal of the United States. When African-Americans sang of freedom, they said, "Go down Moses, way down in Egypt land, tell old Pharaoh, Let my people go."

On 3 April 1968, Martin Luther King delivered a sermon in a church in Memphis, Tennessee. At the end of his address, he referred to the last day of Moses' life, when the man who had led his people to freedom was taken by God to the top of a mountain from which he could see in the distance the land he was not destined to enter. That, said King, was how he felt that night. "I just want to do God's will. And He's allowed me to go up to the mountain. And I've looked over. And I've seen the promised land. I may not get there with you. But I want you to know tonight that we, as a people, will get to the promised land." That night was the last of his life. The next day he was assassinated. Forty years later, for the first time in history, an African-American was elected president of the United States.

No story has been more influential in shaping the inner landscape of liberty, teaching successive generations that oppression is not inevitable, that it is not woven into the fabric of history. There can be another place, another kind of society, a different way of living. What happened once can happen again for those who have faith in the God who had faith in humankind. The God of freedom calls on us to be free.

Nietzsche, the great atheist, put it best. He called Judaism "the slave revolt in morals."[1] He understood that it was the faith of the powerless. Nietzsche believed in the opposite: "the will to power." Knowing as we do what happened in the century after Nietzsche's death – the bloodiest century since humans first walked the earth – we are entitled to conclude that Nietzsche was wrong, as wrong as it is possible to be. Power destroys the powerless and powerful alike, oppressing the one while corrupting the other. If we are to build a society with a human face, we must always choose the way of Exodus, with its message of hope and human dignity.

From Family to Nation

As we move from Genesis to Exodus, the entire biblical landscape changes, and the Jewish project takes on substance and form. For the

---

1. Nietzsche made this point in *Beyond Good and Evil* (1886), part 5, para. 195. He developed the argument further in *On the Genealogy of Morals* (1887), *Twilight of the Idols* and *The Anti-Christ* (1888).

first time, politics enters the narrative, centre-stage. God intervenes in history in a series of miracles and wonders that have no precedent and no real sequels.[2] For the first time we encounter law in all its nuances – Torah, *mitzva*, *hok* and *mishpat* – as the substance of the divine will. And for the first time we encounter a transformative leader, Moses, who emerges from the shadows of a strange, improbable childhood to become, despite his many hesitations, the man who was to leave his mark on the Jewish people from that day to this.

The reason for all these changes is the appearance, early in the first chapter of Exodus, of one word we have not heard before in connection with the covenantal family: the word *Am*, "people" (1:9). Not accidentally, it is an outsider who uses it first, Pharaoh, ruler of Egypt, for it is he who first realises the change that has come about. What had been, at the end of Genesis, a family, has become a nation, just as God had said it would in his first words to Abraham: "I will make you a great nation" (Genesis 12:2). With that, the very terms of Israel's existence are transformed.

Genesis was about individuals and their relationships: husbands and wives, parents and children, brothers and their sibling rivalries. One of its recurring themes was the difficulty the matriarchs – Sarah, Rebecca and Rachel – had in conceiving children. Despite the grandiose promises to the patriarchs – that they would have as many children as the stars of the sky, the sand of the seashore and the dust of the earth – having even a single child turned out to be difficult, even miraculous. Yet as we turn the page and begin the new book, all of that vanishes, and a family of seventy members becomes a nation with six hundred thousand adult males. The Israelites, we are told in a cascade of verbs, "were fruitful, and increased abundantly, and multiplied, and waxed exceeding mighty; and the land was filled with them" (Exodus 1:7). Even the attempt by Pharaoh to limit childbirth by subjecting the Israelites to hard labour,

---

2. There are miracles recorded in later books: the Jordan divides for Joshua and the Israelites (Joshua 3), there are miraculous victories at Jericho and Gibeon (Joshua 6, 10), and the prophets Elijah and Elisha have miraculous powers. But the tendency throughout the biblical books is a progressive move from the supernatural to the natural.

failed completely: "The more they afflicted them, the more they multiplied and grew" (Exodus 1:12).

Exodus is about *the birth of a nation*, described variously as an *am* (people), *goy* (nation), *kahal* (congregation), and *edah* (community). No sooner do we see this than we understand what the Jewish project was intended from the very outset to be. It is about politics, society, and the principles on which a people can come together to form associations. It is about justice, freedom and the rule of law. It is about the sanctity of life and human dignity. Ultimately it is about the use and misuse of power. Exodus places frankly before us the risks inherent in power. It can be used to oppress, enslave and, *in extremis*, to kill. That is what Pharaoh proposes at the beginning of Exodus.

It is important to understand precisely what is being argued in these opening pages. Pharaoh is not portrayed as the embodiment of evil. He is not a Haman. His people are not the Amalekites. Later in the Torah, Moses will command his people not to hold lingering resentment against their former oppressors: "Do not abhor an Egyptian, for you were strangers in his land" (Deuteronomy 23:7). Pharaoh is driven by political motives, not hate: "The Israelites have become much too numerous for us. Come, let us deal wisely with them or they will become even more numerous and, if war breaks out, will join our enemies, fight against us and leave the country" (Exodus 1:10).

The Exodus narrative is not a simple story of good versus evil. It is a critique of the politics of power, empires, hierarchical societies and the division of populations into free human beings and slaves. Lord Acton summed it up in his famous dictum that "all power tends to corrupt and absolute power corrupts absolutely."[3] In its place, the Torah proposes a different kind of politics, based not on power but on covenant, the free agreement of a free people who accord absolute sovereignty to God alone. The idea could hardly be more radical, and it has shaped the history of the West. In an age when might triumphed over right, the Torah records one of the great turning points in the human story, when the Creator of heaven and earth intervened in defence of the powerless.

---

3. Lord Acton expressed this in a letter to Bishop Mandell Creighton in 1887.

An Exile Foreseen

Despite the radical differences between Genesis and Exodus, it is clear that the two form a single unit. Exodus is the enactment of what had already been foreshadowed in Genesis, especially in the haunting covenant scene in Genesis 15. Abraham, having been promised by God that "I will make you into a great nation," had still not had a single child. In exasperation, he says to God, "O Sovereign Lord, what can You give me since I remain childless?" God then repeats his promise. Abraham will have children, as many as the stars of the sky, and he will one day have a land. But something else will happen first:

> As the sun was setting, Abram fell into a deep sleep, and a thick and dreadful darkness came over him. Then the Lord said to him, "Know for certain that your descendants will be strangers in a country not their own, and they will be enslaved and mistreated for four hundred years. But I will punish the nation they serve as slaves, and afterwards they will come out with great possessions." (Genesis 15:12–14)

No sooner do we read the opening of Exodus than we know what is happening. This is Abraham's night vision come to pass – the "thick and dreadful darkness." There is nothing random or unscripted in the series of events that led to the exile and enslavement of Abraham's descendants. It is part of the script written by the divine hand, the people's initiation into nationhood and identity. They will become – they were predestined to be – the people born in, and forever after shaped by, the experience of homelessness and oppression.

Genesis 15 is only the most explicit foreshadowing of the events of the Torah's second book. But when we re-read Genesis in the light of Exodus, we catch traces of it everywhere, nowhere more clearly than in Genesis 12, at the very beginning of the Abraham story. Abraham, we recall, has been told by God to leave his land, birthplace and father's house and travel "to the land I will show you." No sooner does he arrive than he is forced by famine to leave and go to Egypt. There (Genesis

12:10–20) he encounters all that his descendants will eventually experience: the need to go to Egypt because of famine in the land of Canaan, the fear that the males will be killed (Abraham fears that they will kill him and take Sarah into the royal harem); the plagues that affect Pharaoh's household; an eventual expulsion at the order of Pharaoh; and Abraham's departure with "great wealth" as the Israelites would eventually do. The Midrash rightly sees Genesis 12 as a prime example of the idea that "everything written in connection with Abraham is written in connection with his children."[4]

In some sense, all the exiles of the patriarchs in Genesis – Abraham's and Isaac's to Gerar (Genesis 20, 26), as well as Jacob's to Laban (Genesis 28–31) – are precursors of the great exile with which Genesis ends and Exodus begins.[5] So we know this about the book of Exodus: that it is not mere history. It is not the story of a sequence of events that just happened. This is the working out of a divine drama, foreseen by God and foretold to Abraham centuries earlier.

Monotheism and the Universality of Justice

On the surface, the most gripping aspect of the narrative is the miracles it recounts: the ten plagues, the division of the Reed Sea, water from a rock, and food (manna) from heaven. But Maimonides rightly notes that the miracles are secondary.[6] What is primary in the book of Exodus is another aspect of monotheism altogether: the idea of a single God whose sovereignty extends everywhere.

In the ancient world, each nation had its gods, and they were territorially limited. They were gods of this place, not that. This is the essential meaning of Pharaoh's remark to Moses when he demands the Israelites' release in the name of God. Pharaoh replies: "Who is the Lord that I should obey him and let Israel go? I do not know the Lord and I

---

4. *Bereshit Raba* 60:6.
5. See David Daube, *The Exodus Pattern in the Bible* (Westport, Conn: Greenwood Press, 1979).
6. Rambam, *Mishneh Torah*, Yesodei HaTorah 8:1.

will not let Israel go" (Exodus 5:2). This does not mean that he did not know who the God of the Israelites was. It means that within Egypt, the gods of Egypt ruled.[7]

The book of Exodus is the first time we hear of a God not territorially bound, a God of anywhere and everywhere. The point of the plagues is precisely to show this. They are not (with the sole exception of the tenth plague) to punish the Egyptians or Pharaoh. They are to show that God – the one God – is everywhere: "that My name might be proclaimed in all the earth" (9:16).

This is the meaning of Moses' remark in Deuteronomy: "Has any god ever tried to take for himself one nation out of another nation?" (Deuteronomy 4:34). Each nation had its gods, but none except Israel worshipped the God of everywhere and everyone, and this is a political point, not just a theological one. It establishes the concept of justice as a universal ideal transcending the idea of national sovereignty. To put the point in the language of today: the exodus represents the first international intervention in the name of human rights.[8]

---

7. The Torah gives partial acknowledgement to this fact. As the Israelites are crossing the Reed Sea, they sing, "until Your people pass by, O Lord, until the people You bought/purchased/acquired pass by" (Exodus 15:16). Taking an object from one domain into another, from that of the seller to the purchaser, was a mode of acquisition in the ancient world. By crossing the sea, the Israelites moved from Egypt – Pharaoh's domain – into the desert (= no man's land). This is not to say that the Israelites did not belong to God before that. God staked a claim on the people at the outset when he told Moses to tell Pharaoh, "My child, my firstborn, Israel" (Exodus 4:22). The crossing of the sea was, however, a publicly recognisable transfer of ownership. On the relationship generally of biblical narrative to legal principles, see David Daube, *Studies in Biblical Law* (Cambridge University Press, 2008).

8. The first time this happened in secular politics was the United Nations intervention in Kosovo, 1999. The point is significant. The moral justification for international intervention is based on the Nuremburg Principles, established after the Holocaust by the United Nations. These included the rule that there are crimes against humanity, for the commission of which it is no excuse for the perpetrator to claim that he or she was "merely obeying orders." This principle – that one is morally bound to disobey an order that involves a crime against humanity – is itself part of the Exodus narrative. The two midwives, Shifrah and Puah, who disobey Pharaoh's order to kill every male Israelite child (1:15–21), represent the first recorded incident of

Moses, Man of Justice

The concept of justice leads us directly to the central human figure of the drama of Exodus, namely Moses. Moses represents a new form of leadership of a kind not found in Genesis. In Genesis the patriarchs are just that: fathers of children, heads of an extended family. With the exception of the war fought by Abraham in Genesis 14, they are not political figures. As soon as the Israelites become a people – 600,000 adult males, a significant force – they need a new kind of leader. That is what Moses was: a unique combination of prophet, liberator and lawgiver, the voice of God to his people, the voice of his people to God, and the representative of both in his long confrontation with Pharaoh.

We are told little of his early life, but every detail and nuance counts. We see him as a young man intervening three times in the cause of justice: first, defending an Israelite against an Egyptian, a second time defending an Israelite against a fellow Israelite, and on the third occasion defending Jethro's daughters against the local Midianite shepherds. With absolute economy, all the permutations are covered. Moses intervenes to protect people against attack, whether the victims or the perpetrators belong to his people or not. The story of the Exodus is about impartial justice, and Moses is a man of justice, prepared to act and take risks for its sake.

Three other details are fundamental. Moses, adopted by Pharaoh's daughter, is brought up in Pharaoh's household. This means, as Ibn Ezra notes,[9] that he has not experienced slavery or internalised its self-abasement. There is nothing hesitant about his manner. He has been brought up in the royal court. He is used to leadership. He is, as far as the Israelites are concerned, an outsider, and perhaps only an outsider can be an agent of change, the transformative leader they need.

Second, he spends most of his adult years far away, as a shepherd

---

civil disobedience. Note here, as elsewhere in the Torah, divine justice and human justice are seen as essentially the same. God has powers and knowledge no human has; but God and humanity are bound by the same moral laws.

9. Ibn Ezra (*Perush ha-Arukh*), commentary to Exodus 2:3.

in Midian. He knows the ways of the desert. He has had time to mature, to reflect, to compare the urban civilization of Pharaoh's court with the nomadic life of the Midianites. He has had his own wilderness years, and this too is part of his apprenticeship as the man who would eventually take the Israelites through their collective wilderness years.

Third is the strange detail of the encounter with God at the burning bush, when Moses says repeatedly that he is "not a man of words," he is "heavy of mouth and of tongue" (Exodus 4:10; 6:12). Whether or not this is to be construed literally, it signals to us that the words Moses speaks are not his own.[10] Just as Sarah, Rebecca and Rachel could not have children naturally, to signify that their children were in some sense the children of God, so Moses cannot naturally speak, to signal that his words are the words of God.

One other feature of Moses' early life should not be overlooked. Though he is the central figure in the drama of the exodus, there is a striking emphasis on the roles of six women, without whom there would not have been a Moses. There is Yocheved, Moses' mother, who had the courage to have a child at a time when all male Israelite children faced death. There is Miriam, Moses' sister, who followed his fate and ensured that he knew who his people were. There are Shifrah and Puah, the two midwives, who defy Pharaoh's decree of genocide. There is Zipporah, Moses' Midianite wife, who accompanies him on his mission and at one stage saves his life. And most remarkably, there is Pharaoh's daughter, who rescues Moses and adopts him, knowing that in doing so she is acting in contravention of her father's will.

These are six stories of outstanding moral courage and they are all about women, at least two of whom, Zipporah and Pharaoh's daughter, are not Israelites (the identity of the midwives is left uncertain, perhaps deliberately so). It is the women who recognise the sanctity of life and refuse to obey orders that desecrate life. It is the women who, fearing

---

10. Compare in this respect Isaiah's "I am a man of unclean lips" (Isaiah 6:5), Jeremiah's "I cannot speak for I am a child" (Jeremiah 1:6), and the passage in which God says to Ezekiel: "I will make your tongue stick to the roof of your mouth so that you will be silent and unable to rebuke ... But when I speak to you, I will open your mouth" (Ezekiel 3:26–27).

God, are fearless in the face of human evil. It is the women who have compassion – and justice without compassion is not justice. It is as if the Torah were telling us that Moses, the supreme embodiment of the passion for justice, is not enough. There must be, in Carol Gilligan's phrase, "a different voice,"[11] the voice of empathy, sympathy and attachment, the values that make us human, if we are to create a society in which justice has a human face.

People of the Covenant

At the heart of Exodus is a monumental event, the covenant at Sinai, to which the entire story of slavery and liberation has merely been a prologue. It is there, in the desert, at the foot of the mountain, that the central event of Judaism takes place. God pledges himself to a people and the people pledge themselves to God.

The idea of covenant was not new. It was a standard device in the politics of the ancient Near East. Essentially it was a non-aggression treaty between two powers, tribes, clans or city-states. Sometimes it was an agreement between a stronger power (suzerain) and a weaker one, whereby the weaker paid tribute to the stronger, in return for which the stronger undertook to protect the weaker.

We have met such covenants in Genesis. Abraham made one with Avimelech, king of Gerar (21:22–34). So, later, did Isaac (26:28–31). Jacob made a treaty with Laban (31:43–54). The Sinai covenant was quite different: unprecedented beforehand and unrivalled since. In it an entire nation committed itself to the sovereignty of God. The revelation that accompanied it was unique: the only time God appeared, not to a prophet, priest or king, but to an entire nation. In essence, it defined the Israelites as God's people. He alone was to be their king, lawgiver and protector. Israel would become a people unlike any other. In the words of Torah, it was to become "a kingdom of priests and a holy

---

11. Carol Gilligan, *In a Different Voice: Psychological Theory and Women's Development* (Cambridge, Mass.: Harvard University Press, 1982).

nation" – the simplest and most challenging mission statement of Jewish existence, then and now.

Three things made the Sinai covenant unique. First was that one of the parties was God Himself. In any other context this would sound absurd. The gods of the ancient world ruled by power, not by the agreement of the people. Second was that the entire nation – not just a king or an elite – were party to this decision. The text twice emphasises that the agreement to accept the covenant was made by "all the people" (Exodus 19:8; 24:3). The third is that the covenant itself was not confined, as were all others in the ancient world, to external relations. It was to govern the internal life of the people as well. It would become their moral and spiritual code, their constitution of liberty.

We have in the Sinai covenant nothing less than *the first-ever statement of a free society*. The first two points establish the principle that, in the words of the American Declaration of Independence, governments derive "their just powers from the consent of the governed," even when the Governor is creator of heaven and earth. God, in the rabbis' phrase, is not a tyrant. He does not impose His will by force. He does not enslave. On the contrary, He is the God who liberates slaves. He becomes Israel's sovereign only when they willingly declare, "All that God has said, we will do and heed" (24:7). *The free God seeks the free worship of free human beings.*

The third point tells us that a free society is a moral achievement. It is not a mere transaction of power. The "ten commandments" with their emphasis on the sanctity of life, the integrity of the family, respect for truth and for the property of others, summarize the essentials of a decent society in so short and simple a way as to be memorized by – engraved on the hearts of – an entire people. They remain the world's most famous moral code.

Covenant, as the late Daniel Elazar showed in a lifetime of scholarship,[12] is a unique form of politics, an alternative to two others that have prevailed elsewhere. There are *hierarchical* societies, divided into

---

12. Daniel J. Elazar (1934–1999), professor of political science at Bar Ilan University, was the major force in rediscovering Jewish political theory and showing how Covenant – the key political concept in the Hebrew Bible – held a key place in

rulers and ruled, with their kings, courts and bureaucratic elites. There are *organic* societies, based on custom, tradition and laws sanctified by time. Covenantal societies are different because of the value they place on consent, the responsibility they place on the citizenship as a whole, and their insistence on dignity, equality and justice. Covenantal societies are moral societies in which might is subservient to right.

This, then, is the culmination of what the Torah has been about all along. In creating human beings and endowing them with freedom, God had, as it were, taken a risk. He had made the one life form capable of defying Him and destroying the entire order of creation itself. The story so far has been of one disappointment after another. Adam and Eve sinned. Cain committed murder. By the time of the Flood, the earth was filled with violence. Even after the Flood, the builders of Babel were capable of monumental hubris. What then could God do to ensure that humanity would not destroy itself?

The Torah's answer is that God lowers His expectations. He makes a covenant with Noah, insisting on the sanctity of human life. He then chooses Abraham to be the forerunner of a new way of life, in a land far from the centres of power in the ancient world: Mesopotamia and Egypt. The patriarchs and matriarchs of Genesis rehearse the demands of difference. Can they live apart from their neighbours? Can they remain uncorrupted by the lax moral standards of their time? Can they stay faithful to God? Not least, can they live peaceably among themselves? Once these things have been established, by the end of Genesis, the time is right for them to become a nation – a nation that would never forget the debt it owed to God, or the bitterness of slavery. That is what the first half of the book of Exodus is about.

The concept of covenant was rediscovered in the West in the wake of the Reformation, where it played a major role in the "birth of the modern" and the emergence of free societies. In the sixteenth century it was influential in Switzerland, Holland and Scotland. In the seventeenth, it was central to the thought of the Puritans who brought about

the history of political ideas in the West, especially from the sixteenth century to the present. He wrote many books on the subject, culminating in the four-volume *Covenant Tradition in Politics*.

the English revolution, together with those who became the Pilgrim Fathers of America. It remains central to American political thought and discourse to this day.

Mutuality

The Sinai covenant was not the first made by God. He had already made one with Noah (Genesis 9), and another with Abraham and his descendants (Genesis 15, 17). There were subsequent covenant renewal ceremonies at the end of Moses' life, in the days of Joshua, during the reigns of Hezekiah and Josiah, and later, after the Babylonian exile, in the age of Ezra and Nehemiah. The covenant at Sinai was, however, the fulcrum on which all else turned. The Noahide and Abrahamic covenants were unilateral initiatives on the part of God. Noah and Abraham were not asked for their agreement. The subsequent ratification ceremonies were all at the initiative of human beings: prophets, kings and scribes. Only the Sinai covenant was fully mutual, a divine initiative that involved and depended on human consent.

It is specifically here, at Sinai, that we find the classic expression of an idea unique to Judaism: that the religious situation is a partnership, a reciprocal relationship, between God and humankind. This is, on the face of it, a paradoxical idea and one that was not fully developed in either of the two daughter religions of Judaism, namely Christianity and Islam. It sounds hubristic, almost blasphemous. In what conceivable way can God, the Creator of the universe, need the partnership of human beings? What is there that human beings can do that God Himself cannot do without human help?

The short answer is: live within the human heart.

Recall that in the ancient world there were many gods. They lived, fought and contended for supremacy. The heavens, to the pagan mind, were densely thronged with a pantheon of deities. In Abrahamic monotheism, with its belief in One God, God's only conversational partner is humanity itself. We are God's only Other. But to be truly other, humanity must be endowed with freedom, exactly as a parent must give a child the freedom to make his or her own choices, and if need be, mistakes, if the child is ever to reach maturity. It is this freedom, this *integrity of otherness*, that is at the heart of covenant. A covenant is a pledge between two or more partners, each of whom respects the freedom and integrity of the other, to be loyal to one another and to do together what neither can achieve alone.

The Israelites could not survive on their own. That is a point the Hebrew Bible makes time and again. Without God, they were no match for their neighbours. They were a small nation surrounded by great empires. But God cannot live within the human situation alone. Adam, Cain, the generation of the Flood and the builders of Babel all failed to be adequate human responses to the existence of God. That now became the mission of the Jewish people. In itself – its history, its fate, its laws, its way of life – it would continually testify to something greater than itself. It would be a signal of transcendence. That is what Isaiah meant when he said: "You are My witnesses – declares the Lord – that I am God" (Isaiah 43:12).

Exodus: Text and Subtext

This leads us to the great subtext of the Exodus narrative. On the surface, it is about how the Israelites were slaves and God brought them to freedom by a series of signs and wonders. The Israelites played no part in this process. They were pawns in the hands of Pharaoh on the one hand, God on the other. History is a script written by God, and it is for us to leave our destiny entirely in His hands. This is the plain sense of the text.

But there is a subtext which is nuanced differently. A careful examination reveals that Exodus contains a number of double narratives, whose significance becomes clear when we put them together. So, for example:

1. There are two battles, one immediately before, the other immediately after, the crossing of the Reed Sea, the first against Pharaoh and his chariots, the second against the Amalekites.
2. There are two sets of stone tablets recording the revelation at Mount Sinai, one before the episode of the Golden Calf (broken

by Moses on his descent from the mountain), the second after the people have been forgiven for the Calf.

3. There are two times that God is revealed in a cloud of glory, once at Mount Sinai (24:15–18), the other, at the end of Exodus, in the Tabernacle (40:34–35).

4. The Sinai covenant was declared twice, once by God (20:1–14), the second time by Moses, reading from "the book of the covenant" he had written to record God's words (24:1–11).

5. There are two accounts of the construction of the Tabernacle, one before (25–30), the other (35–40) after the Golden Calf.

If we examine each pair carefully we will see that they share a common feature. *In each case, the first is the work of God alone, while the second involves a human contribution.* The Israelites did not need to fight against the Egyptians but they did fight against the Amalekites. The first tablets were the work of God alone, but the second involved Moses as well. At Sinai the Israelites did not create the space within which God appeared; in the Tabernacle they did. At Sinai the Israelites heard the voice of God, but so intense was the experience that they said to Moses, "Speak to us yourself and we will listen. But do not have God speak to us or we will die" (Exodus 20:16). After the revelation, Moses wrote down God's words and read them to the people. The first account of the Tabernacle is about God's instructions; the second is about how the people carried out those instructions. In each case, the first of the paired episodes involves an act done by God alone; the second involved human participation.

So Exodus tells a double story. Yes, God delivered the people by a series of miracles. Yet if those miracles were to have a lasting effect on the people, they had to make their own contribution to the process of liberation. There is an eternal message here. A people can be granted freedom by an external cause, in this case divine intervention. But a people sustain freedom by their own efforts. *It is not what God does for us, but what we do for God, that changes us.*

That is the ultimate significance of the politics of covenant, born at Mount Sinai. More than any other type of politics, covenant makes demands of its citizens. A covenantal society is one in which everyone has responsibilities as well as rights; in which everyone is expected to study and understand the law as well as keep it; in which parents are duty bound to tell the story of freedom to their children; in which we are collectively as well as individually responsible for the common good. So while the surface narrative speaks of God's miraculous deliverance, the deeper thrust of the story is about the mutuality and reciprocity between God and human beings. We must earn our freedom if we are to keep it.

A Realistic Utopia

That surely is the enduring power of the book of Exodus. It is utopian in its aspirations. It envisages a society that will be the opposite of Egypt, in which justice prevails, human life is held sacred, and every individual has equal dignity as the image and covenant-partner of God. But it is a realistic utopia.

There is, in Exodus, no attempt to airbrush away the flaws and faults of human beings. The Israelites are portrayed as fickle and short-sighted. They complain. They readily give way to despair. In an age in which rulers wrote history in the form of triumphal inscriptions, the Israelites alone recorded their failures more vividly than their successes.

There is thus every indication in Exodus that freedom will involve a long journey. It is fair to say, thirty-three centuries later, that we have still not arrived at the destination. But freedom is not a blind journey, a road without a map. The destination is clearly signalled, though it lies beyond the horizon. It is the promised land, flowing with milk and honey, the land Moses spent his life leading his people towards but was not privileged himself to enter. One of the underlying themes of the book was best stated in a later age by Rabbi Tarfon: "It is not for you to complete the task but neither are you free to desist from it."[13] The path to freedom is travelled one step, one generation, one era at a time, never losing heart or forgetting our aim.

The key to Exodus politics, as it is to Judaism as a whole, is what elsewhere I have called "Utopia now."[14] That is the significance

13. Mishna, *Avot* 2:21.
14. Jonathan Sacks, *A Letter in the Scroll* (New York: Free Press, 2000), 136–141.

of Shabbat, whose presence looms large in the book. It was the first commandment the Israelites received in the wilderness. It holds a pivotal place in the ten commandments. It is repeated immediately before and after the episode of the Golden Calf. It is central to the politics of freedom.

On Shabbat we rehearse utopia, or what Judaism came later to call the messianic age. One day in seven, all hierarchies of power are suspended. There are no masters and slaves, employers and employees. Even domestic animals cannot be made to work. We are not allowed to exercise control over other forms of life, or even forces of nature. On Shabbat, within the covenantal society, all are equal and all are free. It is the supreme antithesis of Egypt. What a stroke of genius it was to introduce a foretaste of the future into the present, to remind us constantly of our ultimate destination and to be strengthened by it regularly on the way.

So Exodus ends as Genesis began, with the holy day on which God and His image, humankind, find rest at the still point of the turning world, in the midst of the otherwise restless strife of the human condition. The Israelites were called on to be among the nations what Shabbat is in the midst of time – a sign of what ought to be, in the midst of what actually is.

History has no more unlikely heroes than the Israelites of Moses' day. Capricious, fractious, wayward, hardly able to see tomorrow, let alone the unfolding drama of the centuries, they became, in Herman Melville's evocative phrase, the bearers of "the ark of the liberties of the world."[15] The Exodus story is the universal story of what happens when men and women are touched by the call of God, to relinquish their fetters and have the courage to begin travelling the long road to freedom.

---

15. Herman Melville, *White-Jacket* (Oxford University Press, 1967), 153.

Shemot
שמות

With *Shemot*, the defining drama of the Jewish people begins. In exile, in Egypt, they multiply, until they are no longer a family but a nation. Pharaoh, fearing that they pose a threat to Egypt, enslaves them and orders their male children killed. Moses, an Israelite child adopted by Pharaoh's daughter, is chosen by God to confront Pharaoh and lead the people to freedom. Reluctantly, Moses agrees, but his initial intervention only makes things worse, and on this tense note the *parasha* ends.

The four studies that follow focus on the nature of moral courage at a time of crisis. The first is about the midwives, Shifra and Puah, who disobey Pharaoh's decree. The second is about Pharaoh's daughter, who brings Moses up as her own child. The third is about Moses' hesitations in accepting the role of leader. Which of his doubts were legitimate and which not? The fourth offers a radical interpretation of why Moses was "afraid to look at God." On the surface, *Shemot* is about freedom, slavery and the fate of nations, but it is also about the power of individuals, driven by justice or compassion, to defy tyrants and change the course of history.

Civil Disobedience

The opening chapter of Exodus contains an episode that properly deserves a place of honour in the history of morality. Pharaoh has decided on a plan of slow genocide. He tells the midwives, Shifra and Puah, "When you help the Hebrew women in childbirth and observe them on the delivery stool, if it is a boy, kill him; but if it is a girl, let her live" (Exodus 1:16). We then read the following:

> The midwives feared God and did not do what the Egyptian king had commanded. They allowed the infant boys to live. The king of Egypt summoned the midwives and said to them, "Why did you do this? You let the boys live." The midwives replied, "The Hebrew women are not like the Egyptians. They know how to deliver. They can give birth even before a midwife gets to them." God was good to the midwives, and the people increased and became very numerous. Because the midwives feared God, He made them houses [of their own]. (1:17–21)

Who were Shifra and Puah? Midrashic tradition identifies them as Yocheved and Miriam. However, in describing them the Torah uses an ambiguous phrase, *hameyaldot ha'ivriyot*, which could mean either "the Hebrew midwives" or "the midwives to the Hebrews." If we follow the second interpretation, they may not have been Hebrews at all, but Egyptians. This is the view taken by Abrabanel and Samuel David Luzzatto. Luzzatto's reasoning is simple: Could Pharaoh realistically have expected Hebrew women to murder their own people's children?

The Torah's ambiguity on this point is deliberate. We do not know to which people Shifra and Puah belonged because their particular form of moral courage transcends nationality and race. In essence, they were being asked to commit a "crime against humanity," and they refused to do so. Theirs is a story that deserves to be set in its full historical perspective.

One of the landmarks of modern international law was the judgement against Nazi war criminals in the Nuremberg trials of 1946. This established that there are certain crimes in relation to which the claim that "I was obeying orders" is no defence. There are moral laws higher than those of the state. "Crimes against humanity" remain crimes, whatever the law of the land or the orders of a government.[1] There are instructions one is morally bound to disobey; times when civil disobedience is the necessary response. This principle, attributed to the American writer Henry David Thoreau in 1848, inspired many of those who fought for the abolition of slavery in the United States, as well as the late Martin Luther King in his struggle for black civil rights in the 1960s.[2] At stake in the principle of civil disobedience is a theory of the moral limits of the state.

Until modern times, rulers had absolute authority, tempered only by the concessions they had to make to other powerful groups. It was not until the seventeenth century that figures like John Locke began to develop theories of liberty, social contract and human rights. Most religious thought until then was dedicated to justifying existing structures of power. That was the function of myth, and later the concept of

---

1. The principle was set out in advance, in the London Charter of the International Military Tribunal (usually referred to as the Nuremberg Charter) on August 8, 1945.
2. On civil disobedience, see Henry David Thoreau, *Walden and Civil Disobedience* (New York: Signet Classics, 1980); Hugo Bedau, *Civil Disobedience: Theory and Practice,* (Indianapolis: Pegasus, 1969); Ronald Dworkin, *Taking Rights Seriously* (London: Duckworth, 1977), 206–222.

the "divine right of kings."[3] In such societies, the idea that there might be moral limits to power was unthinkable. To challenge the king was to defy reality itself.

Biblical monotheism was a revolution thousands of years ahead of its time. The exodus was more than the liberation of slaves. It was a redrawing of the moral landscape. If the image of God is to be found, not only in kings but in the human person as such, then all power that dehumanizes is ipso facto an abuse of power. Slavery, seen by almost all ancient thinkers as part of the natural order, is for the first time called into question. To be sure, the Torah permits it – it was not banned in Britain and America until the nineteenth century, and even then not without (in America) a civil war – but, by restricting it in many ways (Shabbat, release after seven years, and so on), it prepared the way for its eventual abolition.[4]

When God tells Moses to say to Pharaoh, "My son, My firstborn, Israel" (4:22), He is announcing to the most powerful ruler of the ancient world that these people may be your slaves but they are My children. The story of the exodus is as much political as theological. Theologically, the plagues showed that the Creator of nature is supreme over the forces of nature. Politically it declared that over every human power stands the sovereignty of God, defender and guarantor of the rights of humankind.

In such a worldview, the idea of civil disobedience is not unthinkable but self-evident. The very notion of authority is defined by the transcendence of right over might, morality over power. In one of the world-changing moments of history, social criticism was born in Israel simultaneously with institutionalization of power. No sooner were there kings in Israel, than there were prophets mandated by God to criticize them when they abused their power. As the Talmud puts it: "If there

3. A political and religious doctrine developed in the Middle Ages that asserted that a monarch is subject to no earthly authority, deriving his right to rule directly from the will of God. The king was thus not subject to the will of his people, the aristocracy, or any other estate of the realm, including the church. The doctrine implies that any attempt to depose the king or to restrict his powers runs contrary to the will of God and may constitute heresy.
4. See essay "Time and Social Transformation," p. 97, for an examination of why slavery was not banned totally by the Torah.

is a conflict between the words of the master and the words of the disciple, whose words should one obey?"[5] No human order overrides the commands of God.

How moving it is, therefore, that the first recorded instance of civil disobedience – predating Thoreau by more than three millennia – is the story of Shifra and Puah, two ordinary women defying Pharaoh in the name of simple humanity. All we know about them is that they "feared God and did not do what the Egyptian king had commanded." In those words, a precedent was set that eventually became the basis of the United Nations Declaration of Human Rights. Shifra and Puah, by refusing to obey an immoral order, redefined the moral imagination of the world.

A final note is in place. Though Greek literature does not know of the concept of civil disobedience, it does contain one famous case where an individual defies the king – Sophocles' Antigone, who buries her brother in defiance of King Creon's order that he stay unburied as a traitor. The contrast between Sophocles and the Bible is fascinating. *Antigone* is a tragedy: the eponymous heroine pays for her defiance with her life. The story of Shifra and Puah is not a tragedy. It ends with a curious phrase: God "made them houses."

What does this mean? The Italian commentator Samuel David Luzzatto offered an insightful interpretation. Sometimes women become midwives when they are unable to have children of their own. That, he suggests, was the case with Shifra and Puah. Because they saved children's lives, God rewarded them – measure for measure – with children of their own ("houses" = families). In Judaism the moral life is not inescapably tragic, because neither the universe nor fate is blind. "In reward for the righteous women of that generation, our ancestors were redeemed from Egypt." Shifra and Puah were two of those women, heroines of the spirit, giants in the story of humankind.

5.   *Kiddushin* 42b.

The Light at the Heart of Darkness

She is one of the most unexpected heroes of the Hebrew Bible. Without her, Moses might not have lived. The whole story of the exodus would have been different. Yet she was not an Israelite. She had nothing to gain, and everything to lose, by her courage. Yet she seems to have had no doubt, experienced no misgivings, made no hesitation. If it was Pharaoh who afflicted the children of Israel, it was another member of his own family who saved the decisive vestige of hope: Pharaoh's daughter.

Recall the context. Pharaoh had decreed death for every male Israelite child. Yocheved, Amram's wife, had a baby boy. For three months she was able to conceal his existence, but no longer. Fearing his certain death if she kept him, she set him afloat on the Nile in a basket, hoping against hope that someone might see him and take pity on him. This is what follows:

Pharaoh's daughter went to bathe in the Nile, while her maids walked along the Nile's edge. She saw the box in the reeds and sent her slave-girl to fetch it. Opening it, she saw the boy. The child began to cry, and she had pity on it. "This is one of the Hebrew boys," she said (2:6).

Note the sequence. First she sees that it is a child and has pity on it. A natural, human, compassionate reaction. Only then does it dawn on her who the child must be. Who else would abandon a child? She remembers her father's decree against the Hebrews. Instantly the situation has changed. To save the baby would mean disobeying the royal command. That would be serious enough for an ordinary Egyptian; doubly so for a member of the royal family.[1]

Nor is she alone when the event happens. Her maids are with her; her slave-girl is standing beside her. She must face the risk that one of them, in a fit of pique, or even mere gossip, will tell someone about it. Rumours flourish in royal courts. Yet she does not shift her ground. She does not tell one of her servants to take the baby and hide it with a family far away. She has the courage of her compassion. She does not flinch. Now something extraordinary happens:

> The [child's] sister said to Pharaoh's daughter, "Shall I go and call a Hebrew woman to nurse the child for you?" "Go," replied Pharaoh's daughter. The young girl went and got the child's own mother. "Take this child and nurse it," said Pharaoh's daughter. "I will pay you a fee." The woman took the child and nursed it. (2:7–9)

The simplicity with which this is narrated conceals the astonishing nature of this encounter. First, how does a child – not just a child, but a member of a persecuted people – have the audacity to address a princess? There is no elaborate preamble, no "Your royal highness" or any other formality of the kind we are familiar with elsewhere in biblical narrative. They seem to speak as equals.

Equally pointed are the words left unsaid. "You know and I know," Moses' sister implies, "who this child is; it is my baby brother." She proposes a plan brilliant in its simplicity. If the real mother is able to keep the child in her home to nurse him, we both minimise the danger. You will not have to explain to the court how this child has suddenly appeared.

---

1. "Seeing that she [Pharaoh's daughter] wanted to save Moses, they [her handmaids] said to her, 'Mistress, it is customary that when a king of flesh and blood issues a decree, even if the whole world does not fulfil it, at least his children and the members of his household fulfil it. Yet you transgress your father's decree!'" (*Sota* 12b).

We will be spared the risk of bringing him up: we can say the child is not a Hebrew, and that the mother is not the mother but only a nurse. Miriam's ingenuity is matched by Pharaoh's daughter's instant agreement. She knows; she understands; she gives her consent.

Then comes the final surprise:

> When the child matured, [his mother] brought him to Pharaoh's daughter. She adopted him as her own son, and named him Moses. "I bore him from the water," she said. (2:10)

Pharaoh's daughter did not simply have a moment's compassion. She has not forgotten the child. Nor has the passage of time diminished her sense of responsibility. Not only does she remain committed to his welfare; she adopts the riskiest of strategies. She will adopt him and bring him up as her own son.[2] This is courage of a high order.

Yet the single most surprising detail comes in the last sentence. In the Torah, it is parents who give a child its name, and in the case of a special individual, God himself. It is God who gives the name Isaac to the first Jewish child; God's angel who gives Jacob the name Israel; God who changes the names of Abram and Sarai to Abraham and Sarah. We have already encountered one adoptive name – Tzafenat Pa'neaḥ – the name by which Joseph was known in Egypt; yet Joseph remains Joseph. How surpassingly strange that the hero of the exodus, greatest of all the prophets, should bear not the name Amram and Yocheved have undoubtedly used thus far, but the one given to him by his adoptive mother, an Egyptian princess. A midrash draws our attention to the fact:

> This is the reward for those who do kindness. Although Moses had many names, the only one by which he is known in the whole Torah is the one given to him by the daughter of Pharaoh. Even the Holy One, blessed be He, did not call him by any other name.[3]

---

2. On the adoption of a foundling in the ancient world, see Nahum Sarna, *Exploring Exodus* (New York: Schocken, 1986), 31–32.
3. *Shemot Raba* 1:26.

Indeed Moshe – Meses – is an Egyptian name, meaning "child," as in Ramses (which means child of Ra; Ra was the greatest of the Egyptian gods).

Who then was Pharaoh's daughter? Nowhere is she explicitly named. However the First Book of Chronicles (4:18) mentions a daughter of Pharaoh, named Bitya, and it was she the sages identified as the woman who saved Moses. The name Bitya (sometimes rendered as Batya) means "the daughter of God." From this, the sages drew one of their most striking lessons: "The Holy One, blessed be He, said to her: 'Moses was not your son, yet you called him your son. You are not My daughter, but I shall call you My daughter.'"[4] They added that she was one of the few people (tradition enumerates nine) who were so righteous that they entered paradise in their lifetime.[5]

Instead of "Pharaoh's daughter" read "Hitler's daughter" or "Stalin's daughter" and we see what is at stake. Tyranny cannot destroy humanity. Moral courage can sometimes be found in the heart of darkness. That the Torah itself tells the story the way it does has enormous implications. It means that when it comes to people, we must never generalize, never stereotype. The Egyptians were not all evil: even from Pharaoh himself a heroine was born. Nothing could signal more powerfully that the Torah is not an ethnocentric text; that we must recognise virtue wherever we find it, even among our enemies; and that the basic core of human values – humanity, compassion, courage – is truly universal. Holiness may not be; goodness is.

Outside Yad Vashem, the Holocaust Memorial in Jerusalem, is an avenue dedicated to righteous gentiles. Pharaoh's daughter is a supreme symbol of what they did and what they were. I, for one, am profoundly moved by that encounter on the banks of the Nile between an Egyptian princess and a young Israelite child, Moses' sister Miriam. The contrast between them – in terms of age, culture, status and power – could not be greater. Yet their deep humanity bridges all the differences, all the distance. Two heroines. May they inspire us.

4. *Vayikra Raba* 1:3.
5. *Derekh Eretz Zuta* 1.

The Belief of a Leader

The *parasha* of *Shemot*, in a series of finely etched vignettes, paints a portrait of the life of Moses, culminating in the moment at which God appears to him in the bush that burns without being consumed. It is a key text of the Torah view of leadership, and every detail is significant. I want here to focus on just one verse in the long dialogue in which God summons Moses to undertake the mission of leading the Israelites to freedom – a challenge which Moses declines no less than four times. I am unworthy, he says. I am not a man of words. Send someone else. It is his second refusal which attracted special attention from the sages, and led them to formulate one of their most radical interpretations, and it is this refusal I want to examine. The Torah states:

> Moses replied: "But they will not believe me. They will not listen to me. They will say, 'God did not appear to you.'(Exodus 4:1)

The sages, ultra-sensitive to nuances in the text, noticed two important features of this response. The first is that God had already told Moses, "They will listen to you" (3:18). Moses' reply seems to contradict God's prior assurance. To be sure, the commentators offered various harmonising interpretations. Ibn Ezra suggests that God had told Moses that the elders would listen to him, whereas Moses expressed doubts about the mass of the people. Nahmanides says that Moses did not doubt that they would believe initially, but he thought that they would lose faith as soon as they saw that Pharaoh would not let them go. There are other explanations, but the fact remains that according to this verse, Moses was not satisfied by God's assurance. His own experience of the fickleness of the people (one of them, years earlier, had already said, "Who made you ruler and judge over us?"[1]) made him doubt that they would be easy to lead.

The second detail is that, whereas Moses' other refusals focused on his own sense of inadequacy, here he speaks not about himself but about the people. They will not believe him.

The rabbis put these two details together and connected them to an anomaly in the signs that God gave Moses to authenticate his mission. The first (the staff that turns into a snake) and third (the water that turned into blood) reappear later in the story; they are signs that Moses and Aaron perform not only for the Israelites but also for the Egyptians. The second, however, is never actually used at all. God tells Moses to put his hand in his cloak. When he takes it out he sees that it has become "leprous as snow" (4:6). What is the significance of this particular sign, in view of the fact that it is never used? The sages recalled that later, Miriam was punished with leprosy for speaking negatively about Moses (Numbers 12:10). In general they understood leprosy as a punishment for *lashon hara*, derogatory speech. Had Moses, perhaps, been guilty of the same sin? Was this sign actually a rebuke?

Having connected these three points, the sages arrived at the following comment:

> Resh Lakish said: "He who entertains a suspicion against the innocent will be bodily afflicted, as it is written, 'Moses replied: But they will not believe me.' However, it was known to the Holy One blessed be He, that Israel would believe. He said to Moses: 'They are believers, the children of believers, but you will ulti-

---

1. Exodus 2:14.

mately disbelieve.' They are believers, as it is written, 'and the people believed' (Exodus 4:31). The children of believers [as it is written], 'and he [Abraham] believed in the Lord' (Genesis 15:6). But you will ultimately disbelieve, as it is said, '[And the Lord said to Moses] Because you did not believe in Me' (Numbers 20:12). How do we know that he was afflicted? Because it is written, 'And the Lord said to him, Put your hand inside your cloak...' (Exodus 4:6)."[2]

This is an extraordinary passage. Moses, it now becomes clear, was entitled to have doubts about his own worthiness for the task. What he was not entitled to do was to have doubts about the people. In fact, his doubts were amply justified. The people were fractious. Moses calls them a "stiff-necked people." Time and again during the wilderness years they complained, sinned, and wanted to return to Egypt. Moses was not wrong in his estimate of their character. Yet God reprimanded him; indeed punished him, by making his hand leprous. A fundamental principle of Jewish leadership is intimated here for the first time: a leader does not need faith in himself, but he must have faith in the people he is to lead.

This is an exceptionally important idea. The political philosopher Michael Walzer has written insightfully about social criticism, in particular about two stances the critic may take vis-à-vis those he criticises. On the one hand there is the critic as outsider. At some stage, beginning in ancient Greece:

Detachment was added to defiance in the self-portrait of the hero. The impulse was Platonic; later on it was Stoic and Christian. Now the critical enterprise was said to require that one leave the city, imagined for the sake of the departure as a darkened cave, find one's way, alone, outside, to the illumination of Truth, and only then return to examine and reprove the inhabitants. The critic-who-returns doesn't engage the people as kin; he looks

2. *Shabbat* 97a.

at them with a new objectivity; they are strangers to his new-found Truth.[3]

This is the critic as detached intellectual. The prophets of Israel were quite different. Their message, writes Johannes Lindblom, was "characterized by the principle of solidarity."[4] "They are rooted, for all their anger, in their own societies," agrees Walzer.[5] They lived and worked "among their own people."[6] They spoke, not from outside, but from within. That is what gives their words power. They identify with those to whom they speak. They share their history, their fate, their calling, their covenant. Hence the peculiar pathos of the prophetic calling. The prophets were the voice of God to the people, but they were also the voice of the people to God.

That, according to the sages, was what God was teaching Moses: What matters is not whether they believe in you, but whether you believe in them. Unless you believe in them, you cannot lead in the way a prophet must lead. You must identify with them and have faith in them, seeing not only their surface faults but also their underlying virtues. Otherwise, you will be no better than a detached intellectual – and that is the beginning of the end. If you do not believe in the people, eventually you will not even believe in God. You will think yourself superior to them, and that is a corruption of the soul.

The classic text on this theme is Maimonides' *Epistle on Martyrdom*.[7] Written in 1165, when Maimonides was thirty years old, it was occasioned by a tragic period in medieval Jewish history when an

---

3. Michael Walzer, *The Company of Critics: Social Criticism and Political Community in the Twentieth Century* (London: Peter Halban, 1989), 13.
4. Johannes Lindblom, *Prophecy in Ancient Israel* (Philadelphia: Muhlenberg Press, 1962), 344.
5. Michael Walzer, *Interpretation and Social Criticism* (Harvard University Press, 1987), 81.
6. II Kings 4:13.
7. For an English version with commentary and notes, see Abraham Halkin and David Hartman, *Crisis and Leadership: Epistles of Maimonides* (Philadelphia: Jewish Publication Society of America, 1985), 13–90.

extremist Muslim sect, the Almohads, forced many Jews to convert to Islam under threat of death.

One of the forced converts (they were called *anusim*; literally, "those who are forced") asked a rabbi whether he might gain merit by practising as many of the Torah's commands as he could in secret. The rabbi sent back a dismissive reply. Now that he had forsaken his faith, the rabbi answered, he would achieve nothing by living secretly as a Jew. Any Jewish act he performed would not be a merit but an additional sin.

Maimonides' *Epistle* is a work of surpassing spiritual beauty. He utterly rejects the rabbi's reply. Those who keep Judaism in secret are to be praised, not blamed. He quotes a whole series of rabbinic passages in which God rebukes prophets who criticised the people of Israel, including the one above about Moses. He then writes:

> If this is the sort of punishment meted out to the pillars of the universe – Moses, Elijah, Isaiah, and the ministering angels – because they briefly criticized the Jewish congregation, can one have an idea of the fate of the least among the worthless [i.e., the rabbi who criticized the forced converts] who let his tongue loose against Jewish communities of sages and their disciples, priests and Levites, and called them sinners, evildoers, gentiles, disqualified to testify, and heretics who deny the Lord God of Israel?[8]

The *Epistle* is a definitive expression of the prophetic task: to speak out of love for one's people; to defend them, see the good in them, and raise them to higher achievements through praise, not condemnation.

Who is a leader? To this, the Jewish answer is, one who identifies with his or her people, mindful of their faults, to be sure, but convinced also of their potential greatness and their preciousness in the sight of God. In effect, God said to Moses: Those people of whom you have doubts are believers, the children of believers. They are My people, and they are your people. Just as you believe in Me, so you must believe in them.

---

8. Ibid., 19.

Of What Was Moses Afraid?

I
t was, it could be said, the most fateful encounter in Jewish history. Moses is in Midian, having escaped from Egypt, where he had intervened to protect an Israelite slave from being beaten by an Egyptian taskmaster. His true identity is unknown. Moses looks, speaks, and dresses like an Egyptian. Jethro's daughters, whom he rescues from rough treatment at the hands of local shepherds, tell their father that "An Egyptian man saved us" (2:19). He marries one of Jethro's daughters and settles down to the life of a shepherd, quiet, anonymous, and far from Pharaoh and the Israelites. It is the slow movement in the symphony of his life.

Yet his memories do not leave him alone. They come into sudden focus as he is tending his sheep and his eye catches sight of a strange phenomenon:

> Now Moses was tending the flock of Jethro his father-in-law, the priest of Midian, and he led the flock to the far side of the desert and came to Horeb, the mountain of God. There the angel of the Lord appeared to him in flames of fire from within a bush. Moses saw that though the bush was on fire it did not burn up.

So Moses thought, "I will go over and see this strange sight – why the bush does not burn up."

When the Lord saw that he had gone over to look, God called to him from within the bush, "Moses! Moses!" And Moses said, "Here I am."

"Do not come any closer," God said. "Take off your sandals, for the place where you are standing is holy ground." Then he said, "I am the God of your father, the God of Abraham, the God of Isaac and the God of Jacob."

At this, Moses hid his face, because he was afraid to look at God. (3:1–6)

God tells him that the moment has come. He has heard the cries of the Israelites. In response both to their cries and to the promise He made with the patriarchs, He is about to bring them out of slavery and He calls on Moses to lead them. The drama of the exodus is about to begin.

The sages noticed a similarity between the last sentence of this passage – "At this, Moses hid his face, because he was afraid to look at God" – and a later passage, after the Golden Calf, when Moses comes down from the mountain having secured forgiveness for the people, with new tablets to replace those he had broken when he first saw the calf. The text reads:

When Moses came down from Mount Sinai with the two tablets of the Testimony in his hands, he was not aware that his face was radiant because he had spoken with the Lord. When Aaron and all the Israelites saw Moses, his face was radiant, and they were afraid to come near him. (34:29–30)

The sages commented:

Rabbi Shmuel ben Naḥmani said in the name of Rabbi Yonatan: in reward for three [pious acts], Moses was privileged to receive three [forms of reward]. In reward for "and Moses hid his face," he was given a radiant face. In reward for "he was afraid," he merited that "they were afraid to come near him." In reward for "to look upon God," he merited that "he sees the form of the Lord."[1]

It is a lovely idea. Moses, who came closer to God than any other human being before or since, took on some of the characteristics of God himself – not that he became Godlike (Moses, like every other figure in the Hebrew Bible, remains human, not divine) but that his face shone from the encounter.

One detail in the sages' commentary, however, is strange. The first two rewards are straightforward – a kind of measure for measure. Because he hid his face, his face became radiant. Because he was awe-struck by the burning bush, he became awe-inspiring (the Israelites were "afraid to come near him"). But what about the third – because he was afraid to look at God, he was rewarded by seeing God? Either it is right or wrong to "look at God." If it is right, why was Moses afraid? And if it is wrong, why was he later rewarded with something that should not have happened?

I was privileged to hear a remarkable answer from my teacher, Rabbi Nahum Rabinovitch, one of the great Maimonidean scholars of our time.[2] One question, according to the sages, troubled Moses. Why do the innocent suffer? Why is there evil in the world? Moses burned with a sense of justice. When he saw a slave beaten, or two people fighting, or young women being roughly treated by shepherds, he intervened. Later, when his mission to Pharaoh initially made things worse for the Israelites, not better, he said to God: "O Lord, why have You brought trouble to this people … You have not rescued Your people at all" (5:22–23). Moses belonged to the tradition of Abraham, who said to God, "Shall the judge of all the earth not do justice?" (Genesis 18:25).

This is the question of questions for biblical faith. Paganism then, like secularism now, had no such doubt. Why should anyone expect justice in the world? The gods fought. They were indifferent to mankind.

1. *Berakhot* 7a.
2. It has been published in Nahum Rabinovitch, *Darkhah shel Torah* (Jerusalem: Ma'aliyot, 1999), 185–191.

The universe was not moral. It was an arena of conflict. The strong win, the weak suffer, and the wise keep far from the fray. If there is no God or (what amounts to the same thing) many gods, there is no reason to expect justice. The question does not arise.

But for biblical faith, it does. God, the supreme power of powers, is just. Was this not why He chose Abraham in the first place, so that he would teach his children and his household to "keep the way of the Lord by doing what is right and just" (Genesis 18:19)? Why then do the good suffer, while evil men prosper? It is a question that reverberates through the centuries, in Jeremiah, the book of Job, ancient rabbinic midrash, the *kinot* ("laments") of the Middle Ages, and post-Holocaust literature. It was this question that stayed with Moses and gave him no rest. Why are the Israelites enslaved? What wrong did they do to warrant it? Why is the brutal regime of Egypt so strong? Where is the justice in the world?

Pain, harm, suffering are evils. Yet there are circumstances in which we make our peace with them – when we know that they are necessary for some good. To be a parent is to be troubled by the cry of a child in distress, yet we willingly give a child medicine, and put up with its cries, when we know it will cure the illness from which the child is suffering. A surgeon must, at a certain point, treat the patient on the operating table as an object rather than a person, for were it otherwise he could not perform the surgery. A political leader may have to make a decision that will have a disastrous impact on some people – thrown out of work as a result of stringent economic policies, even killed on the battlefield as the consequence of a decision to go to war. One who shrinks from these choices because of a strong sense of compassion may be a good human being but a wholly inadequate leader, because the long-term result of a failure to make tough choices may be far worse. There are times when we must silence our most human instincts if we are to bring about good in the long run.

It was just this of which Moses was afraid. If he could "look at the face of God," if he could understand history from the perspective of heaven, he would have to make his peace with the suffering of human beings. He would know why pain here was necessary for gain there; why bad now was essential to good later on. He would understand the ultimate justice of history.

That is what Moses refused to do, because the price of such knowledge is simply too high. He would have understood the course of history from the vantage point of God, but only at the cost of ceasing to be human. How could he still be moved by the cry of slaves, the anguish of the oppressed, if he understood its place in the scheme of things, if he knew that it was necessary in the long run? Such knowledge is divine, not human – and to have it means saying goodbye to our most human instincts: compassion, sympathy, identification with the plight of the innocent, the wronged, the afflicted and oppressed. If to "look at the face of God" is to understand why suffering is sometimes necessary, then Moses was afraid to look – afraid that it would rob him of the one thing he felt in his very bones, the thing that made him the leader he was: his anger at the sight of evil, which drove him, time and again, to intervene in the name of justice.

Moses was afraid to "look at the face of God." But there are two primary names of God in the Bible: *Elokim* and *Hashem* (literally "The Name," used in place of the four-letter name, the so-called tetragrammaton, Y-H-V-H, that we may not pronounce). *Elokim*, say the sages, refers to God's attribute of justice. *Hashem* refers to His compassion, His mercy, His kindness. At the burning bush, Moses was afraid to look at *Elokim*. His reward, years later, was that he saw "the form of *Hashem*." He understood God's compassion. He did not understand – he was afraid to understand – God's attribute of justice. He preferred to fight injustice as he saw it, than to accept it by seeing its role in the script of eternity. When it came to kindness and mercy, Moses was inspired by heaven. But when it came to justice, Moses preferred to be human than divine.

So it was throughout history. Jews, however deeply they believed in God and divine providence, never made their peace with what seemed to them to be injustice. Albert Einstein spoke of the "almost fanatical love of justice" that made him "thank his stars" that he belonged to the Jewish tradition.[3]

Nowhere is this clearer than in the book of Job. Job protests the injustice of his fate. His comforters tell him he is wrong. God is just, therefore there is a reason for the tragedies that have befallen him.

3.   Albert Einstein, *The World As I See It* (New York: Citadel Press, 2006), 103.

Throughout the long dialogue we sense that Job is on the brink of blasphemy, that it is his comforters who speak the truth. Yet at the conclusion of the book our expectations are suddenly overturned. God says to Eliphaz and his colleagues: "I am angry with you and your two friends, because you have not spoken as you ought about Me, as My servant Job has done" (Job 42:7).

It is an astonishing volte-face. Better the protests of Job than the acceptance of fate on the part of his friends. Yes, there is an ultimate justice in the affairs of mankind. But we may not aspire to such knowledge – not because we cannot (because, being human, our minds are too limited, our horizons too short) but because we morally must not, for we would then accept evil and not fight against it. God wants us to be human, not divine. He seeks our protest against evil, our passion for justice, our refusal to come to terms with a world in which the innocent suffer and the evil have power.

It is that refusal – born not out of a lack of faith but precisely the opposite, the conviction that God wants us to be active in pursuit of justice – that drove Abraham, Jeremiah and Job; that drove successive generations of those inspired by the Bible to fight slavery, tyranny, poverty and disease; that moves us to become God's partners in the work of redemption. Faced with the opportunity to understand the troubling aspects of history from the vantage point of God, Moses was afraid to look. He was right, and for this he was rewarded. God does not want us to understand the suffering of the innocent but to fight for a world in which the innocent no longer suffer. To that, Moses dedicated his life. Can we, his disciples, do less?

Va'era
ואָרֵא

In *Va'era*, the story of the exodus begins in earnest, with an unprecedented series of divine interventions into history. Time and again plagues hit the Egyptians. Moses repeatedly asks Pharaoh to release the people. Repeatedly, Pharaoh refuses. An immense drama is taking place. All the power of imperial Egypt is powerless against the God of creation and redemption.

In the essays that follow, the first examines the four (or is it five?) expressions of redemption, and the missing "fifth cup" of the Seder service. The second looks at God's "hardening" of Pharaoh's heart. Does this imply that Pharaoh kept or lost his freedom? The third analyzes the satirical subplot in the third plague, of lice. The fourth is a study of the revolutionary change implicit in the exodus narrative. This was, in a profound sense, the "birth of history," the first appearance in civilization of the idea of time as an arena of change.

The Cup of Hope

As a child, I used to be fascinated by the cup of Elijah at the Pesaḥ Seder table. Would the prophet come when we opened the door after the meal? Would he be visible or invisible? Did the level of the wine go down, however imperceptibly? The idea of the prophet who did not die, but went to heaven in a chariot of fire (II Kings 2:11), and who would one day return to bring the good news of redemption was intensely dramatic. Only later did I discover the real significance of Elijah's cup, and found, as so often, that the truth is no less moving than the stories we learned as children.

The Mishna in *Pesaḥim* speaks of four cups of wine.[1] These are the basic requirements of the Seder, and the community must ensure that even the poorest person has sufficient wine to drink these cups. According to the Jerusalem Talmud,[2] they represent the four stages of redemption at the beginning of our *parasha*. God assures Moses that despite the fact that his intervention with Pharaoh has initially made things worse, liberation will indeed come:

1. Mishna, *Pesaḥim* 10:1.
2. Talmud Yerushalmi, *Pesaḥim* 10:1.

"Therefore, say to the Israelites: 'I am the Lord, and I will bring you out from under the yoke of the Egyptians. I will free you from being slaves to them, and I will redeem you with an outstretched arm and with mighty acts of judgment. I will take you as My own people, and I will be your God.'" (Exodus 6:6–7)

The first cup corresponds to "I will bring you out," the second to "I will free you," the third to "I will redeem you," and the fourth to "I will take you." Geographically, God will take the Israelites out of Egypt, physically He will save them from oppression, legally He will liberate them from Pharaoh's rule, and spiritually He will take them under His own protection and tutelage. Each of the four cups is a stage on the way to freedom, a way of pausing and giving thanks.

In the Babylonian Talmud, however, there is a strange statement:

The fifth cup: over this, one completes Hallel and says Hallel Hagadol (Psalm 136: "Gives thanks to the Lord, His love endures forever"). These are the words of Rabbi Tarfon.[3]

Rashi is puzzled by these words. Thus far, the discussion has been about four cups, not five. He is therefore driven to the conclusion that the text is a scribal error. He believes it should say, "the fourth cup."[4]

Maimonides, however, accepts the text as it stands. He writes that after drinking the four cups and completing Hallel:

One may pour a fifth cup and say over it Hallel Hagadol...This cup is not obligatory, unlike the four cups.[5]

Ravad (R. Avraham ibn Daud), a contemporary of Maimonides, takes a slightly different view. For him it is a mitzva to drink a fifth cup.[6] There is a difference between mitzva and *hova*. The latter is an obligation,

3. *Pesaḥim* 118a.
4. Rashi, commentary to *Pesaḥim*, ad loc.
5. *Mishneh Torah*, Ḥametz u'Matza, 8:10.
6. Ravad, commentary to *Ba'al HaMe'or*, 794.

the former an act which, though not obligatory, constitutes a positive religious deed.

Two questions arise on the views of Maimonides and Ravad. The first is: why does the Mishna speak about four cups if there are in fact five? To this the answer is straightforward: The four cups are obligatory, unlike the fifth. That is why the community must provide the poor with the means of fulfilling their obligation, but they do not have to make provision for the fifth cup, which according to Maimonides is optional, and according to Ravad is desirable but not absolutely necessary.

The second question seems stronger. When God speaks to Moses, He uses four expressions of deliverance, not five. Hence, the four cups. Asking this question, however, takes us back to the text at the beginning of our *parasha*. It is then that we discover, to our surprise, that there is in fact a fifth expression of deliverance:

> "And I will bring you to the land I swore with uplifted hand to give to Abraham, to Isaac and to Jacob. I will give it to you as a possession. I am the Lord." (Exodus 6:8)

The drama of the fifth cup now becomes apparent. Pesaḥ represents the start of the great journey of Jewish history, from slavery to freedom, Egypt to the promised land. The fifth cup stands for the destination, the "land flowing with milk and honey" (Exodus 3:8). What then became of it after the destruction of the Second Temple, the failure of the Bar Kochba rebellion, the Hadrianic persecutions and the long, tragic series of events that led to the greatest exile-and-dispersion of Jewish history? Could Jews, no longer a sovereign people in their own land, celebrate freedom under such circumstances?

The pathos of this question is evident in the opening words of the Seder: "This is the bread of affliction our ancestors ate in the land of Egypt." The very festival that spoke of liberty gained became – for almost two thousand years – a poignant reminder of what the Jewish people had lost: freedom, a land, a home. A new phrase was born: next year. "This year we are slaves; next year we will be free. This year we are here; next year in Israel." The past became the future. Memory was transfigured into hope. It is not too much to call the Jewish people "the people of hope." What had happened once would happen again. As the prophets of exile – Jeremiah and Ezekiel – said: there would be a second exodus. The loss was only temporary. The divine promise was forever.[7]

It was in this context that the debate over the fifth cup arose. Jews could speak about the four preliminary stages of redemption – but could they celebrate the fifth: "I will bring you to the land"? That is the debate between Rashi, Maimonides and Ravad. Rashi says one should not drink a fifth cup; Maimonides says one may; Ravad says one should.

Hence the extra cup at the Seder table. Out of respect for Maimonides and Ravad, we pour it. Out of respect for Rashi, we do not drink it. According to the sages, unresolved halakhic disputes will one day be resolved by Elijah (the word *Teyku*, "Let it stand [undecided]," refers to Elijah: "The Tishbite [Elijah] will come and answer questions and problems"). Hence the fifth cup became known as the cup of Elijah.

In our times, the Jewish people have returned to the land. According to one sage (the late Rabbi Menahem Kasher), we should now drink the fifth cup. Be that as it may, it is no less moving to think back to the eleventh and twelfth centuries – the age of Rashi, Maimonides and Ravad – and know that in the darkest night of exile, the only question was: how far, in the present, do we celebrate hope for the future? Four-fifths? Or all five? The promise God gave Moses at the beginning of this *parasha* spoke not just to that time, but to all time. Pesaḥ kept hope alive. Hope kept the Jewish people alive.

---

7. "This is what the Lord says, He who appoints the sun to shine by day, who decrees the moon and stars to shine by night, who stirs up the sea so that its waves roar – the Lord Almighty is His name – 'Only if these decrees vanish from My sight,' declares the Lord, 'will the descendants of Israel ever cease to be a nation before Me'" (Jeremiah 31:35–36).

    "'As surely as I live,' declares the Sovereign Lord, 'I will rule over you with a mighty hand and an outstretched arm and with outpoured wrath. I will bring you from the nations and gather you from the countries where you have been scattered'" (Ezekiel 20:33–34).

The Hardened Heart

I t is one of the classic philosophical conundrums. In the *parasha* of *Va'era*, before even the first plague has struck Egypt, God tells Moses:

> "But I will harden Pharaoh's heart, and multiply My miraculous signs and wonders in Egypt. He will not listen to you. Then I will lay My hand on Egypt and with mighty acts of judgment I will bring out My troops, My people the Israelites. And the Egyptians will know that I am the Lord when I stretch out My hand against Egypt and bring the Israelites out of it." (Exodus 7:3–5)

The problem is obvious. If it was God who hardened Pharaoh's heart, where then was his freedom? Either the Egyptian ruler had a genuine choice, or he did not. If he did, it was Pharaoh, not God, who was responsible for the hardness of his heart. If he did not – if it was God acting upon him, controlling his responses, determining his reactions – then how could Pharaoh be guilty and worthy of punishment? As Maimonides puts it: If there were no free will, what room what would there be for the whole of the Torah? By what right or justice could God punish the wicked or reward the righteous? "Shall not the judge of all the earth act justly?"[1]

Punishing Pharaoh for something he could not help doing is, simply, unjust.

The general outline of an answer – however we construe its details – is already implicit in the precise wording of the biblical narrative. After each of the first five plagues, the Torah tells us that Pharaoh hardened his own heart. So, for example, we read: "Pharaoh's heart was hard" (7:13, 22; 8:15), "he hardened his heart" (8:11), "Pharaoh hardened his heart this time too" (8:28), and "Pharaoh's heart was unyielding" (9:7). It is only from the sixth plague onwards that his hard-heartedness is attributed to God:

Plague 6, Boils: "But the Lord hardened Pharaoh's heart and he would not listen to Moses and Aaron, just as the Lord had said to Moses." (Exodus 9:12)

Plague 7, Hail: "Then the Lord said to Moses, 'Go to Pharaoh, for I have hardened his heart and the hearts of his officials so that I may perform My miraculous signs among them.'" (10:1)

Plague 8, Locusts: "But the Lord hardened Pharaoh's heart, and he would not let the Israelites go." (10:20)

Plague 9, Darkness: "But the Lord hardened Pharaoh's heart, and he was not willing to let them go." (10:26)

Plague 10, Death of the Firstborn: "Moses and Aaron performed all these wonders before Pharaoh, but the Lord hardened Pharaoh's heart, and he would not let the Israelites go out of his country." (11:20)

Rashi understands the hardening of Pharaoh's heart in the last five

1. Genesis 18:25; *Mishneh Torah*, Hilkhot Teshuva 5:6.

plagues as a form of punishment for the first five, when it was Pharaoh's own obstinacy that led him to refuse to let the people go.[2]

Maimonides interprets God's hardening of Pharaoh's heart as meaning that "repentance was withheld from him, and the liberty to turn from his wickedness was not accorded to him."[3]

Albo and Sforno offer the opposite interpretation. God hardened Pharaoh's heart precisely to restore his free will. After the succession of plagues that had devastated the land, Pharaoh was under overwhelming pressure to let the Israelites go. Had he done so, it would not have been out of free choice, but rather under force majeure. God therefore toughened, strengthened, Pharaoh's heart so that even after the first five plagues he was genuinely free to say yes or no.[4]

Simplest and most profound are the words of the Talmudic sages about the *yetser hara*, the evil impulse:

> Rav Assi said: At first the evil impulse is as thin as a spider's gossamer, but in the end it is as thick as a cart-rope.[5]
>
> Rava said: At first the evil impulse is called a "wayfarer," then a "guest," then finally a "master."[6]

Evil has two faces. The first – turned to the outside world – is what it does to its victim. The second – turned within – is what it does to its perpetrator. Evil traps the evildoer in its mesh. Slowly but surely he or she loses freedom and becomes not evil's master but its slave.

Pharaoh is in fact (and this is rare in Tanakh) a tragic figure like Lady Macbeth, or like Captain Ahab in Melville's *Moby Dick*, trapped in an obsession which may have had rational beginnings, right or wrong, but which has taken hold of him, bringing not only him but those around him to their ruin. This is signalled, simply but deftly, early in the following *parasha*, *Bo*, when Pharaoh's own advisors say to him: "Let the people

---

2. Rashi, commentary to Exodus 7:3.
3. *Mishneh Torah*, Hilkhot Teshuva 6:3.
4. Albo, *Ikkarim* 4:25; Sforno, commentary to Exodus 7:3.
5. *Sukka* 52a.
6. *Sukka* 52b.

go so that they may worship the Lord their God. Do you not yet realize that Egypt is ruined?" (10:7). But Pharaoh has left rationality behind. He can no longer hear them.

It is a compelling narrative, and helps us understand not only Pharaoh, but Hitler, Stalin and other tyrants in modern times. It also contains a hint – and this really is fundamental to understanding what makes the Torah unique in religious literature – of why the Torah teaches its moral truths through narrative, rather than through philosophical or quasi-scientific discourse on the one hand, myth or parable on the other.

Compare the Torah's treatment of free will with that of the great philosophical or scientific theories. For these other systems, freedom is almost invariably an either/or: either we are always free or we never are. Some systems assert the first. Many – those that believe in social, economic or genetic determinism, or historical inevitability – claim the second. Both are too crude to portray the inner life as it really is.[7]

The belief that freedom is an all-or-nothing phenomenon – that we have it either all the time or none of the time – blinds us to the fact that there are degrees of freedom. It can be won and lost, and its loss is gradual. Unless the will is constantly exercised, it atrophies and dies. We then become objects, not subjects, swept along by tides of fashion, or the caprice of desire, or the passion that becomes an obsession. Only narrative can portray the subtlety of Pharaoh's slow descent into a self-destructive madness. That, I believe, is what makes Torah truer to the human condition than its philosophical or scientific counterparts.

Pharaoh is everyman writ large. The ruler of the ancient world's greatest empire, he ruled everyone except himself. It was not the Hebrews but he who was the real slave: to his obstinate insistence that he, not God, ruled history. Hence the profound insight of Ben Zoma

7. For further reading, see Daniel O'Connor, *Free Will* (New York: Anchor Books, 1971); Gerald Dworkin, ed., *Determinism, Free Will and Moral Responsibility* (Prentice-Hall, 1970); Jennifer Trusted, *Free Will and Responsibility* (Oxford University Press, 1984); Robert Kane, ed., *The Oxford Handbook of Free Will* (Oxford, 2002); Daniel Dennett, *Freedom Evolves* (Allen Lane, 2003). For Jewish views, see Charles Manekin and Menachem Kellner, eds., *Freedom and Moral Responsibility: General and Jewish Perspectives* (University Press of Maryland, 1997); Yitzhak Berger and David Shatz, eds., *Judaism, Science and Moral Responsibility* (Rowman and Littlefield, 2006).

(*Avot* 4:1): "Who is mighty?" Not one who can conquer his enemies but "One who can conquer himself."

Many things influence us – our genes, our parents, our early childhood, our race, creed, culture, class, and the persuasions and pressures of our environment. But influence is not control. Causes do not compel. It was a survivor of Auschwitz, the late Viktor Frankl, who discovered in that nightmare kingdom the truth to which he subsequently devoted his life. He said: The Nazis tried to rob us of every vestige of our humanity, but there was one freedom they could not take away from us, the freedom to decide how to respond:

> We who lived in concentration camps can remember the men who walked through the huts comforting others, giving away their last piece of bread. They may have been few in number, but they offer sufficient proof that everything can be taken from a man but one thing: the last of the human freedoms – to choose one's attitude in any given set of circumstances, to choose one's own way.[8]

At the heart of Judaism is faith in freedom: Our faith in God's freedom, and God's faith in ours.

Judaism is, among other things, a sustained tutorial in freedom: in the ability to say no; to conquer instinct by conscience; to resist the madness of crowds and their idols. That needs discipline, and the ability to stand a little apart from society, even while contributing to it. To be a Jew is to know that though we are here, we are also elsewhere. We live in time, but we are addressed by the voice of One who is beyond time.

Pharaoh was born free but became his own slave. Moses was born into a nation of slaves but led them to freedom. Easily lost, hard to sustain, freedom is our most precious gift. But it must be exercised if it is to be retained. Its greatest discipline is to let God's will challenge ours. That is the path to freedom and the cure for hardness of heart.

8. Victor Frankl, *Man's Search for Meaning* (Boston: Beacon Press, 1992), 75.

A Handful of Dust

The third plague seems like all the others: an affliction, a turning of nature against the Egyptians who themselves had turned against the Israelites. The story is told simply and briefly:

> Throughout all Egypt the dust turned into lice. But when the magicians tried to produce lice by their secret arts, they could not. The lice attacked men and animals alike. The magicians said to Pharaoh, "This is the finger of God." But Pharaoh's heart was hard and he would not listen. (Exodus 8:13–15)

There is, however, a hidden depth in this episode. To understand it we need to focus on a phenomenon to which too little attention has been paid: the use of humour in the Torah. Its most significant form is the use of satire to mock the pretensions of human beings who think they can emulate God. One thing makes God laugh – the sight of humanity attempting to defy heaven:

> The kings of the earth take their stand,
> And the rulers gather together against the Lord

and His anointed one.
"Let us break our chains," they say,
"and throw off their fetters."
He who sits in heaven laughs,
God scoffs at them. (Psalm 2:2–4)

There is a marvellous example in the story of the Tower of Babel. The people in the plain of Shinar decide to build a city with a tower that "will reach heaven" (Genesis 11:1–9). This is an act of defiance against the divinely given order of nature ("The heavens are the heavens of God: the earth He has given to the children of men" Psalm 115:16). The Torah then says, "But God came down to see the city and the tower…" (Genesis 11:5). Down on earth, the builders thought their tower would reach heaven. From the vantage point of heaven, however, it was so miniscule that God had to "come down" to see it.

Satire is essential to understanding at least some of the plagues. The Egyptians worshipped a multiplicity of gods, most of whom represented forces of nature. By their "secret arts" the magicians believed that they could control these forces. Magic is the equivalent in an era of myth to technology in an age of science. A civilization that believes it can manipulate the gods, believes likewise that it can exercise coercion over human beings. In such a culture, the concept of freedom is unknown.

The response of the Egyptians to the first two plagues is to see them within their own frame of reference. Plagues, for them, are forms of magic, not miracles. To Pharaoh's magicians, Moses and Aaron are people like themselves who practice secret arts. So they replicate them: they show that they too can turn water into blood and generate a horde of frogs. The irony here is very close to the surface. So intent are the Egyptian magicians on proving that they can do what Moses and Aaron have done, that they entirely fail to realise that far from making matters better for the Egyptians, they are making them worse: more blood, more frogs.

This brings us to the third plague, lice. One of the purposes of this plague was to produce an effect which the magicians could not replicate. They try. They fail. Immediately they conclude, "This is the finger of God" (8:15).

This is the first appearance in the Torah of an idea, surprisingly persistent in religious thinking even today, called "the god of the gaps." This holds that a miracle is something for which we cannot yet find a scientific explanation. Science is natural; religion is supernatural. An "act of God" is something we cannot account for rationally. What magicians (or technocrats) cannot reproduce must be the result of divine intervention. This leads inevitably to the conclusion that religion and science are opposed. The more we can explain scientifically or control technologically, the less need we have for faith. As the scope of science expands, the place of God progressively diminishes to vanishing point.

What the Torah is intimating is that this is a pagan mode of thought, not a Jewish one. The Egyptians admitted that Moses and Aaron were genuine prophets when they performed wonders beyond the scope of their own magic. But this is not why we believe in Moses and Aaron. On this, Maimonides is unequivocal:

> Israel did not believe in Moses our teacher because of the signs he performed. When faith is predicated on signs, a lurking doubt always remains that these signs may have been performed with the aid of occult arts and witchcraft. All the signs Moses performed in the wilderness, he did because they were necessary, not to authenticate his status as a prophet.... When we needed food, he brought down manna. When the people were thirsty, he cleaved the rock. When Korach's supporters denied his authority, the earth swallowed them up. So too with all the other signs. What then were our grounds for believing in him? The revelation at Sinai, in which we saw with our own eyes and heard with our own ears....[1]

The primary way in which we encounter God is not through miracles but through His word – the revelation – Torah – which is the Jewish people's constitution as a nation under the sovereignty of God. To be sure, God is in the events which, seeming to defy nature, we call miracles. But He is also in nature itself. Science does not displace God: it reveals, in ever more intricate and wondrous ways, the design within

---

1. *Mishneh Torah*, Hilkhot Yesodei HaTorah 8:1.

nature itself. Far from diminishing our religious sense, science (rightly understood) should enlarge it, teaching us to see "How great are Your works, O God; You have made them all with wisdom" (Psalm 104:24). Above all, God is to be found in the voice heard at Sinai, teaching us how to construct a society that will be the opposite of Egypt: in which the few do not enslave the many, nor are strangers mistreated.

The best argument against the world of ancient Egypt was divine humour. The cultic priests and magicians who thought they could control the sun and the Nile discovered that they could not even produce a louse. Pharaohs like Ramses II demonstrated their godlike status by creating monumental architecture: the great temples, palaces and pyramids whose immensity seemed to betoken divine grandeur (the Gemara explains that Egyptian magic could not function on very small things[2]). God mocks them by revealing His presence in the tiniest of creatures. It is a moment that recalls T.S. Eliot's famous lines in *The Waste Land*:

> And I will show you something different from either
> Your shadow at morning striding behind you
> Or your shadow at evening rising to meet to you;
> I will show you fear in a handful of dust.[3]

What the Egyptian magicians (and their latter-day successors) did not understand is that power over nature is not an end in itself, but solely the means to *ethical* ends. The lice were God's joke at the expense of the magicians who believed that because they controlled the forces of nature, they were masters of human destiny. They were wrong.

Technological prowess has led human beings, time and again, to believe that they were like gods. They could scale the heavens, bend nature to their purposes, and construct vast edifices to their glory. Yet in their wake they left a trail of devastation, and the civilizations they built declined and died, to be remembered only in relics and ruins.

---

2. *Sanhedrin* 67b: "Rabbi Elazar said: 'This proves that a magician cannot produce a creature less than a barley corn in size.'"
3. T.S. Eliot, *Collected Poems* (London: Faber and Faber, 1963), 63.

Humility is the only antidote to hubris. However great we are, we are small in the scheme of things. That is what God showed the Egyptians in the plague of lice.

The God Who Acts in History

The Israelites are at their lowest ebb. They have been enslaved. A decree has been issued that every male child is to be killed. Moses is sent to liberate them, but the first effect of his intervention is to make matters worse, not better. Their quota of brick-making remains unchanged, but now they also have to provide their own straw. Initially they had believed Moses when he performed the various signs God had given him, and told them that God was about to rescue them. Now they turn on Moses and Aaron, accusing them:

> When they left Pharaoh, they found Moses and Aaron waiting to meet them, and they said, "May the Lord look upon you and judge you! You have made us a stench to Pharaoh and his officials and have put a sword in their hand to kill us." (Exodus 5:20–21)

At this point Moses – who had been so reluctant to take on the mission – turns to God in protest and anguish:

> Moses returned to the Lord and said, "O Lord, why have You brought trouble upon this people? Is this why You sent me? Ever

since I went to Pharaoh to speak in Your name, he has brought trouble upon this people, and You have not rescued Your people at all." (Exodus 5:22)

None of this, however, has been accidental. The Torah is preparing the ground for one of its most monumental propositions: It is in the darkest night that Israel has its greatest visions. Hope is born at the very edge of the abyss of despair. There is nothing natural about this, nothing inevitable. No logic can give rise to hope; no law of history charts a path from slavery to redemption, exile to return. The entire sequence of events has been a prelude to the single most formative moment in the history of Israel: the intervention of God in history – the supreme Power intervening on behalf of the supremely powerless, not (as in every other culture) to endorse the status quo, but to overturn it.

The speech that follows, in Exodus 6:2–8, is breathtaking in its grandeur and literary structure. As Nechama Leibowitz and others point out, it takes the form of a chiasmus:[4]

God said to Moses

[A] **I am God.**

[B] I appeared to Abraham, to Isaac, and to Jacob as the Lord Almighty, but by My name God I was not known to them.

[C] I also established My covenant with them to give them the land of Canaan, where they lived as aliens.

[D] Moreover, I have heard the groaning of the Israelites, whom the Egyptians are enslaving, and have remembered My covenant.

[E] Therefore say to the Israelites,

---

4. A chiasmus is a literary form that displays mirror-image symmetry – ABCBA – such that the second half repeats the first in reverse.

I am God

[D1] and I will bring you out from under the yoke of the Egyptians. I will free you from being slaves to them, and will redeem you with an outstretched arm and with mighty acts of judgments. I will take you as My own people, and I will be your God. Then you will know that I am the Lord your God who brought you out from under the yoke of the Egyptians.

[C1] And I will bring you to the land I swore with uplifted hands to give

[B1] to Abraham, to Isaac, and to Jacob. I will give it to you as a possession.

[A1] **I am God.**

The structure is worked out in extraordinary detail. The first and second halves of the speech each contain exactly fifty words in the Hebrew text. B and B1 are about the patriarchs; C and C1 about the land; D and D1 about Egypt and slavery. The first half is about the past, the second about the future. The first half refers to the Israelites in the third person ("them"), the second in the second person ("you"). The entire speech turns on the threefold repetition of "I am God" – at the beginning, end and middle of the speech. (The phrase actually appears four times, the extra mention occurring in D1. It is not impossible that this is linked to the fact that the name – which is, as we will see, the central theme of the speech – has four letters, the so-called tetragrammaton.)

The entire speech is full of interest, but what will concern us – as it has successive generations of interpreters – is the proposition signalled at the outset: "I appeared to Abraham, to Isaac, and to Jacob as the Lord Almighty, but by My name God I was not known to them." A fundamental distinction is being made between the experience the patriarchs had of God, and the experience the Israelites are about to have. Something new, unprecedented, is about to happen. What is it?

Clearly it has to do with the names by which God is known. The verse distinguishes between E-l Shaddai ("the Lord Almighty") and the four-letter name of God which, because of its sanctity, Jewish tradition referred to simply as *Hashem* – "the name" par excellence (which is translated above simply as "God").

As the classic Jewish commentators point out, the verse must be read with great care. It does not say that the patriarchs "did not know" this name; nor does it say that God did not "make this name known" to them. The four-letter name appears no less than 165 times in the book of Genesis. God Himself uses the phrase "I am *Hashem*" to both Abraham (Genesis 15:7) and Jacob (28:13). Rashi's explanation is the simplest and most elegant:

> It is not written here, "[My name, *Hashem*] I did not make known to them" but rather "[By the name, *Hashem*] I was not known to them" – meaning, I was not recognized by them in My attribute of "keeping faith," by reason of which My name is "*Hashem*," namely that I am faithful to fulfil My word, for I made promises to them but I did not fulfil them [during their lifetime].[5]

What then is the difference between the other names of God and *Hashem*? For the sages of the Midrash, *Hashem* signified the divine attribute of compassion:

> God said to Moses, "You wish to know My name? I am called according to My deeds...When I judge creatures, I am called Elokim. When I wage war against the wicked I am called 'Lord of hosts.' When I suspend judgment for man's sins I am called E-l Shaddai. When I am merciful towards My world I am called *Hashem*."[6]

For Judah Halevi and Nahmanides, the key difference has to do with God's acts within and beyond nature. This is how Halevi puts it in *The Kuzari*:

5. Rashi, commentary to Exodus 6:3.
6. *Shemot Raba* 3:6.

This is perhaps what the Bible means when it says, "and I appeared to Abraham … as E-l Shaddai," namely, in the way of power and dominion…. He did not, however, perform any miracle for the patriarchs as he did for Moses … for the wonders done for Moses and the Israelites left no manner of doubt in their souls that the creator of the world also created these things which He brought into existence immediately by His will, such as the plagues of Egypt, the division of the Reed Sea, the manna, the pillar of cloud, and the like.[7]

Similarly, Nahmanides writes:

Thus God said to Moses, "I have appeared to the patriarchs with the might of My arm with which I prevail over the constellations and help those whom I have chosen, but with My name *Hashem*, with which all existence came into being, I was not made known to them, that is, to create new things for them by the open change of nature."[8]

Thus, for the Midrash, the key to the new revelation of God in the days of Moses was his compassion in responding to the cries of the oppressed Israelites. For Judah Halevi and Nahmanides it was the fact that the exodus was accompanied by supernatural events (what Nahmanides calls "revealed" as opposed to "hidden" miracles).[9]

The simplest and most cogent explanation, however, is that of Rashi. Something was about to change. The patriarchs had received the covenantal promise. They would become a nation. They would inherit a land. None of this, however, happened in their lifetime. To the contrary, as the book of Genesis reaches its close, the family of the patriarchs

---

7. Judah Halevi, *Kuzari* 2:2.
8. Ramban, commentary to Exodus 6:2.
9. See Ramban, commentary to Genesis 17:1; Charles Chavel, *Ramban, His Life and Teachings* (New York: Feldheim, 1960), 84–88. For Nahmanides, all events are miraculous, since they are the will of God. Those, however, that involve no suspension of natural law are "hidden" miracles, since their miraculous nature is not self-evident.

numbers a mere seventy souls and they are in exile in Egypt. Now, the fulfilment is about to begin. Already, in the first chapter of Exodus, we hear, for the first time, the phrase *am bnei Yisrael*, "the people of the children of Israel" (1:9). Israel has at last become, not merely a family, but a nation. Moses at the burning bush has been told, by God, that He will bring them to "a good and spacious land, a land flowing with milk and honey" (3:8). *Hashem* therefore means the God who acts in history to fulfil His promises.

Throughout these essays I have tried to convey the world-changing character of this idea. What is revolutionary in Judaism is not simply the concept of monotheism – that the universe is not a blind clash of conflicting powers but the result of a single creative will. It is that God is *involved* in His creation. God is not simply the force that brought the universe into being, nor is He reached only in the private recesses of the soul. At a certain point He intervened in history, to rescue His people from slavery and set them on the path to freedom. This was the revolution, at once political and intellectual.

At the heart of most visions of the human condition is what Mircea Eliade (in his book *Cosmos and History*) calls "the terror of history."[10] The passage of time, with its disasters, its apparent randomness, its radical contingency, is profoundly threatening to the human search for order and coherence. There seems to be no meaning in history. We live, we die, and it is as if we had never been. The universe gives no sign of any interest in our existence. If that was so in ancient times, when people believed in the existence of gods, how much more so is it true today for those neo-Darwinians who see life as no more than the operation of "chance and necessity" (Jacques Monod) or "the blind watchmaker" (Richard Dawkins).[11] Time seems to obliterate all meaning. Nothing lasts. Nothing endures. The author of Ecclesiastes is obsessed with this fact: "Man's fate is like that of the animals; the same fate awaits them both; as one dies so does the other.... Everything is meaningless" (Ecclesiastes 3:19).

It is against this background that myth and ritual arise as the

---

10. Mircea Eliade, *Cosmos and History* (New York: Harper & Row, 1959), 139.
11. Jacques Monod, *Chance and Necessity* (New York: Vintage, 1972); Richard Dawkins, *The Blind Watchmaker* (New York: Norton, 1996).

attempt to endow the human condition with significance. Both aim at giving us a sense of eternity. Myth tells us how things were before the birth of time. Rituals are acts through which people are transposed to time beyond time, and space beyond space. In Eliade's words: "an object or an act becomes real only in so far as it imitates or repeats an archetype. Thus reality is acquired solely through repetition or participation... any repetition of an archetypal gesture suspends duration, abolishes profane time, and participates in mythical time."[12] Ritual is endless repetition. It is how things were and always will be. Myth gives us the structure of a reality that never changes. The mythic imagination is an attempt to escape from history and the vicissitudes of time.

In ancient Israel, by contrast, "for the first time, the prophets placed a value on history...For the first time, we find affirmed and increasingly accepted the idea that historical events have a value in themselves, insofar as they are determined by the will of God... Historical facts thus become situations of man in respect to God, and as such they acquire a religious value that nothing had previously been able to confer on them. It may, then, be said with truth that the Hebrews were the first to discover the meaning of history as the epiphany of God."[13] Judaism is the escape into history, the unique attempt to endow events with meaning, and to see in the chronicles of mankind something more than a mere succession of happenings – to see them as nothing less than a drama of redemption in which the fate of a nation reflects its loyalty or otherwise to a covenant with God.

It is hard to recapture this turning point in the human imagination, just as it is hard for us to imagine what it was like for people first to encounter Copernicus' and Galileo's discovery that the earth went round the sun. It must once have been a terrifying, destabilizing threat to all who believed that the earth did not move; that it was the one stable point in a shifting universe. So it was with time. The ancients believed that nothing really changed. Time was, in Plato's lovely phrase, no more than the "moving image of eternity." That was the certainty that gave

---

12. Eliade, *Cosmos and History*, 34–36.
13. Ibid., 104.

people solace. The times may be out of joint, but eventually order will be restored. Things will return to the way they were.

To think of history as an arena of change is terrifying likewise. It means that we have only one life to live; that what happened once may never happen again; that we are embarked on a journey with no assurance that we will ever return to where we began. It is what Milan Kundera meant in his phrase, "the unbearable lightness of being."[14] Only profound faith – a new kind of faith, breaking with the entire world of ancient mythology – could give people the courage to set out on a journey to the unknown. Eliade's conclusion is worth quoting at length:

> Basically, the horizon of archetypes and repetition cannot be transcended with impunity unless we accept a philosophy of freedom that does not exclude God...Faith, in this context, as in many others, means absolute emancipation from any kind of natural "law" and hence the highest freedom that man can imagine: freedom to intervene even in the ontological constitution of the universe. It is, consequently, a preeminently creative freedom. In other words, it constitutes a new formula for man's collaboration with the creation – the first, but also the only such formula accorded to him since the traditional horizon of archetypes and repetition was transcended. Only such a freedom...is able to defend modern man from the terror of history – a freedom, that is, which has its source and finds its guarantee and support in God. Every other modern freedom, whatever satisfactions it may procure to him who possesses it, is powerless to justify history; and this, for every man who is sincere with himself, is equivalent to the terror of history... Any other situation of modern man leads, in the end, to despair.[15]

Not just then, in other words, but at all times including the present, the ultimate choice lies between faith in the God of history (who invites

---

14. Milan Kundera, *The Unbearable Lightness of Being* (London: Faber, 1984).
15. Eliade, *Cosmos and History*, 160–162.

human beings to become His partners in the work of redemption), or the "terror of history" from which the only refuge is myth.

Where is God? It is a mark of how deeply influenced we have been by ancient Greece that we tend to answer this question in philosophical terms, by referring to proofs from logic or nature. Many Jewish thinkers themselves – Maimonides is the most famous example – did likewise. Judah Halevi, however, thought otherwise. The ten commandments begin – he pointed out – not with the words "I am the Lord your God who created heaven and earth," but "I am the Lord your God who brought you out from Egypt, from the house of slavery." God – the One we call *Hashem* – is to be found not primarily in creation (that is another face of God to which we give the name *Elokim*), but in history.

I find it moving that this is precisely what non-Jewish observers concluded. Pascal, for example, wrote:

> It is certain that in certain parts of the world we can see a peculiar people, separated from the other peoples of the world, and this is called the Jewish people … This people is not only of remarkable antiquity but has also lasted for a singularly long time … For whereas the peoples of Greece and Italy, of Sparta, Athens and Rome, and others who came so much later have perished so long ago, these still exist, despite the efforts of so many powerful kings who have tried a hundred times to wipe them out, as their historians testify, and as can easily be judged by the natural order of things over such a long spell of years. They have always been preserved, however, and their preservation was foretold … My encounter with this people amazes me … [16]

The once-Marxist Russian thinker Nikolai Berdyaev came to a similar conclusion:

> I remember how the materialist interpretation of history, when I attempted in my youth to verify it by applying it to the destinies of peoples, broke down in the case of the Jews, where destiny

16. Pascal, *Pensées*, trans. A.J. Krailsheimer (Harmondsworth: Penguin, 1968), 171, 176–7.

seemed absolutely inexplicable from the materialistic stand-
point ... Its survival is a mysterious and wonderful phenomenon
demonstrating that the life of this people is governed by a special predetermination, transcending the processes of adaptation
expounded by the materialistic interpretation of history. The survival of the Jews, their resistance to destruction, their endurance
under absolutely peculiar conditions and the fateful role played
by them in history: all these point to the particular and mysterious foundations of their destiny.[17]

More recently, the historian Barbara Tuchman wrote:

The history of the Jews is ... intensely peculiar in the fact of having
given the western world its concept of origins and monotheism,
its ethical traditions, and the founder of its prevailing religion,
yet suffering dispersion, statelessness and ceaseless persecution,
and finally in our times nearly successful genocide, dramatically
followed by fulfilment of the never-relinquished dream of return
to the homeland. Viewing this strange and singular history, one
cannot escape the impression that it must contain some special
significance for the history of mankind, that in some way, whether
one believes in divine purpose or inscrutable circumstance, the
Jews have been singled out to carry the tale of human fate.[18]

Some 3,300 years ago, God told Moses that He would intervene
in the arena of time, not only (though primarily) to rescue the Israelites
but also "so that My name may be declared throughout the world" (9:16).
The script of history would bear the mark of a hand – not human, but
divine. And it began with these words: "Therefore say to the Israelites: I
am God, and I will bring you out from under the yoke of the Egyptians."

17. Nicolai Berdyaev, *The Meaning of History* (1936), 86–87.
18. Barbara Tuchman, *Bible and Sword* (New York: Ballantine, 1984), ix–x.

Bo
בא

The *parasha* of Bo details the last three of the plagues and the institution of Passover, both at the time of the exodus itself and as it was subsequently to be celebrated. The long exile was at an end. The Israelites had begun their journey to freedom.

The first of the following essays focuses on the ninth plague, darkness. What was its significance and symbolism? The second explores Moses' concern that the story of redemption be taught to future generations. What is the connection between education and freedom? The third looks at the "wicked child" of the Haggada and what this passage teaches about the collective nature of Jewish identity. The fourth analyzes the extraordinary detail of God's insistence that the Israelites, before they leave, take vessels of silver and gold from the Egyptians as part payment for their work as slaves. Why was this so important as a preparation for freedom?

Heart of Darkness

The ninth plague – darkness – comes shrouded in a darkness of its own.

What is this plague doing here? It seems out of sequence. Thus far there have been eight plagues, and they have become steadily, inexorably, more serious. The first two, the Nile turning blood-red and the infestation of frogs, seemed more like omens than anything else. The third and fourth, gnats and flies, caused discomfort, not crisis. The fifth, the plague that killed livestock, affected animals, not human beings.

The sixth, boils, was again a discomfort, but a serious one, no longer an external nuisance but a bodily affliction. (Remember that Job lost everything he had, but did not start cursing his fate until his body was covered with sores: Job 2.) The seventh and eighth, hail and locusts, destroyed the Egyptian grain. Now – with the loss of grain added to the loss of livestock in the fifth plague – there was no food. Still to come was the tenth plague, the death of the firstborn, in retribution for Pharaoh's murder of Israelite children. It would be this that eventually broke Pharaoh's resolve.

So we would expect the ninth plague to be very serious indeed, something that threatened, even if it did not immediately take, human life. Instead we read what seems like an anticlimax:

> Then the Lord said to Moses, "Stretch out your hand towards the sky so that darkness will spread over Egypt – darkness that can be felt." So Moses stretched out his hand towards the sky, and total darkness covered all Egypt for three days. No one could see anyone else or leave his place for three days. Yet all the Israelites had light in the places where they lived. (Exodus 10:21–23)

Darkness is a nuisance, but no more. The phrase "darkness that can be felt" suggests what happened: a khamsin, a sandstorm of a kind not unfamiliar in Egypt, which can last for several days, producing sand- and dust-filled air that obliterates the light of the sun. A khamsin is usually produced by a southern wind that blows into Egypt from the Sahara desert. The worst sandstorm is usually the first of the season, in March. This fits the dating of the plague which happened shortly before the death of the firstborn, on Pesah.

The ninth plague was doubtless unusual in its intensity, but it was not an event of a kind wholly unknown to the Egyptians, then or now. Why then does it figure in the plague narrative, immediately prior to its climax? Why did it not happen nearer the beginning, as one of the less severe plagues?

The answer lies in a line from "Dayyenu," the song we sing as part of the Haggada: "If God had executed judgment against them [the Egyptians] but had not done so against their gods, it would have been sufficient." Twice the Torah itself refers to this dimension of the plagues:

> "I will pass through Egypt on that night, and I will kill every first-born in Egypt, man and animal. I will perform acts of judgment against all the gods of Egypt: I (alone) am God." (Exodus 12:12)

> The Egyptians were burying all their firstborn, struck down by the Lord; and against their gods, the Lord had executed judgment. (Numbers 33:4)

Not all the plagues were directed, in the first instance, against the Egyptians. Some were directed against things they worshipped as gods. That is the case in the first two plagues. The Nile was personified in ancient Egypt as the god Hapi and was worshipped as the source of fertility in an otherwise desert region. Offerings were made to it at times of inundation. The inundations themselves were attributed to one of the major Egyptian deities, Osiris. The plague of frogs would have been associated by the Egyptians with Heket, the goddess who was believed to attend births as a midwife, and who was depicted as a woman with the head of a frog.

The plagues were not only intended to punish Pharaoh and his people for their mistreatment of the Israelites, but also to show them the powerlessness of the gods in which they believed. What is at stake in this confrontation is the difference between myth – in which the gods are mere powers, to be tamed, propitiated or manipulated – and biblical monotheism, in which ethics (justice, compassion, human dignity) constitute the meeting point of God and mankind.

The symbolism of these plagues, often lost on us, would have been immediately apparent to the Egyptians. Two things now become clear. The first is why the Egyptian magicians declared, "This is the finger of God" (Exodus 8:15) only after the third plague, lice. The first two plagues would not have surprised them at all. They would have understood them as the work of Egyptian deities who, they believed, were sometimes angry with the people and took their revenge.

The second is the quite different symbolism the first two plagues were meant to have for the Israelites, and for us. As with the tenth plague, these were no mere miracles intended to demonstrate the power of the God of Israel, as if religion were a gladiatorial arena in which the strongest god wins. Their meaning was moral. They represented the most fundamental of all ethical principles, stated in the Noahide covenant in the words "He who sheds the blood of man, by man shall his blood be shed" (Genesis 9:6). This is the rule of retributive justice, measure for measure: As you do, so shall you be done to.

By first ordering the midwives to kill all male Israelite babies, and then, when that failed, by commanding, "Every boy who is born must be cast into the Nile" (Exodus 1:22), Pharaoh had turned what should have been symbols of life (the Nile, which fed Egyptian agriculture, and midwives) into agents of death. The river that turned to blood, and the Heket-like frogs that infested the land, were not afflictions as such, but rather coded communications, as if to say to the Egyptians: reality has an ethical structure. See what it feels like when the gods you turned against the Israelites turn on you. If used for evil ends, the powers of nature will turn against man, so that what he does will be done to him in turn. There is justice in history.

Hence the tenth plague, to which all the others were a mere prelude. Unlike all the other plagues, its significance was disclosed to Moses even before he set out on his mission, while he was still living with Jethro in Midian:

> You shall say to Pharaoh: This is what the Lord says. "Israel is My son, My firstborn. I have told you to let My son go, that he may worship Me. If you refuse to let him go, I will kill your own firstborn son." (Exodus 4:22–23)

Whereas the first two plagues were symbolic representations of the Egyptian murder of Israelite children, the tenth plague was the enactment of retributive justice, as if heaven was saying to the Egyptians: You committed, or supported, or passively accepted the murder of innocent children. There is only one way you will ever realize the wrong you did, namely, if you yourself suffer what you did to others.

This too helps explain the difference between the two words the Torah regularly uses to describe what God did in Egypt: *otot u'moftim,* "signs and wonders." These two words are not two ways of describing the same thing – miracles. They describe quite different things. A *mofet,* a wonder, is indeed a miracle. An *ot,* a sign, is something else: a symbol (like tefillin or circumcision, both of which are called *ot*), that is to say, a coded communication, a message.

The significance of the ninth plague is now obvious. The greatest god in the Egyptian pantheon was Ra or Re, the sun god. The name of the Pharaoh often associated with the exodus, Ramses II, means *meses,* "son of" (as in the name Moses) Ra, the god of the sun. Egypt – so its people believed – was ruled by the sun. Its human ruler, or Pharaoh, was semi-divine, the child of the sun god.

In the beginning of time, according to Egyptian myth, the sun god ruled together with Nun, the primeval waters. Eventually there were many deities. Ra then created human beings from his tears. Seeing, however, that they were deceitful, he sent the goddess Hathor to destroy them; only a few survived.

The plague of darkness was not a *mofet* but an *ot*, a sign. The obliteration of the sun signalled that there is a power greater than Ra. Yet what the plague represented was less the power of God over the sun, but the rejection by God of a civilization that turned one man, Pharaoh, into an absolute ruler (son of the sun god) with the ability to enslave other human beings – and of a culture that could tolerate the murder of children because that is what Ra himself did.

When God told Moses to say to Pharaoh, "My son, My firstborn, Israel," He was saying: I am the God who cares for His children, not one who kills His children. The ninth plague was a divine act of communication that said: there is not only physical darkness but also moral darkness. The best test of a civilization is to see how it treats children, its own and others'. In an age of broken families, neglected and impoverished children, and worse – the use of children as instruments of war – that is a lesson we still need to learn.

Schools of Freedom

> *"And you shall explain to your child on that day,*
> *'It is because of what the Lord did for me when I*
> *went free from Egypt.'" (Exodus 13:8)*

I t was the moment for which they had been waiting for more than two hundred years. The Israelites, slaves in Egypt, were about to go free. Ten plagues had struck the country. The people were the first to understand; Pharaoh was the last. God was on the side of freedom and human dignity. You cannot build a nation, however strong your police and army, by enslaving some for the benefit of others. History will turn against you, as it has against every tyranny known to mankind.

And now the time had arrived. The Israelites were on the brink of their release. Moses, their leader, gathered them together and prepared to address them. What would he speak about at this fateful juncture, the birth of a people? He could have spoken about many things. He might have talked about liberty, the breaking of their chains, and the end of slavery. He might have talked about the destination to which they were about to travel, the "land flowing with milk and honey" (Exodus 3:17).

Or he might have chosen a more sombre theme: the journey that lay ahead, the dangers they would face: what Nelson Mandela called "the long walk to freedom." Any one of these would have been the speech of a great leader sensing an historic moment in the destiny of Israel.

Moses did none of these things. Instead he spoke about children, and the distant future, and the duty to pass on memory to generations yet unborn. Three times in the *parasha* of *Bo* he turns to the theme:

> When you enter the land that the Lord will give you as He promised, observe this ceremony. And when your children say to you, "What does this ceremony mean to you?" then tell them, "It is the Passover sacrifice to the Lord, who passed over the houses of the Israelites in Egypt and spared our homes when He struck down the Egyptians." (Exodus 12:26–27)

> On that day tell your son, "I do this because of what the Lord did for me when I came out of Egypt." (Exodus 13:8)

> In days to come, when your son asks you, "What does this mean?" say to him, "With a mighty hand the Lord brought us out of Egypt, out of the land of slavery." (Exodus 13:14)

About to gain their freedom, the Israelites were told that they had to become a nation of educators. That is what made Moses not just a great leader, but a unique one. What the Torah is teaching is that freedom is won, not on the battlefield, nor in the political arena, nor in the courts, national or international, but in the human imagination and will. To defend a country you need an army. But to defend a free society you need schools. You need families and an educational system in which ideals are passed on from one generation to the next, and never lost, or despaired of, or obscured. There has never been a more profound understanding of freedom. It is not difficult, Moses was saying, to gain liberty, but to sustain it is the work of a hundred generations. Forget it and you lose it.

Freedom needs three institutions: parenthood, education and memory. You must tell your children about slavery and the long journey to liberation. They must annually taste the bread of affliction and the bitter herbs of slave labour. They must know what oppression feels like if they are to fight against it in every age. So Jews became the people whose passion was education, whose citadels were schools and whose heroes were teachers.

The result was that by the time the Second Temple was destroyed, Jews had constructed the world's first system of universal compulsory education, paid for by public funds:

> Remember for good the man Yehoshua ben Gamla, because were it not for him the Torah would have been forgotten from Israel. At first a child was taught by his father, and as a result orphans were left uneducated. It was then resolved that teachers of children should be appointed in Jerusalem, and a father [who lived outside the city] would bring his child there and have him taught, but the orphan was still left without tuition. Then it was resolved to appoint teachers in each district, and boys of the age of sixteen and seventeen were placed under them; but when the teacher was angry with a pupil, he would rebel and leave. Finally Yehoshua ben Gamla came and instituted that teachers be appointed in every province and every city, and children from the age of six or seven were placed under their charge.[1]

By contrast, England did not institute universal compulsory education until 1870. In America it took from 1852 (Massachusetts) until 1918 (Mississippi). The seriousness the sages attached to education can be measured by the following two passages:

> If a city has made no provision for the education of the young, its inhabitants are placed under a ban, until teachers have been engaged. If they persistently neglect this duty, the city is excommunicated, for the world only survives by the merit of the breath of schoolchildren.[2]

1. *Bava Batra* 21a.
2. Rambam, *Mishneh Torah*, Hilkhot Talmud Torah 2:1.

Rabbi Yehudah the Prince sent R. Ḥiyya and R. Issi and R. Ami on a mission through the towns of Israel to establish teachers in every place. They came to a town where there were no teachers. They said to the inhabitants, "Bring us the defenders of the town." They brought them the military guard. The rabbis said, "These are not the protectors of the town but its destroyers." "Who then are the protectors?" asked the inhabitants. They answered, "The teachers."[3]

No other faith has attached a higher value to study. None has given it a higher position in the scale of communal priorities. From the very outset Israel knew that freedom cannot be created by legislation, nor can it be sustained by political structures alone. As the American justice Judge Learned Hand put it:

> Liberty lies in the hearts of men and women; when it dies there, no constitution, no law, no court can save it; no constitution, no law, no court can even do much to help it. And what is this liberty which must lie in the hearts of men and women? It is not the ruthless, the unbridled will; it is not freedom to do as one likes. That is the denial of liberty, and leads straight to its overthrow. A society in which men recognize no check upon their freedom soon becomes a society where freedom is the possession of only a savage few; as we have learned to our sorrow.[4]

That is the truth epitomized in a remarkable exegesis given by the sages. They based it on the following verse about the tablets Moses received at Sinai:

> The tablets were the work of God; the writing was the writing of God, engraved [*ḥarut*] on the tablets. (Exodus 32:16)

They reinterpreted it as follows:

3. Talmud Yerushalmi, *Hagiga* 1:6.
4. Speech at Central Park, New York, 21 May 1944.

Read not *ḥarut*, engraved, but *ḥerut*, freedom, for there is none so free as one who occupies himself with the study of Torah.[5]

What they meant was that if the law is engraved on the hearts of the people, it does not need to be enforced by police. True freedom – *cherut* – is the ability to control oneself without having to be controlled by others. Without accepting voluntarily a code of moral and ethical restraints, liberty becomes license and society itself a battleground of warring instincts and desires.

This idea, fateful in its implications, was first articulated by Moses in this *parasha*, in his words to the assembled Israelites. He was telling them that freedom is more than a moment of political triumph. It is a constant endeavour, throughout the ages, to teach those who come after us the battles our ancestors fought, and why, so that my freedom is never sacrificed to yours, or purchased at the cost of someone else's. That is why, to this day, on Passover we eat matza, the unleavened bread of affliction, and taste *maror*, the bitter herbs of slavery, to remember the sharp taste of affliction and never be tempted to afflict others.

The oldest and most tragic phenomenon in history is that empires, which once bestrode the narrow world like a colossus, eventually decline and disappear. Freedom becomes individualism – "each doing what was right in his own eyes,"[6] individualism becomes chaos, chaos becomes the search for order, and the search for order becomes a new tyranny imposing its will by the use of force. What, thanks to Torah, Jews never forgot, is that freedom is a never-ending effort of education in which parents, teachers, homes and schools are all partners in the dialogue between the generations. Learning, *talmud Torah*, is the very foundation of Judaism, the guardian of our heritage and hope. That is why, when tradition conferred on Moses the greatest honor, it did not call him "our hero," "our prophet" or "our king." It called him, simply, Moshe Rabbenu, Moses our teacher. For it is in the arena of education that the battle for the good society is lost or won.

5. Mishna, *Avot* 6:2.
6. Judges 21:25.

The Covenant of Fate

I n the last essay, I examined the profound idea found in the *para-sha* of *Bo*, that freedom is only possible in the long term if you educate your children in your history. Freedom is not, as so many have thought, a matter of military victories or political structures alone. It involves "habits of the heart." Unless children know how freedom was fought for and won – in the case of Judaism, unless they remember Egypt and the exodus – they will not understand the entire concept of law-governed liberty. They will not grasp the fact that Judaism is an infinitely subtle set of laws designed to create a society of free individuals serving the free God in and through the responsible exercise of freedom. Freedom lies in what we teach our children. That is what Moses told the Israelites on the brink of their release.

We noted that Moses spoke about this subject in *Bo* three times. There is a later, fourth passage in *Va'et-ḥanan*, in the book of Deuteronomy:

> In the future, when your son asks you, "What is the meaning of the stipulations, decrees and laws the Lord our God has commanded you?" tell him: "We were slaves of Pharaoh in Egypt, but

> the Lord brought us out of Egypt with a mighty hand. (Deuteronomy 6:20–21)

Famously, these four passages became the basis of the four sons of the Haggada. I want to focus in this essay on one of those sons: the *rasha*, the wicked or rebellious child. This is how the Haggada portrays him:

> What does the wicked son say? "What does this ceremony mean to you?" To you, not to him. Because he excludes himself from the community and denies a fundamental principle of faith, you shall set his teeth on edge and say to him, "I do this because of what the Lord did for me when I came out of Egypt" – for me, not for him. If he had been there he would not have been saved.[1]

What is going on in this passage? What was it in the nature of the question that led the sages to conclude that the child was rebellious? On the face of it, the query seems innocent. The child is presumably not yet bar mitzva.[2] He does not yet have obligations in Jewish law. He is therefore asking, rightly, "What does this law, to which you are obligated but I am not, mean?"

There are other perplexing features. What is the fundamental principle of faith the child denies? What, in any case, is wrong with asking? Judaism embodies the profound insight that it is only through the questions we ask, that we learn. How then can it be right to condemn a child for merely making a query, even if it is badly phrased? And how can any parent be so heartless as to say to a child: "if you had been there you would not have been saved?" Clearly, there is more going on in this passage than a superficial reading would suggest.

Rabbi Meir Simcha of Dvinsk, in his commentary *Meshekh Ḥokhma*,[3] makes a profound observation. What is significant, he says, is

---

1. Haggada of Pesaḥ, an expanded version of the text in *Mekhilta*, commentary to *Bo*, 18.
2. The standard meaning of the word "son" (*ben*) in the context of Jewish education is of a minor (below the age of thirteen in the case of boys, twelve in the case of girls).
3. *Meshekh Ḥokhma*, commentary to Exodus 13:14.

not so much the question, as the verb with which it is introduced. In the other cases, the child is described as *asking*. In this case he is described as *saying*. You ask a question, you do not say one. It is therefore clear that the child does not wish to know. Instead he wishes *not* to know. His question is rhetorical. He is not asking, but expressing cynicism: "What is this strange and meaningless ritual?" R. Meir Simcha's close reading of the text helps us understand why the sages – in attributing this verse to the rebellious child – were in fact listening carefully to the nuances of the verse itself.

The Talmud offers another approach. It translates the question, "What does this ceremony mean to you?" as "What is this burdensome effort that you impose on us each year?"[4] I suspect that the sages were responding to yet another word in the verse, namely *avoda*, "ceremony." *Avoda* has a range of meanings often lost in translation. On the one hand it means service – what we are commanded to do for God. On the other, it means slavery – what the Israelites were forced to do for the Egyptians. *Avoda* is a key word in the opening chapter of Exodus:

> So they, Egypt, made the children of Israel subservient with crushing labour. They embittered their lives with hard servitude in loam and in bricks and with all kinds of servitude in the field – all their service in which they made them subservient with crushing labour. (Exodus 1:13–14)

In these two verses alone, the word *avoda*, in noun or verb form, appears no less than five times (seven times in all in Exodus 1–2; a sevenfold repetition is always a sign that the text is signalling a key term). It is what robbed the Israelites of their freedom. Yet the same word is also cited as the key to their liberation:

> And God said, "I will be with you. And this will be the sign to you that it is I who have sent you: When you have brought the people out of Egypt, you will worship God on this mountain." (Exodus 3:12)

4. Talmud Yerushalmi, *Pesaḥim* 10:4.

And again:

> Then say to Pharaoh, 'This is what the Lord says: Israel is My firstborn son, and I told you, "Let My son go, so he may worship Me."' (Exodus 4:22)

In both cases the term used for "worship" is *avoda*. The meaning of the explanation in the Talmud is now clear. The son is saying: "What advantage did we gain by the exodus? In Egypt we were *avadim*, slaves. Leaving Egypt we became *avadim*, servants. The only difference is a change of master. Then we served Pharaoh. Now we serve God. But that is a distinction without a difference. Either way, we are not free. Either way, we carry the weight of burdensome effort. Then we were subject to Pharaoh's law, now we are subject to God's law. But do not tell me that *avoda* means freedom. It means the opposite."

This too is a profound insight. The word *avoda* in the child's question is significant (especially in contrast to the "wise" son's terms, "stipulations, decrees and laws," which focus on the positive aspects of Jewish law in its several varieties). Moreover the Talmud is placing in the mouth of the rebellious child the classic argument that leads, eventually, to the downfall of societies, namely that the only freedom that counts is the freedom to do what you like. That is not freedom but anarchy; not liberty but lawlessness.

It is the point classically made by Edmund Burke: "Men are qualified for civil liberty, in exact proportion to their disposition to put moral chains upon their appetites." Society depends on a system of restraints, and these can be imposed from the outside by police, or from within, in the form of conscience. The less law is internalized as conscience, the more society – if it is to avoid anarchy – will resemble a police state. "It is ordained in the eternal constitution of things, that men of intemperate minds cannot be free. Their passions form their fetters."[5]

Freud said much the same in his *Civilization and Its Discontents*. Civilization, he argued, is the capacity to defer the gratification of instinct,

---

5. Edmund Burke, *Reflections on the Revolution in France* (Oxford University Press, 1993), 289.

and the way this is achieved is by internalizing external authority through conscience or what he called the super-ego.[6] That is one of the central features of a life lived according to halakha.

There is however one source which sheds a new light on the whole passage. It occurs in the *Mekhilta*, a midrashic commentary on Exodus dating from the period of the Mishna:

> "I do this because of what the Lord did for me…" Why is this said? Because it says, "What does this ceremony mean to you?" This refers to a wicked child who excludes himself from the community, and because he excludes himself from the community, you too should exclude him from the community by saying, "I do this because of what the Lord did for me when I came out of Egypt." Me, not you. And because you have excluded yourself from the community, had you been there [in Egypt] you would not have been saved.[7]

What is striking about this passage is that it only mentions the rebellious child, not the other three. The fact that the source is a very early one suggests that there was a time when the passage relating to the wicked son stood on its own, and was only later incorporated into a larger passage, dealing with four sons, as it appears in the Haggada.

If so, we can place the text in a highly specific historical and halakhic context. There was a time, under both the Greeks and the Romans, during which Hellenistic culture had an enormous appeal for many Jews. They assimilated. They were drawn to Greek art and drama. They took part in athletic competitions. For them Hellenism was cosmopolitan, Judaism merely parochial. Both periods (the Greek in the second century BCE, the Roman in the first century CE) represented crises of Jewish identity, not unlike the one Diaspora Jewry is going through today.

What principle was at stake? During the medieval periods of

---

6. Sigmund Freud, "Civilization and Its Discontents," in *The Complete Psychological Works of Sigmund Freud*, vol XXI (London: Vintage, 2001), esp. 23–133.
7. *Mekhilta*, commentary to *Bo*, 17. A shorter version can be found in *Mekhilta de-Rabbi Shimon bar Yochai*, ed. Epstein, 26.

forced conversions, under Christianity and Islam, the principle was clear. It was apostasy, changing one's religion. By contrast, Greek and Roman culture – like secular culture today – were not religions (to be sure, they had gods and religious rites, but these did not appeal to Jews. On the contrary, many Romans admired Judaism and adopted aspects of it themselves). What was at stake were styles of behaviour, not modes of belief: assimilation, not apostasy. The individuals concerned were not so much giving up Jewish practice, though doubtless they did that as well, but abandoning Jewish identity. They no longer saw themselves as Jews but as Greek or Roman citizens, Hellenes.

This explains a remarkable ruling of Maimonides. In the course of listing the various categories of sinners, heretics and apostates who "have no share in the world to come" he adds the following:

> One who separates himself from the community, even if he does not commit a transgression, but only holds aloof from the congregation of Israel, does not fulfil religious precepts in common with his people, shows himself indifferent when they are in distress, does not observe their fasts, but goes his own way as if he were one of the Gentiles and did not belong to the Jewish people – such a person has no share in the world to come.[8]

Almost certainly, this ruling and the passage from the *Mekhilta* refer to the same phenomenon, namely, assimilation as the abandonment of Jewish identity.

Both should be read in the context of yet another passage, this time from the Talmud. The context is conversion – a would-be proselyte who comes to the *Beit Din* (rabbinical court) wishing to become a Jew:

> Our rabbis taught: nowadays, if a person desires to become a proselyte, he is to be addressed as follows: "What reason have you for desiring to become a proselyte? Do you not know that Israel at the present time is persecuted and oppressed, despised, harassed and overcome by afflictions?" If he replies, "I know and

---

8. Rambam, *Mishneh Torah*, Hilkhot Teshuva, 3:11.

yet am unworthy," he is accepted immediately…. He is also to be addressed thus: "Do you not know that before you came to this condition, if you had eaten suet you would not have been punishable with *karet* [excision, the most severe form of divine punishment]; if you had profaned the Sabbath you would not have been punishable with stoning. But now, were you to eat suet you would be punished with *karet*, and were you to profane the Sabbath, you would be punished with stoning."[9]

What is clear from this passage is that there are two components of Jewish belonging, not one. There is the acceptance of Jewish law (forbidden foods, the Sabbath and so on). There is also, separately, the acceptance of Jewish identity, namely a willingness to be part of the often tragic terms of Jewish history ("persecuted and oppressed"). The late Rabbi Joseph B. Soloveitchik called these, respectively, *brit ye'ud* (the covenant of destiny) and *brit goral* (the covenant of fate).[10] Destiny is what we do. Fate is what happens to us. One is a code of action, halakha. The other is a form of imagination, the story we tell ourselves as to who we are and where we belong.

There is an abandonment of Judaism that consists in giving up its laws of conduct. But there is another kind of abandonment – no longer seeing oneself as part of the Jewish people, sharing its fate and hope or identifying with the plight of other Jews. That is what Maimonides means by "separating oneself from the community," and its classic source is the passage in the *Mekhilta* about the "wicked child." When this passage was incorporated into the Haggada and became part of an exposition about four kinds of children sitting around the Seder table, it became less easy to understand. The children of the Haggada are, after all, young. They are participating in a religious event. It becomes difficult to understand why one should be singled out for such rebuke. But once we recover the original context – a mature individual who has abandoned his people

9. *Yevamot* 47a.
10. Rabbi Joseph Soloveitchik, *Kol Dodi Dofek*. English translation in Bernhard Rosenberg and Fred Heuman, eds., *Theological and Halakhic Reflections on the Holocaust* (New York: Ktav, 1992), 51–118.

and become no longer a Jew but a Roman – the text makes sense. It also tells us something profound about Jewish identity.

Judaism is a communal faith. This is the "principle" that the rebellious child denies. Judaism is not addressed to individuals. Nor is it addressed to humanity as a whole. God chose a people, a nation, and asked them at Mount Sinai to pledge themselves, not only to Him but also to one another. *Emuna*, that key word of Judaism, usually translated as "faith," more properly means loyalty – to God, but also to the people He has chosen as the carriers of His mission, the witnesses to His presence. To be sure, Jews are sometimes exasperating. Rashi, commenting on Moses' charge to his successor Joshua, says that he told him: "Know that they [the people you are about to lead] are troublesome and contentious."[11] But he also told him: "You are fortunate for you will have the privilege of leading the children of God Himself."[12]

In this fundamental idea there is a measure of hope. To be sure, not all Jews today obey Jewish law. But many who do not, nevertheless identify with Israel and the Jewish people. They plead its case. They support its cause. When Israel suffers, they too feel pain. They are implicated in the fate of the people. They know only too well that "Israel at the present time are persecuted and oppressed, despised, harassed and overcome by afflictions" but they do not walk away. They may not be religiously observant, but they are loyal – and loyalty is an essential part (if only a part) of what Jewish faith is.

From the negative, therefore, we can infer the positive: that a Jew who does not say "You" when Jews or Israel are under attack, but "Us," has made a fundamental affirmation – to be part of a people, sharing in its responsibilities, identifying with its hopes and fears, celebrations and griefs. That is the covenant of fate, and it still summons us today.

11. Rashi, commentary to Numbers 27:19.
12. Rashi, commentary to Numbers 27:18.

Letting Go of Hate

There is a detail in the story of the exodus that is highly empha-sised in the Torah, yet at first sight it appears almost unintelligible. Here is the command:

> Now the Lord had said to Moses, "I will bring one more plague on Pharaoh and on Egypt. After that, he will let you go from here, and when he does, he will drive you out completely. Tell the people that men and women alike are to ask their neighbours for articles of silver and gold." (Exodus 11:1–2)

And here is its fulfilment:

> The Egyptians urged the people to hurry and leave the country. "For otherwise," they said, "we will all die!" So the people took their dough before the yeast was added, and carried it on their shoulders in kneading troughs wrapped in clothing. The Israelites did as Moses instructed and asked the Egyptians for articles of silver and gold and for clothing. The Lord had made the Egyptians

favourably disposed towards the people, and they gave them what they asked for; so they plundered the Egyptians. (12:33–36)

Why the silver and gold? The Israelites were in such a hurry to leave, and the Egyptians so hasty in urging their departure, that they did not even have time for the dough to rise. Why then was God so insistent that they take the time to ask for these parting gifts? What conceivable use did they have for them in the long journey across the wilderness?

Our perplexity is made all the more acute when we remember what they actually did with the gold. They used it to commit the worst sin of those years: the making of a Golden Calf. The Talmud says that Moses referred to this fact in defending Israel. In effect, he said to God: Had you not told them to take gold from Egypt, they would not have had the materials with which to make the calf![1]

Yet we cannot doubt that this detail is fundamental to the story, because God refers to it in his first encounter with Moses, at the burning bush, before the exodus had begun – long before Moses had returned to Egypt:

> "And I will make the Egyptians favorably disposed towards this people, so that when you leave you will not go empty-handed. Every woman is to ask her neighbour and any woman living in her house for articles of silver and gold and for clothing, which you will put on your sons and daughters. And so you will plunder [*venitzaltem*] the Egyptians." (Exodus 3:21–22)

Why was this so important?

It is not until we reach the end of the Mosaic books that we can begin to understand it, only in retrospect. Two details from the book of Deuteronomy provide the key. The first has to do with the liberation of slaves:

> If a fellow Hebrew, a man or a woman, sells himself to you and serves you six years, in the seventh year you must let him go free.

---

1.   *Berakhot* 32a.

And when you release him, do not send him away empty-handed. Supply him liberally from your flock, your threshing floor and your winepress. Give to him as the Lord your God has blessed you. Remember that you were slaves in Egypt and the Lord your God redeemed you. That is why I give you this command today. (Deuteronomy 15:12–15)

The second is one of the most striking commands of all. Moses insists:

Do not hate an Edomite, for he is your brother. Do not hate an Egyptian, because you were a stranger in his land. (23:7)

This is remarkable. The Israelites had been enslaved by the Egyptians. They owed them no debt of gratitude. On the contrary, they were entitled to feel a lingering resentment. Yet Moses insists that they should not do so. They should bear the Egyptians no ill will. Why? In this brief command we have one of the most profound insights into the nature of a free society.

A people driven by hate are not – cannot be – free. Had the people carried with them a burden of hatred and a desire for revenge, Moses would have taken the Israelites out of Egypt, but he would not have taken Egypt out of the Israelites. They would still be there, bound by chains of anger as restricting as any metal. To be free you have to let go of hate.

There is a fundamental difference between living *with* the past and living *in* the past. Judaism is a religion of memory. We remember the exodus annually, even daily. But we do so for the sake of the future, not the past. "Do not oppress the stranger," says the Torah, "because you know what it feels like to be a stranger." In other words: what you suffered, do not inflict. Memory is a moral tutorial. In Santayana's famous words: "Those who cannot remember the past, are destined to repeat it."[2] Israel remembers its past precisely in order *not* to repeat it. Moses' message is: remember, but not in order to hate.

That means drawing a line over the resentments of the past. That

---

2. George Santayana, *The Life of Reason*, vol. 1, *Reason in Common Sense* (Scribner's, 1905), 284.

is why, when a slave went free, his master had to give him gifts. This was not to compensate for the fact of slavery. There is no way of giving back the years spent in servitude. But there is a way of ensuring that the parting is done with goodwill, with some symbolic compensation. The gifts allow the former slave to reach emotional closure; to feel that a new chapter is beginning; to leave without anger and a sense of humiliation. One who has received gifts finds it hard to hate.

That is the significance of the silver and gold taken from the Egyptians by the Israelites at the express command of God. The early twentieth-century commentator Benno Jacob translated the word *venitzaltem* in Exodus 3:22 as "You shall save," not "You shall plunder" the Egyptians. The gifts they took from their neighbours were intended, Jacob argues, to persuade the Israelites that it was not the Egyptians as a whole, but only Pharaoh and the leadership, who were responsible for their enslavement.[3] They were meant to save the Egyptians from any possible future revenge by Israel.

The message could not be more germane to our situation in the early twenty-first century. In an age riven by ethnic and religious conflict, the message of the Torah rings true in our time. To be free, you have to let go of hate.

3. Cited in Chief Rabbi J.H. Hertz, *The Pentateuch and Haftorahs* (London: Soncino, 1977), 217.

Beshallaḥ
בשלח

The Israelites leave Egypt. God deliberately leads them on a circuitous route. They come up against the Reed Sea. Pharaoh, having changed his mind about letting them go, pursues them with horses and chariots. The people come close to despair. Then, in one of the supreme miracles of history, the sea divides. The Israelites pass through and sing a momentous song of faith and deliverance. But their troubles are not over. They lack drinkable water, and food. God sends both: oasis springs and then water from a rock, and manna from heaven. The *parasha* ends as it began, with the prospect of war, this time against the Amalekites.

In the first of the following studies we look at Maimonides' view as to why God did not lead the people directly to the promised land. The second analyzes a striking feature of the narrative of the division of the sea. The Torah tells the story two ways, one natural, the other supernatural, giving us two perspectives on the nature of the miraculous. The third explores a rabbinic debate about the way Moses and the Israelites sang the song at the sea – a debate that turns on four different views of the nature of leadership. The fourth looks at the crossing of the sea as a turning point in the relationship between God and the people, from one in which God fights the people's battles, to one in which He gives them the courage to fight their own.

Time and Social Transformation

> Now when Pharaoh let the people go, God did not
> lead them by the way of the land of the Philistines,
> although it was nearer; for God said, "The people
> may have a change of heart when they see war,
> and return to Egypt." So God led the people
> roundabout, by way of the wilderness at the Sea
> of Reeds. (Exodus 13:17–18)

So begins the *parasha* of *Beshallaḥ*. On the face of it, this is a
minor detail in the larger story of the exodus. Yet it is the key text in one
of the most fascinating chapters in medieval Jewish thought. The man
who wrote it was Moses Maimonides, in his great philosophical work,
The Guide for the Perplexed.[1]

The context in which it is discussed is deeply controversial. In *The*

---

1. There are two good English translations: M. Friedlander, *The Guide for the Perplexed*
(London: Kegan Paul, 2006), and Shlomo Pines, *The Guide of the Perplexed*, 2 vols.
(University of Chicago Press, 1963).

Guide, Maimonides poses a fundamental question. Why, if the sacrificial system is so central to Judaism, were the prophets so critical of it?[2] He does not ask a second question, but we should: if sacrifices are the primary form of worshipping God, how did Judaism survive without them for twenty centuries from the destruction of the Second Temple until today?

Maimonides' answer is that sacrifices are secondary; prayer – the uniting of the soul of the individual with the mind of God – is primary. Judaism could thus survive the loss of the outer form of worship, because the inner form – prayer – remained intact.

Maimonides recognises that this idea is open to an obvious challenge. If sacrifices are secondary, and prayer primary, why did God not dispense with sacrifices altogether and immediately? His answer – it was, and remains, deeply controversial – is that the Israelites of Moses' day could not conceive of a form of worship that did not involve sacrifice. That was the norm in the ancient world. God is beyond time, but human beings live within time. We cannot take ourselves out of, say, the twenty-first century and project ourselves a thousand years from now. Inescapably, we live in the now, not eternity.

This leads Maimonides to his fundamental assertion.[3] There is no such thing as sudden, drastic, revolutionary change in the world we inhabit. Trees take time to grow. The seasons shade imperceptibly into one another. Day fades into night. Processes take time, and there are no shortcuts.

If this is true of nature, it is all the more so of human nature. There can be little doubt that from the outset, the Torah is opposed to slavery. The free God desires the free worship of free human beings. That one person should own and control another is an offence against human dignity. Yet the Torah permits slavery, while at the same time

---

2. Maimonides' prooftexts are "Does the Lord delight in burnt offerings and sacrifices as much as in obeying the voice of the Lord?" (1 Samuel 15:22); "The multitude of your sacrifices – what are they to Me? says the Lord." (Isaiah 1:11); and "For when I brought your forefathers out of Egypt and spoke to them, I did not command them about burnt offerings and sacrifices, but I commanded them this: Obey me, and I will be your God and you will be My people" (Jeremiah 7:22–23).

3. Rambam, *The Guide for the Perplexed,* III:32.

restricting and humanizing it. Looking back with the full perspective of history, we know that slavery was not abolished in Britain and America until the nineteenth century – and in the case of America, not without a civil war. Change takes time.

This leads to a deeper question. Why did God not circumvent human nature? Why did He not simply intervene and *make* the Israelites of Moses' day see that various practices of the ancient world were wrong? Here, Maimonides states a truth he saw as fundamental to Judaism. God sometimes intervenes to change nature. We call these interventions miracles. But God never intervenes to change human nature. To do so would be to compromise human free will. That is something God, on principle, never does.[4]

To put it simply: it would have been easy for God to create a billion computers programmed to sing His praises continually. But that would not be worship. Freedom of the will is not accidental to human existence as Judaism conceives it. It is of its very essence. Worship is not worship if it is coerced. Virtue is not virtue if we are compelled by inner or outer forces over which we have no control. In creating humanity, God, as it were, placed Himself under a statute of self limitation. He had to be patient. He could not force the pace of the moral development of mankind without destroying the very thing He had created. This self limitation – what the kabbalists called *tzimtzum* – was God's greatest act of love. He gave humanity the freedom to grow. But that inevitably meant that change in the affairs of mankind would be slow.

Maimonides' prooftext for this assertion is the verse with which our *parasha* begins: "Now when Pharaoh let the people go, God did not lead them by the way of the land of the Philistines." God feared that, seeing war, the Israelites would panic and want to go back. Why did God not put courage into their hearts? Because God does not intervene in human nature. Maimonides, however, goes further. It was no accident that the generation that left Egypt was not the generation to cross the Jordan and enter the promised land. That privilege belonged to their children:

---

4. See essay "The Hardened Heart," p. 47, for a discussion of the case of God hardening Pharaoh's heart, which seems to contradict this idea.

It was the result of God's wisdom that the Israelites were led about in the wilderness until they acquired courage. For it is a well-known fact that travelling in the wilderness, deprived of bodily enjoyments like bathing, produces courage…Besides, another generation arose during the wanderings, that had not been accustomed to degradation and slavery.[5]

In other words: it takes a generation born in freedom to build a society of freedom.

It is hard to overemphasise the importance of this insight. The modern world was formed through four revolutions: the British (1640), the American (1776), the French (1789) and the Russian (1917). Two – the British and the American – led to a slow but genuine transformation towards democracy, universal franchise, and respect for human dignity. The French and Russian revolutions, however, led to regimes that were even worse than those they replaced: the "Terror" in France, and Stalinist communism in Russia.[6]

The difference was that the British and American revolutions, led by the Puritans, were inspired by the Hebrew Bible.[7] The French and Russian revolutions were inspired by philosophy: Rousseau's in the first, Karl Marx's in the second. Tanakh understands the role of time in human affairs. Change is slow and evolutionary. Philosophy lacks that understanding of time, and tends to promote revolution. What makes revolutions fail is the belief that by changing structures of power, you can change human behaviour. There is some truth in this, but also a signifi-

---

5. Rambam, *The Guide for the Perplexed*, III:32.
6. One of the major differences was that the English and American revolutions focused on the limits of state action and governmental power. The French and Russian aimed at a total transformation of society, through the instrumentality of the state. See J.L. Talmon, *The Origins of Totalitarian Democracy* (London: Secker and Warburg, 1952).
7. For the role of the Bible in the English revolution, see Michael Walzer, *Revolution of the Saints* (New York: Atheneum, 1968); Christopher Hill, *The English Bible and the Seventeenth-Century Revolution* (London: Allen Lane, 1993). For its role in the American revolution, see Perry Miller, *The New England Mind: The Seventeenth Century* (Harvard University Press, 1963). More generally, see Michael Walzer, *Exodus and Revolution* (New York: Basic Books, 1985).

cant falsehood. Political change can be rapid. Changing human nature is very slow indeed. It takes generations, even centuries and millennia.

The shape of the modern world would have been very different if France and Russia had understood the significance of the opening verse of *Beshallaḥ*. Change takes time. Even God himself does not force the pace. That is why He led the Israelites on a circuitous route, knowing that they could not face the full challenge of liberty immediately. There are no shortcuts on the long walk to freedom.

The Divided Sea: Natural or Supernatural?

The splitting of the Reed Sea is engraved in Jewish memory. We recite it daily during the morning service, at the transition from the Verses of Praise to the beginning of communal prayer. We speak of it again after the Shema, just before the *Amida*. It was the supreme miracle of the exodus. But in what sense?

If we listen carefully to the narratives, we can distinguish two perspectives. This is the first:

> The waters were divided, and the Israelites went through the sea on dry ground, with a wall of water on their right and on their left... The water flowed back and covered the chariots and horsemen – the entire army of Pharaoh that had followed the Israelites into the sea. Not one of them survived. But the Israelites went through the sea on dry ground, with a wall of water on their right and on their left. (Exodus 14:22, 28–29)

The same note is struck in the Song at the Sea:

> By the blast of Your nostrils

the waters piled up.
The surging waters stood firm like a wall;
the deep waters congealed in the heart of the sea.

(Exodus 15:8)

The emphasis here is on the supernatural dimension of what happened. Water, which normally flows, stood upright. The sea parted to expose dry land. The laws of nature were suspended. Something happened for which there can be no scientific explanation.

However, if we listen carefully, we can also hear a different note:

Then Moses stretched out his hand over the sea, and all that night the Lord drove the sea back with a strong east wind and turned it into dry land. (Exodus 14:21)

Here there is not a sudden change in the behaviour of water, with no apparent cause. God brings a wind that, in the course of several hours, drives the waters back. Or consider this passage:

During the last watch of the night the Lord looked down from the pillar of fire and cloud at the Egyptian army and threw it into confusion. He made the wheels of their chariots come off so that they had difficulty driving. The Egyptians said, "Let's get away from the Israelites! The Lord is fighting for them against Egypt." (*Exodus* 14:24–25).

The emphasis here is less on miracle than on irony. The great military assets of the Egyptians – making them almost invulnerable in their day – were their horses and chariots. These were Egypt's specialty. They still were, in the time of Solomon, five centuries later:

Solomon accumulated chariots and horses; he had fourteen hundred chariots and twelve thousand horses, which he kept in the chariot cities and also with him in Jerusalem … They imported a chariot from Egypt for six hundred shekels of silver, and a horse for a hundred and fifty. (1 Kings 10:26–29)

Viewed from this perspective, the events that took place could be described as follows: The Israelites had arrived at the Reed Sea at a point at which it was shallow. Possibly there was a ridge in the sea bed, normally covered by water, but occasionally – when, for example, a fierce east wind blows – exposed. This is how the Cambridge University physicist Colin Humphreys puts it in his *The Miracles of Exodus*:

> Wind tides are well known to oceanographers. For example, a strong wind blowing along Lake Erie, one of the Great Lakes, has produced water elevation differences of as much as sixteen feet between Toledo, Ohio, on the west, and Buffalo, New York, on the east…There are reports that Napoleon was almost killed by a "sudden high tide" while he was crossing shallow water near the head of the Gulf of Suez.[1]

In the case of the wind that exposed the ridge in the bed of the sea, the consequences were dramatic. Suddenly the Israelites, travelling on foot, had an immense advantage over the Egyptian chariots that were pursuing them. Their wheels became stuck in the mud. The charioteers made ferocious efforts to free them, only to find that they quickly became mired again. The Egyptian army could neither advance nor retreat. So intent were they on the trapped wheels, and so reluctant were they to abandon their prized war machines, the chariots, that they failed to notice that the wind had dropped and the water was returning. By the time they realized what was happening, they were trapped. The ridge was now covered with sea water in either direction, and the island of dry land in the middle was shrinking by the minute. The mightiest army of the ancient world was defeated, and its warriors drowned, not by a superior army, not by human opposition at all, but by their own folly in being so focused on capturing the Israelites that they ignored the fact that they were driving into mud where their chariots could not go.

We have here two ways of seeing the same events: one natural, the

---

1. Colin Humphreys, *The Miracles of Exodus* (Continuum, 2003), 247–48. For a similar analysis, see James K. Hoffmeier, *Israel in Egypt: The Evidence for the Authenticity of the Exodus Tradition* (Oxford University Press: 1996), 199–215.

other supernatural. The supernatural explanation – that the waters stood upright – is immensely powerful, and so it entered Jewish memory. But the natural explanation is no less compelling. The Egyptians' strength proved to be their weakness. The weakness of the Israelites became their strength. On this reading, what was significant was less the supernatural, than the moral dimension of what happened. God visits the sins on the sinners. He mocks those who mock Him. He showed the Egyptian army, which revelled in its might, that the weak were stronger than they – just as He later did with the pagan prophet Bilaam, who prided himself in his prophetic powers and was then shown that his donkey (who could see the angel Bilaam could not see) was a better prophet than he was.

To put it another way: a miracle is not necessarily something that suspends natural law. It is, rather, an event for which there may be a natural explanation, but which – happening when, where and how it did – evokes wonder, such that even the most hardened sceptic senses that God has intervened in history. The weak are saved; those in danger, delivered. More significant still is the moral message such an event conveys: that hubris is punished by nemesis; that the proud are humbled and the humble given pride; that there is justice in history, often hidden but sometimes gloriously revealed.

This idea can be taken further. Emil Fackenheim has spoken of "epoch-making events" that transform the course of history.[2] More obscurely, but along similar lines, the French philosopher Alain Badiou has proposed the concept of an "event" as a "rupture in ontology" through which individuals are brought face to face with a truth that changes them and their world.[3] It is as if all normal perception fades away and we know that we are in the presence of something momentous, to which we sense we must remain faithful for the rest of our lives. "The appropriation of Presence is mediated by an event."[4] It is through transformative events that we feel ourselves addressed, summoned, by something beyond history, breaking through into history. In this sense, the division of the Reed Sea was something other and deeper than a

2. Emil Fackenheim, *To Mend the World* (New York: Schocken, 1982), 14–20.
3. Alain Badiou, *Being and Event*, trans. Oliver Feltham (Continuum, 2006).
4. Ibid., 255.

suspension of the laws of nature. It was the transformative moment at which the people "believed in the Lord and in Moses His servant" (14:31) and called themselves "the people You acquired" (15:16).

Not all Jewish thinkers focused on the supernatural dimension of God's involvement in human history. Indeed, Maimonides insisted that "Israel did not believe in Moses our teacher because of the signs he performed."[5]

What made Moses the greatest of the prophets, for Maimonides, is not that he performed supernatural deeds but that, at Mount Sinai, he brought the people the word of God.

In general, the sages tended to downplay the dimension of the miraculous, even in the case of the greatest miracle of all, the division of the sea. That is the meaning of the following midrash, commenting on the verse, "Moses stretched out his hand over the sea, and at daybreak the sea went back to its full flow [*le'eitano*]" (Exodus 14:27):

> Rabbi Jonathan said: "The Holy One, blessed be He, made a condition with the sea [at the beginning of creation], that it should split asunder for the Israelites. That is the meaning of 'the sea went back to its full flow' – [read not *le-eitano* but] *letenao*, "the condition" that God had earlier stipulated."[6]

The implication is that the division of the sea was, as it were, programmed into creation from the outset.[7] It was less a suspension of nature than an event written into nature from the beginning, to be triggered at the appropriate moment in the unfolding of history.

We even find an extraordinary debate among the sages as to whether miracles are a sign of merit or the opposite. The Talmud tells the story of a man whose wife died, leaving a nursing child. The father was too poor to be able to afford a wet-nurse, so a miracle occurred and

---

5. Rambam, *Mishneh Torah*, Yesodei HaTorah 8:1.
6. *Bereshit Raba* 5:5.
7. In general, the sages said that all future miracles were created at twilight at the end of the six days of creation (Mishna, *Avot* 5:6).

he himself gave milk until the child was weaned. On this, the Talmud records the following difference of opinion:

> Rav Joseph said: "Come and see how great was this man that such a miracle was wrought for him." Abbaye said to him: "On the contrary, how inferior was this man, that the natural order was changed for him." [8]

According to Abbaye, greater are those to whom good things happen without the need for miracles. The genius of the biblical narrative of the crossing of the Reed Sea is that it does not resolve the issue one way or another. It gives us both perspectives. To some, the miracle was the suspension of the laws of nature. To others, the fact that there was a naturalistic explanation did not make the event any less miraculous. That the Israelites should arrive at the sea precisely where the waters were unexpectedly shallow, that a strong east wind should blow when and how it did, and that the Egyptians' greatest military asset should have proved their undoing – all these things were wonders, and we have never forgotten them.

8.   *Shabbat* 53b.

Four Models of Leadership

> *"That day, God saved Israel from the hands of the Egyptians... The Israelites saw the great power God had displayed against the Egyptians, and the people were in awe of God. They believed in God and in His servant Moses. Moses and the Israelites then sang this song to God and said, saying... "*
> *(Exodus 14:30–15:1)*

The Song at the Sea was one of the great epiphanies of history. The sages said that even the humblest of Jews saw at that moment what even the greatest of prophets who lived afterwards was not privileged to see.[1] For the first time they broke into collective song – a song we still recite every day. There is a fascinating discussion among the sages

---

1. *Mekhilta*, commentary to Exodus 15:2, Horowitz-Rabin edition (Jerusalem: 1970), 126.

as to how exactly they sang. On this, there were four opinions. Three appear in the tractate of *Sota*:[2]

> Our rabbis taught: On that day Rabbi Akiva expounded: When the Israelites came up from the Reed Sea, they wanted to sing a song. How did they sing it? Like an adult who reads the Hallel [for the congregation] and they respond after him with the leading word. Moses said, "I will sing to the Lord," and they responded, "I will sing to the Lord." Moses said, "For He has triumphed gloriously," and they responded, "I will sing to the Lord."
>
> R. Eliezer son of R. Yose the Galilean said: It was like a child who reads the Hallel [for a congregation] and they repeat after him all that he says. Moses said, "I will sing to the Lord," and they responded, "I will sing to the Lord." Moses said, "For He has triumphed gloriously," and they responded, "For He has triumphed gloriously."
>
> R. Neḥemia said: It was like a schoolteacher who recites the Shema in the synagogue. He begins first and they respond after him.

According to Rabbi Akiva, Moses sang the song phrase by phrase, and after each phrase the people responded, "I will sing to the Lord" – their way, as it were, of saying Amen to each line.

According to Rabbi Eliezer son of Rabbi Yose the Galilean, Moses recited the song phrase by phrase, and they repeated each phrase after he had said it.

According to Rabbi Nehemiah, Moses and the people sang the whole song together. Rashi explains that all the people were seized by divine inspiration and miraculously, the same words came into their minds at the same time.[3] There is a fourth view, found in the *Mekhilta*:[4]

2. *Sota* 30b.
3. Rashi to *Sota*, ad loc., based on *Mekhilta*, commentary to Exodus 15:1, Horowitz-Rabin edition, 115.
4. Ibid., 119.

R. Eliezer ben Taddai said, Moses began [each verse] and the Israelites repeated what he had said and then completed the verse. Moses began by saying, "I will sing to the Lord, for He has triumphed gloriously," and the Israelites repeated what he had said, and then completed the verse with him, saying, "I will sing to the Lord, for He has triumphed gloriously, the horse and its rider He hurled into the sea." Moses began [the next verse] saying, "The Lord is my strength and my song," and the Israelites repeated and then completed the verse with him, saying, "The Lord is my strength and my song; He has become my salvation." Moses began [the next verse] saying, "The Lord is a warrior," and the Israelites repeated and then completed the verse with him, saying, "The Lord is a warrior, Lord is His name."

Technically, as the Talmud explains, the sages are debating the implication of the (apparently) superfluous words *vayomru lemor*, "and said, saying," which they understood to mean "repeating." What did the Israelites repeat? For Rabbi Akiva it was the first words of the song only, which they repeated as a litany. For Rabbi Eliezer son of Rabbi Yose the Galilean they repeated the whole song, phrase by phrase. For Rabbi Nehemiah they recited the entire song in unison. For Rabbi Eliezer ben Taddai they repeated the opening phrase of each line, but then completed the whole verse without Moses having to teach it to them.

Read thus, we have before us a localised debate on the meaning of a biblical verse. There is, however, a deeper issue at stake. To understand this, we must look at another Talmudic passage, on the face of it unrelated to the passage in *Sota*. It appears in the tractate of *Kiddushin*, and poses a fascinating question.

There are various people we are commanded to honour: a parent, a teacher (i.e., a rabbi), the Nasi (religious head of the Jewish community), and a king. May any of these four types renounce the honour that is their due?

R. Yitzhak ben Shila said in the name of R. Mattena, in the name of R. Hisda: If a father renounces the honour due to him, it is renounced, but if a rabbi renounces the honour due to him it is not renounced. R. Yosef ruled: Even if a rabbi renounces his honour, it is renounced...

R. Ashi said: Even on the view that a rabbi may renounce his honour, if a Nasi renounces his honour, the renunciation is invalid... [An objection to this view is then brought by the Talmud].

Rather, if [the teaching of R. Ashi] was stated, it was stated thus: Even on the view that a Nasi may renounce his honour, yet a king may not renounce his honour, as it is said, You shall surely set a king over you, meaning, his authority [literally "fear"] should be over you.[5]

Each of these people exercises a leadership role: parent to child, teacher to disciple, Nasi to the community and king to the nation. Analysed in depth, the passages makes it clear that these four roles occupy different places on the spectrum between authority predicated on the person, and authority vested in the holder of an office.[6] The more the relationship is personal, the more easily honour can be renounced. At one extreme is the role of a parent (intensely personal), at the other that of king (wholly official).

I suggest that this was the issue at stake in the argument over how Moses and the Israelites sang the Song at the Sea. For Rabbi Akiva, Moses was like a king. He spoke, and the people merely answered Amen (in this case, the words "I will sing to the Lord.") For Rabbi Eliezer son of Rabbi Yose the Galilean, he was like a teacher. Moses spoke, and the Israelites repeated, phrase by phrase, what he had said. For Rabbi Nehemiah, he was like a Nasi among his rabbinical colleagues (the passage in Kiddushin, which holds that a Nasi may renounce his honour, makes it clear that this is only among his fellow rabbis). The relationship was collegial: Moses began, but thereafter, they sung in unison. For Rabbi

5. See the passage in full in Kiddushin 32a–b; for reasons of space I have only quoted a fragment here.

6. Max Weber famously called this the distinction between charismatic and bureaucratic authority. See Max Weber, The Theory of Social and Economic Organisation (New York: Free Press, 1964).

Eliezer ben Taddai, Moses was like a father. He began, but allowed the Israelites to complete each verse. This is the great truth about parenthood, made clear in the first glimpse we have of Abraham:

> Terach took his son Abram, his grandson Lot son of Haran, and his daughter-in-law Sarai, the wife of Abram, and together they set out from Ur of the Chaldeans to go to Canaan. But when they came to Haran, they settled there. (Genesis 31:11)

Abraham completed the journey his father began. To be a parent is to want one's children to go further than you did. That too, for Rabbi Eliezer ben Taddai, was Moses' relationship to the Israelites.

The prelude to the Song at the Sea states that the people "believed in God and in his servant Moses" – the first time they are described as believing in Moses' leadership. On this, the sages asked: What is it to be a leader of the Jewish people? Is it to hold official authority, of which the supreme example is a king ("The rabbis are called kings"[7])? Is it to have the kind of personal relationship with one's followers that rests not on honour and deference but on encouraging people to grow, accept responsibility and continue the journey you have begun? Or is it something in between?

There is no single answer. At times, Moses asserted his authority (for example, during the Korach rebellion). At another, he said, "Would that all God's people were prophets" (Numbers 11:29). There are times when it is important to show that "There is only one leader for the generation, not two,"[8] and others when the highest mark of leadership is inviting others to share in it.[9]

Judaism is a complex faith. There is no one Torah model of leadership. We are each called on to fill a number of leadership roles: as parents, teachers, friends, team members and team leaders. There is no doubt,

---

7. *Gittin* 62a.
8. *Sanhedrin* 8a.
9. *Sanhedrin*, ad loc. According to the sages, this was the difference between Moses, and God's advice to Joshua in Deuteronomy 31:7, 23. See Rashi, commentary to Deuteronomy 31:7.

however, that Judaism favours as an ideal the role of parent, encouraging those we lead to continue the journey we have begun, and go further than we did.[10] A good leader creates followers. A great leader creates leaders. That was Moses' greatest achievement – that he left behind him a people willing, in each generation, to accept responsibility for taking further the great task he had begun.

10. See Rashi, commentary to Genesis 6:9.

The Turning Point

T he *parasha* of *Beshallaḥ* is beautifully constructed. It begins with a battle; it ends with a battle; and in the middle is the great miracle, the turning point – the crossing of the Reed Sea. As so often in the Mosaic books, we are presented with a chiasmus, a literary structure of the form ABCBA, in which the end is a mirror image of the beginning, and the climax is at the centre.

Occupying the central role in *Beshallaḥ* is the episode of the Reed Sea, which turns out to be a division in more than one sense. Literally, the waters are divided. But metaphorically the fate of the Israelites is also divided: into a before and after. Before, they are still in Egyptian territory, still – that is to say – under the sway of Pharaoh. It is no accident that Pharaoh and his chariots pursue the Israelites to the very edge of their territory. Anywhere within Egypt Pharaoh rules; or at least, he believes he does.

Once across the sea, however, the Israelites have traversed a boundary. They are now in no-man's-land, the desert. Again it is no accident that here, where no king rules, they can experience with pristine clarity the sovereignty of God. Israel becomes the first – historically, the only – people to be ruled directly by God. The Reed Sea is what anthropologist Victor Turner called "liminal space," a boundary between two domains that must be traversed if one is to enter into a new mode of being[1] – in this case the boundary between human and divine rule. Once crossed, there is no going back.

The symbolism of the Sea does not end there however. It reminds us of the ancient ceremony of covenant-making. The key verb of covenant is "to cut." An animal, or several animals, were divided, and the parties to the covenant stood or sat between them. The division of things normally united or whole stood as symbol of the unification of entities (persons, tribes, nations) previously divided. In this context a key passage is the covenant "cut" between God and Abraham in Genesis 15:

> So the Lord said to him, "Bring Me a heifer, a goat and a ram, each three years old, along with a dove and a young pigeon." Abram brought all these to Him, cut them in two and arranged the halves opposite each other; the birds, however, he did not cut in half... As the sun was setting, Abram fell into a deep sleep, and a thick and dreadful darkness came over him. Then the Lord said to him, "Know for certain that your descendants will be strangers in a country not their own, and they will be enslaved and mistreated four hundred years. But I will punish the nation they serve as slaves, and afterwards they will come out with great possessions. You, however, will go to your fathers in peace and be buried at a good old age. In the fourth generation your descendants will come back here, for the sin of the Amorites has not yet reached its full measure." When the sun had set and darkness had fallen, a smoking firepot with a blazing torch appeared and passed between the pieces. On that day the Lord made (literally "cut") a covenant with Abram... (Genesis 15:9–18)

---

1. Turner expounded his views in "Betwixt and Between: The Liminal Period in *Rites de Passage*," in *The Forest of Symbols* (Ithaca, N.Y: Cornell University Press, 1967); "Liminality and Communitas," in *The Ritual Process* (Chicago: Aldine, 1969), and "Passages, Margins, and Poverty: Religious Symbols of Communitas," in *Dramas, Fields, and Metaphors* (Ithaca, N.Y: Cornell University Press, 1974).

So at the Reed Sea the Israelites passed "between the pieces" (the waters, rather than the halves of animals) in a ratification of the covenant with Abraham. They passed from one domain to another, from being slaves – *avadim* – to Pharaoh to becoming servants – *avadim* – to God. This surely is the meaning of the phrase, in the Song at the Sea:

> …until Your people pass by, O Lord, until the people You have acquired pass by. (Exodus 15:16)

The crossing of the sea is both an act of covenant-making and a transfer of possession. The Israelites are now God's possession rather than Pharaoh's. They have entered new territory, not just geographically but also existentially. What does this mean? What difference does it make? The answer is surprising, counter-intuitive. To understand it, we must compare the two battles, one before, the other after, the Sea.

The first is marked by extreme passivity. Having let the Israelites go, the Egyptians then change their minds. Pharaoh decides to pursue them and assembles a force of six hundred chariots. We have to think ourselves back to an age in which the horse-drawn chariot was the ultimate weapon of war. As we saw earlier, in biblical times, Egypt was famous for its horses. No other nation could rival them. This meant that they could out-manoeuvre any rival military force. Horses gave them speed, and chariots gave them protection. They were impregnable, and the sight of six hundred of them approaching would have been terrifying to a well-drilled army, let alone an unruly, disorganised group of slaves. Predictably, the Israelites lose heart and blame Moses for bringing them out of Egypt to die in the wilderness.

Moses' reply is short and sharp:

> Moses answered the people, "Do not be afraid. Stand firm and you will see the deliverance the Lord will bring you today. The Egyptians you see today you will never see again. The Lord will fight for you, but you must remain silent." (Exodus 14:13–14)

He says, in effect, do nothing. God will do it all. The sages, their ears ever attuned to nuance, detected four responses in Moses' words:

Our ancestors were divided into four groups at the Sea. One group said, "Let us throw ourselves into the sea." Another said, "Let us go back to Egypt." A third said, "Let us wage war against them." A fourth said, "Let us cry out against them." To the first, who said, "Let us throw ourselves into the sea," Moses said, "Stand firm and you will see the deliverance the Lord will bring." To the second, who said, "Let us go back to Egypt," he said, "The Egyptians you see today you will never see again." To the third, who said, "Let us wage war against them," he said, "The Lord will fight for you." To the fourth, who said, "Let us cry out against them," he said, "you must remain silent."[2]

The battle against the Egyptians was a divine act, not a human one.

Not so the Amalekites, a battle that was fought after the crossing. Here the battle is fought by the Israelites themselves:

The Amalekites came and attacked the Israelites at Rephidim. Moses said to Joshua, "Choose some of our men and go out to fight the Amalekites. Tomorrow I will stand on top of the hill with the staff of God in my hands." So Joshua fought the Amalekites as Moses had ordered, and Moses, Aaron and Hur went to the top of the hill. As long as Moses held up his hands, the Israelites were winning, but whenever he lowered his hands, the Amalekites were winning. When Moses' hands grew tired, they took a stone and put it under him and he sat on it. Aaron and Hur held his hands up – one on one side, one on the other – so that his hands remained steady till sunset. So Joshua overcame the Amalekite army with the sword. (Exodus 17:8–13)

There is no hint here of a miracle. The Israelites fought; the Israelites won. The only hint of a supernatural presence is the reference to Moses' hands. Somehow, they held the key to victory. When Moses lifted them, the Israelites prevailed. When he lowered them, the tide turned against them. Strangely, but significantly, the Mishna makes a comment on

2. Talmud Yerushalmi, *Ta'anit* 2:5.

this passage. The Mishna is a law code. It is not a book of biblical interpretation. It is therefore very rare for a biblical exegesis to appear in the Mishna – all the more so given its content. The sages, far from emphasising the supernatural factor in the battle against Amalek, went out of their way to minimise it:

> It is written, "As long as Moses held up his hands, the Israelites were winning." Now did the hands of Moses wage war or crush the enemy? Not so. The text signifies that so long as Israel turned their thoughts above and subjected their hearts to their Father in heaven they prevailed, but otherwise they fell.[3]

God, implies the Mishna, makes a difference not "out there" but "in here." Moses' hands did not perform a miracle. They merely pointed upwards. They directed the eyes, and thus the minds, of the Israelites to heaven. That gave them the courage, the inner strength, the hope and faith to prevail.

This transition – as we will see, it forms the underlying argument of the book of Exodus – is signalled in an extraordinarily subtle verse immediately prior to the battle against Amalek.

God had performed a miracle for the Israelites of the most majestic kind. For them, He had divided the waters of the sea – and for once, the Israelites believed. "The Israelites saw the great power that God had unleashed against Egypt, and the people were in awe of God. They believed in God and in His servant Moses" (Exodus 14:31). But the change of heart did not last. Three days later they were complaining about the water. Then they complained about the lack of food. Miracle follows miracle. The water is made drinkable. God sends manna from heaven. They move on to Rephidim, and again there is no water. Again the people complain. This time Moses comes close to despair. "What am I to do with these people?" he says to God, "They are almost ready to stone me" (17:4). God then sends water from a rock. But the memory of the Israelites' ingratitude remains. Moses incorporates it into a place name:

3. Mishna, *Rosh HaShana* 3:8.

And he called the place Massa ["testing"] and Meriba ["quarrel-ing"] because the Israelites quarrelled and because they tested the Lord saying, "Is the Lord among us (*bekirbenu*) or not?" (17:7)

Immediately thereafter we read that "The Amalekites came and attacked the Israelites at Rephidim" (17:8). There is an obvious con-nection. The Israelites' doubt is punished. Having protected them throughout, God gives them a glimpse of what life is like without his protection. They will be exposed to great dangers. This is on the surface of the narrative.

However, beneath the surface is a surpassing irony. The Hebrew word *bekirbenu* can mean two things. It can mean "among us" (a spatial sense) but it can also mean "within us" (a psychological sense). The real meaning of the battle against Amalek, as understood by the Mishna, is that it showed the inner, psychological, spiritual and emotional dimen-sion of the Divine Presence. The Israelites won not because God fought the battle for them, but because God gave them the strength to fight the battle for themselves. God was not "among" them but "within" them. That was the crucial change between before and after the crossing of the Reed Sea.

One of the most remarkable features of Judaism – in this respect it is supreme among religious faiths – is its call to human responsibility. God wants us to fight our own battles. This is not abandonment. It does not mean – God forbid – that we are alone. God is with us whenever and wherever we are with Him. "Yea, though I walk through the Valley of the shadow of death, I will fear no evil, for You are with me" (Psalm 23:4). What it means is that God calls on us to exercise those qualities – con-fidence, courage, choice, imagination, determination and will – which allow us to reach our full stature as beings in the image of God.

The book of Exodus teaches this lesson in the form of three nar-ratives, of which the division of the Reed Sea is the first. The others are the epiphany of God at Mount Sinai and later in the Tabernacle, and the first and second tablets Moses brings down from the mountain. In all three cases we have a double narrative, a before and after. In each, the first is an act performed entirely by God – the drowning of the Egyp-tians, the revelation at Sinai, and the first tablets. The second involves a partnership between God and human beings (the battle against the Amalekites, the construction of the Tabernacle, and the second tablets, carved by Moses and inscribed by God). The difference is immense. In the first of each pair of events, what is evident is the power of God and the passivity of man. In the second, what counts is the will of God internalised by man. God is transformed from doer to teacher. In the process, human beings are transformed from dependency to interdependency.

This is the astonishing message contained within a single Hebrew word, *eved*, which can mean either "servant" or "slave." In Egypt, the Israelites were Pharaoh's *avadim*. Leaving Egypt they became God's *avadim*. The difference, however, is no mere change of masters. The slave of a human being is one who lacks freedom. The servant of God is one who is called to freedom – a specific kind of freedom, namely one that respects the freedom of others and the integrity of the created world (the difference, as seventeenth- and eighteenth-century writers used to put it, between liberty and licence, between freedom with and without responsibility[4]). At the heart of the Hebrew Bible is a specific view of humanity, set out in the first chapters of Genesis. Human beings are not incurably evil, tainted by original sin. Nor are we inescapably good. Instead we are defined by the ability to choose. If we choose well we are "little lower than the angels" (Psalm 8:5). If we choose badly, we are worse than the beasts. We are not condemned to a perpetual condition of arrested development in which we are utterly dependent on a parent figure, human or divine. Such a view fails to accord with the concept of parenthood as articulated in the Hebrew Bible and the rabbinic literature.

Genesis, which is about families, is a series of variations on the theme of human parents and children. Exodus, about the birth of a nation, is about a divine parent and his human children (God's first command to Moses is, "Then say to Pharaoh, 'This is what the Lord says: Israel is My firstborn son, and I told you, "Let My son go, so he may worship Me," Exodus 4:22).

Neither parenthood nor childhood are – the Torah teaches –

---

4. The distinction between liberty and licence was made by John Locke in the second of his *Two Treatises of Government* (bk. II, chap. II, par. 6). See essay "The Covenant of Fate," p. 83, for a similar statement by Edmund Burke.

static conditions. They are developmental. In its early years, a child really is dependent. Without the attentiveness of a parent, it would not survive. But over the course of time, it develops those capacities that allow it to mature. During that period, a parent learns progressively to make space for the child to act on its own. This can be doubly heartbreaking. Not only does it involve letting go, which is always a form of bereavement. It also demands that a parent be strong and self-restrained enough to allow the child to walk, knowing that it will fall; to choose, knowing that it will make mistakes; to travel, knowing that it will take wrong paths and false turns.

The "anger" of God, so often expressed in the Hebrew Bible, is actually not anger but anguish: the anguish of a parent who sees a child do wrong but knows that he or she may not intervene if the child is ever to grow, to learn, to mature, to change, to become responsible.

That is the turning point marked by the battles before and after the division of the Sea. The opening and closing verses of *Beshallah* both contain as their key word, *milhama*, "war." The opening verse states:

> When Pharaoh let the people go, God did not lead them on the road through the Philistine country, though that was shorter. For God said, "If they face war, they might change their minds and return to Egypt." (13:17)

The closing verse says:

> The Lord will be at war against the Amalekites from generation to generation. (17:16)

The difference between them is between the war God fights for us, and the war we fight for God. The first is miraculous, the second only metaphorically so. The war God fights changes nature, even to the point of dividing a sea. But the war we fight changes us – and that is something God cannot do for us. We can only do it for ourselves. As long as the Israelites were totally dependent on God, they remained querulous and quarrelsome, in a state of arrested development. Only when they fought their own battles did they eventually – and painfully slowly – begin to acknowledge God.

A true parent is one who fights battles on our behalf when we are young and defenceless, but who, once we have matured, gives us the inner strength to fight for ourselves. That is the difference between the war before and the war after the crossing of the Reed Sea.

Yitro
יתרו

The *parasha* of *Yitro* (Jethro) is divided into two episodes. In the first (chapter 18), Israel receives its first system of governance – devolved to leaders of thousands, hundreds, fifties and tens – at the advice of Jethro, Moses' father-in-law, whose name the *parasha* bears. In the second (chapters 19–20), it receives its eternal constitution by way of covenant with God. A brief summation of its key elements is given by the voice of God Himself in the form of the Ten Commandments (or Utterances).

The first of the following essays examines the tension between strict justice and peace as modes of conflict resolution. The second and third look at the two elements of the mission statement of the Jewish people as "a kingdom of priests and as holy nation." The fourth argues that the revelation at Sinai and the political order it instituted hold a key place in the history of liberty.

Justice or Peace?

The *parasha* of *Yitro*, which contains the account of the greatest divine revelation in history, at Mount Sinai, begins on a note that is human, all too human. Yitro (Jethro[1]), priest of Midian, has come to see how his son-in-law Moses and the people he leads are faring. It begins by telling us what Jethro heard (the details of the exodus and its attendant miracles). It goes on to describe what Jethro saw, and tells us that this gave him cause for concern.

He saw Moses leading the people alone. The result was bad for Moses and bad for the people. This is what Jethro said:

> Moses' father-in-law said, "What you are doing is not good. You and these people who come to you will wear yourselves out. The work is too heavy for you; you cannot handle it alone. Listen now to me and I will give you advice, and may God be with you. You must be the people's representative before God and bring their

---

1. I've kept to the Hebrew spelling for the name of the *parasha*, while – as in other cases – using the anglicized version of Moses' father-in-law's name, since that is better known.

disputes to Him. Teach them the decrees and laws, and show them the way to live and the duties they are to perform. But select capable men from all the people – men who fear God, trustworthy men who hate dishonest gain – and appoint them as officials over thousands, hundreds, fifties and tens. Have them serve as judges for the people at all times, but have them bring every difficult case to you; the simple cases they can decide themselves. That will make your load lighter, because they will share it with you. If you do this and God so commands, you will be able to stand the strain, and so too all these people will reach their place in peace." (Exodus 18:17–23)

Moses must learn to delegate and share the burden of leadership. Interestingly, the sentence "What you are doing is not good (*lo tov*)" is one of only two places in the Torah where the phrase "not good" occurs. The other (Genesis 2:18) is "It is not good for man to be alone." We cannot lead alone; we cannot live alone. That is one of the axioms of biblical anthropology. The Hebrew word for life, *ḥayim*, is in the plural, as if to signify that life is essentially shared. Dean Inge once defined religion as "what an individual does with his own solitude." That is not a Jewish view.

However, it was the great nineteenth-century scholar Netziv (Rabbi Naftali Zvi Yehuda Berlin) who made an unexpected, even counter-intuitive observation on this passage. He begins by raising the following question. It is easy to understand how Jethro's advice helped Moses. The work was too much. He was becoming exhausted, and he needed help. What is less easy to understand is his final comment: if, with God's permission, you delegate, "so too all these people will reach their place in peace." The people were not exhausted; Moses was. How then would they gain by a system of delegation? Their cases would still be heard – but not by Moses. How was this to their advantage?[2]

Netziv begins by quoting a passage from the Talmud.[3] The passage is about what the sages called *bitzua*, or what later became known as *peshara*, compromise. This is a decision on the part of a judge in a

2. *Harḥev Davar*, commentary to Exodus 18:23.
3. *Sanhedrin* 6b.

civil case to seek a solution based on equity rather than strict application of the law. It is not wholly unlike mediation, in which the parties agree to a resolution that they both consider fair, regardless of whether or not it is based on statute or precedent. From a different perspective, it is a mode of conflict resolution in which both sides gain, rather than the pure administration of justice, in which one side wins, the other loses. The Talmud wants to know: is this good or bad? To be adopted or avoided? This is part of the debate:

> Rabbi Eliezer, son of R. Yose the Galilean, said: it is forbidden to mediate ... Instead, let the law pierce the mountain [a saying similar to: "Let the chips fall where they may."] And so Moses' motto was: Let the law pierce the mountain. Aaron, however, loved peace and pursued peace and made peace between people ... R. Yehudah ben Korḥa said: it is good to mediate, for it is written (Zechariah 8:16), "Execute the judgment of truth and peace in your gates." Surely where there is strict justice, there is no peace, and where there is peace, there is no strict justice! What then is the justice that coexists with peace? We must say: mediation.

The law follows Rabbi Judah ben Korcha. It is permissible, even preferable, to mediate, with one proviso: that the judge does not yet know who is right and who is wrong. It is precisely this uncertainty at the early stages of a hearing that allows an equitable resolution to be favoured over a strictly legal one. If the judge has already reached a clear verdict, it would be a suppression of justice on his part to favour a compromise solution.

Ingeniously applying this principle to the Israelites in Moses' day, Netziv points out that – as the Talmud says – Moses preferred strict justice to peace. He was not a man to compromise or mediate. In addition, as the greatest of the prophets, he knew almost instantly which of the parties before him was innocent and which guilty; who had right on his side and who did not. It was therefore impossible for him to mediate, since this is only permitted before the judge has reached a verdict, which in Moses' case was almost immediately.

Hence Netziv's remarkable conclusion. By delegating the judicial function downwards, Moses would bring ordinary people – with no special prophetic or legal gifts – into the seats of judgment. Precisely because they *lacked* Moses' intuitive knowledge of law and justice, they were able to propose equitable solutions, and an equitable solution is one in which both sides feel they have been heard. Both gain; both believe the result is fair. That, as the Talmud says above, is the only kind of justice that at the same time creates peace. That is why the delegation of judgment would not only help Moses avoid total exhaustion; it would also help "all these people" to "reach their place in peace."

What a profound idea this is. Moses was the *Ish HaElokim* (Psalm 90:1), the supreme man of God. Yet there was, Netziv implies, one thing he could not do, which others – less great in every other respect – could achieve. They could bring peace between contending parties. They could create non-violent, non-coercive forms of conflict resolution. Not knowing the law with the depth that Moses did, not having his intuitive sense of truth, they had instead to exercise patience. They had to listen to both sides. They had to arrive at an equitable verdict that both parties could see as fair. A mediator has different gifts from a prophet, a liberator, a law-giver – more modest perhaps, but sometimes no less necessary.

It is not that one character type is to be preferred to another. No one – certainly not Netziv – regarded Moses as anything less than the greatest leader and prophet Israel has ever had. It is, rather, that no one individual can embody all the virtues necessary to sustain a people. A priest is not a prophet (though a few, like Samuel and Ezekiel, were both). A king needs different virtues than a saint. A military leader is not (though in later life he can become) a man of peace.

What emerges at the end of the train of thought Netziv sets in motion is the deep significance of the idea that we can neither live nor lead alone. Judaism is not a faith transacted in the privacy of the believer's soul. It is a social faith. It is about networks of relationship. It is about families, communities, and ultimately a nation, in which each of us, great or small, has a role to play. "Despise no one and disdain nothing," said Ben Azzai (*Avot* 4:3), "for there is no one who does not have his hour, and nothing that does not have its place." There was something ordinary individuals (heads of thousands, hundreds, tens) could achieve that even Moses in all his glory could not achieve. That is why a nation is greater than any individual, and why each of us has something to give.

A Kingdom of Priests

Immediately prior to the revelation at Mount Sinai, God instructs Moses to communicate His proposal to the people. Through Moses, God invites them to enter into a covenant with Him that will define their identity for all time:

> "You yourselves have seen what I did to Egypt, and how I carried you on eagles' wings and brought you to Me. And now, if you truly heed My voice and keep My covenant, you will become for Me a special treasure among all the peoples, for all the earth is Mine. As for you, you will be to Me a kingdom of priests and a holy nation." (Exodus 19:4–6)

This phrase – "a kingdom of priests and a holy nation" – a mere four words in the original Hebrew, was to become the shortest, simplest, most challenging mission statement of the Jewish people. Indeed, with the possible exception of the United States, the Jewish people is the only nation ever to have had a mission statement. Most are defined in terms of language, geography, political structure, long association and the like. Jews became a nation by adopting a task, by covenanting with God. Absent that, and it is hard to say what it is to be a Jew.

Yet the words themselves are difficult to understand. In this essay I want to look at the first part of the phrase: "a kingdom of priests." Construed literally, it leads to obvious problems. First, Jews never were a kingdom of priests. Priesthood fell to Aaron and his sons. Even Moses was not a priest. There was a time when Moses said, "Would that all God's people were prophets" (Numbers 11:29), but neither he nor anyone else said, "Would that all God's people were priests."[1]

What is more, priesthood as such is not seen by the Torah as a distinctively Jewish or Israelite phenomenon. Melchizedek, Abraham's contemporary, is described as "a priest of the most high God" (Genesis 14:18). Jethro, Moses' father in law, is described at the beginning of the *parasha* as "a Midianite priest" (Exodus 18:1). All ancient religions had priests.

The classic commentators are divided. Some – Ibn Ezra, Nahmanides – interpret the word to mean "servants." A priest is one consecrated to the service of God. That was now to be the task of the Israelites as a whole. Others – Saadia Gaon, Rashi, Rashbam – understand it to mean "princes," based on the verse (11 Samuel 8:18) in which David's sons are described as *kohanim*, which cannot mean priests, and must mean royalty, noblemen, princes. Since God is the supreme King of kings, and since He had described the Israelites as "My son, My firstborn child" (Exodus 4:22), it followed that the Israelites were children of the king – royalty.

The most interesting suggestion is that of Ovadia Sforno, who interprets the phrase to mean that the Israelites stand in relation to the rest of humanity as the children of Aaron stood vis-à-vis the Israelites. They are, as it were, the world's priests, whose task is to "teach the entire human race that all shall call in the name of God and serve Him with one accord, as indeed will be the role of Israel in the future."[2] It is notable that Sforno (Italy, 1470–1550) – writing in the Italian Renais-

---

1. To be sure, Korach argued for equality, and also sought to be a priest (Numbers 16), but that is a complex narrative in the course of which there appear to have been several different claims by the various groups that took part in the rebellion.
2. Sforno, commentary to Exodus 19:6. His comment on the previous verse is equally

sance – provides the most universalistic of interpretations. For it was in Renaissance Italy that Jews and Judaism were more integrated into the wider society than elsewhere.[3]

I want, however, to suggest a different kind of interpretation altogether, by looking at the wider context of the ancient world and the background against which the biblical narrative is set. It begins with the proposition that the most profound transformations of the human situation take place when there is a change in information technology – in the way human beings record and transmit what they know. Other technological advances have localised impact. They change the way things are done. Information technology has systemic impact. It affects the way people think.[4]

One obvious example, which was to change the face of Europe, was Gutenberg's invention of printing in the mid-fifteenth century.[5] When Luther initiated the Reformation, his works spread like wildfire across Europe, setting in motion a series of revolutions that led, in the course of time, to the phenomenon we know as "the birth of the modern." Yet most of Luther's ideas had already been formulated two centuries earlier, in Oxford, by John Wycliffe. The difference was that in Wycliffe's time the printing press did not exist, so his impact remained local. By Luther's day there were more than two hundred printing presses in Europe. Soon they began producing Luther's writings, and Bibles in vernacular translations, in the hundreds of thousands. It was a tide impossible to control, and it transformed the politics and culture of Europe.

The first technological invention was the birth of writing, in

striking. He interprets the phrase "a special treasure among all the peoples," to mean that though Jews are beloved of God, so too are the righteous of all peoples since "all the earth is Mine."

3. Sforno was a man of wide humanistic scholarship. He studied mathematics, philology, philosophy and medicine. Between 1498 and 1500 he taught Hebrew to the Christian humanist Johannes Reuchlin.

4. On the way literacy "restructures consciousness," see Walter J. Ong, *The Presence of the Word* (Yale University Press: 1967), and *Orality and Literacy* (New York: Routledge, 1982). See also Jack Goody, *The Logic of Writing and the Organization of Society* (Cambridge University Press, 1986).

5. The Chinese, of course, had invented it earlier, but the technology had not yet reached Europe.

Mesopotamia, some five thousand years ago.[6] This was the birth of civilization. Although writing was first used for trade and administrative purposes – recording who owed what to whom – its larger possibilities were soon exploited, to record myth and the victories of kings. For the first time, human beings could accumulate knowledge beyond the scope of unaided human memory. Nothing else so accelerated the pace of human progress.

Writing was invented independently at least seven times, in Mesopotamia (cuneiform), ancient Egypt (hieroglyphics), the Indus Valley (Indus script), China (ideograms), Crete (the Minoan script known as Linear-B), and the Americas (by both the Mayans and the Aztecs). The first writing systems usually took the form of pictograms, stylized representations of the objects the symbols denoted, or ideograms, standing for qualities or concepts. Some became syllabaries, each symbol representing a syllable.

The earliest writing systems, however, involved an obvious problem. The number of symbols involved was large. In Chinese, there are some sixty thousand. They could take years to master. The result was that in each society where there was writing, there was a literate elite, a knowledge class, often involved in administration. Pictographic or ideographic societies were hierarchical. Only the few had access to knowledge – and knowledge, said Francis Bacon,[7] is power.

It was the second revolution that led to possibilities hitherto unknown: the invention of the alphabet. It was this that reduced the number of symbols needed to be learned to less than thirty. The first alphabetic inscriptions, in what has come to be known as proto-Semitic, were discovered by the British archaeologist William Flinders Petrie at Serabit el-Khadem in the Sinai desert in 1905. He surmised that they were made by the Israelites on their way from Egypt to the Promised Land. Their full significance was not realised until 1916, when they were

6. On the history of writing and the alphabet, two recent books are David Sacks, *The Alphabet* (Arrow Books, 2004); John Man, *Alpha Beta* (Headline Books, 2000). On the Hebrew alphabet specifically, a classic work is David Diringer, *The Story of the Aleph Bet* (Lincolns-Prager, 1958).

7. Sir Francis Bacon, *Religious Meditations, "Of Heresies"* (1597).

decoded by British Egyptologist Alan Gardiner, who was the first to grasp that they were, in fact, alphabetical. A second, similar discovery, was made in the mid-1990s by Yale Egyptologist John Darnell, at Wadi el-Hol (the Valley of Terror) near Luxor.

Both Flinders Petrie and Darnell noted that the alphabet was developed from Egyptian hieroglyphics by truncating a word or syllable into its initial sound. Both were convinced that the creators of the first alphabets were not themselves Egyptians, but Semitic workers, traders, slaves or their supervisors. We cannot give a precise date to the first alphabet – some time between 1,800 and 2,000 BCE seems likely. But unlike the pre-alphabetical scripts, the alphabet seems to have been invented only once. All the hundreds of scripts that exist are direct or indirect descendants of the proto-Semitic writing from the Sinai desert. The word *alphabet* itself comes from the first two letters of the Hebrew script *aleph-bet*. The first script to include vowels was Greek, but this too derived from earlier Sinaitic/Canaanite/Phoenician systems, as we can see from its first four letters. Alpha, beta, gamma, delta in Greek correspond to *aleph, bet, gimmel* and *daled* in Hebrew.

The connection between this and the development of the faith of Israel is unmistakable, even if we can only speculate about its precise form. As John Man writes: "Both new God and new script worked together to forge a new nation and disseminate an idea that would change the world."[8] The alphabet created the book that created the people of the book. Was it divine providence that led to this invention becoming available at exactly the right time and place to be used by the Israelites for the holiest of purposes, namely, recording the divine word? Or was it this new development that allowed the Israelites to develop the consciousness – the high levels of abstraction, essential to monotheism, made possible by literacy – that allowed them to decipher the word of the One God?

One way or another, the alphabet created a possibility that never existed before, namely of a society of mass, even universal, literacy. With only twenty-two symbols, it could be taught, in a relatively short time, to everyone. We see evidence of this at many places in Tanakh, the Hebrew

---

8. John Man, *Alpha Beta: How 26 Letters Shaped the Western World* (Wiley, 2001), 129.

Bible. Isaiah says "All your children shall be taught of the Lord and great shall be the peace of your children" (Isaiah 54:13), implying universal education. In the book of Judges, before the first of Israel's kings, we read that Gideon "caught a young man of Sukkot and questioned him, and the young man wrote down for him the names of the seventy-seven officials of Sukkot, the elders of the town" (Judges 8:14). Gideon took it for granted that a young man, selected at random, could read and write.

After the revelation at Mount Sinai, Moses "took the book of the covenant and read it in the hearing of the people" (Exodus 24:7). Was this a parchment scroll? A stone inscription? We have no way of knowing. But it is surely no coincidence that Israel became the first – indeed the only – nation in history to receive its laws before its land. A law that could be easily written and read, and that could be transported anywhere, was the expression of the God who was everywhere, in the desert as well as in the land.

Above all, the idea of a society of universal literacy was world-changing because it heralded the possibility of a non-hierarchical society, in which everyone had equal access to knowledge. This was the momentous change, summed up in the radical statement of the sages:

> The crown of the Torah is for all Israel, as it is said, "Moses commanded us a law, an inheritance of the congregation of Jacob" (Deuteronomy 33:4). Whoever desires it can win it. Do not suppose that the other two crowns [of kingship and priesthood] are greater than the crown of the Torah, for it is said, "By me [the Torah], kings reign and princes decree justice; by me princes rule" (Proverbs 8:15–16). Hence it follows that the crown of the Torah is greater than the other two crowns.[9]

Equality is the holy grail of revolutionary politics. It has often been sought, but never achieved. The two best-known attempts have been equality of wealth (through communism or socialism) or equality of power (through participative, as opposed to representative, democracy). It is unlikely that any such system will endure, because wealth

9. Rambam, *Mishneh Torah*, Talmud Torah 3:1.

and power are essentially contested goods. The more you have, the less I have. Therefore my gain is your loss.

Knowledge is different. If I give all I know to you, I will not thereby know less. I may know more. Equality of dignity based on universal access to knowledge is the only equality likely to last in the long run. All the more so is this true if the knowledge at stake, as it is in Judaism, is of the law, and the source of the law, God Himself. That is the knowledge on which citizenship is based. At Mount Sinai, all Israel became partners to the covenant. God spoke to everyone – the only recorded revelation, not to a prophet or a group of initiates but to an entire people. Everyone was party to the law, because, potentially, everyone could read it and know it. All were equal citizens in the nation of faith under the sovereignty of God. That is what happened at Sinai.

What does this have to do with the phrase "a kingdom of priests"? Normally we think of a priest in terms of his duties, ministering to God in a holy place. But priests also had certain capacities. The word "hieroglyphics" means "priestly script" – because only the priests could read and write. The English word "clerical" means (a) pertaining to the clergy, ministers of religion, and (b) office staff who type letters and keep records. The reason one word means two such different things is because, throughout the Middle Ages, ministers of religion were almost the only literate class. The first universities were primarily for the teaching of religious officials.

Functionally, a priest in the ancient world was one who could read and write. A kingdom of priests is therefore *a nation of universal literacy*. Understood this way, the nature of the covenant, and of Israel's mission, becomes clear. The law God was about to reveal at Mount Sinai would become the possession of every member of the nation. He or she could know it, read it, study it, internalize it and make it their own. The Jewish people was summoned to become, as it were, a nation of constitutional lawyers. That, to a remarkable extent, is what they became, at least in the rabbinic period.

Torah – God's law and teaching – was not a code written by a distant king, to be imposed by force. Nor was it an esoteric mystery understood by only a scholarly elite. It was to be available to, and intelligible by, everyone. God was to become a teacher, Israel His pupils, and the Torah the text that bound them to one another. In the words of the Psalm, "He has revealed His word to Jacob, His laws and decrees to Israel. He has done this for no other nation; they do not know His laws. Halleluya!" (Psalm 147:19–20).

There is nothing quite like this in the annals of the religious experience of humankind. Eventually, within Judaism study would become a religious experience higher even than prayer.[10] Jews would be educated when most of Europe was sunk in illiteracy. It was through study that Jews created a new and still-compelling form of human dignity and equality, and it was made possible through the birth of the alphabet. That is how Jews became "a kingdom of priests."

10. See *Shabbat* 10a.

A Holy Nation

I n the previous essay, I examined the first half of Israel's mission statement as the people of the covenant: "a kingdom of priests." Here I turn to the second half: "a holy nation." What, exactly, is holiness in Judaism, and how does it apply not to this person or that, but to an entire nation?

Rudolf Otto, in his book *The Idea of the Holy*, famously defined the holy as the *mysterium tremendum et fascinans*, a sense of being in the presence of something vast and awe inspiring.[1] There is doubtless much truth in this idea, but the late Eliezer Berkovits argued the opposite: that whenever we encounter the word holy in relation to God it refers to His involvement with humanity, not His transcendence or mystery.[2]

However, these analyses do not go far enough in explaining what the word "holy" means in the Torah. Its most obvious appearances in the Mosaic books are twofold, the first in relation to Shabbat – the day God Himself proclaimed holy – and the second in relation to the inner

1. Rudolf Otto, *The Idea of the Holy* (Oxford University Press, 1958).
2. Eliezer Berkovits, *Essential Essays on Judaism*, ed. David Hazony (Jerusalem: Shalem, 2002), 247–314.

chamber of the Sanctuary, which was known as the holy of holies.[3] It is in these contexts that we are best able to learn what holiness means when applied to a people.

Lurianic Kabbala – the school of mysticism associated with Rabbi Isaac Luria and his circle in sixteenth-century Safed[4] – gave Judaism one of its most glorious concepts – an idea, to be sure, that had been present from the outset, but had never been articulated as simply before. The idea was *tzimtzum*, divine "contraction" or "self-effacement."

Behind the idea of *tzimtzum* is the realization that there is a contradiction between the infinite and the finite. If God is everywhere, how can anything else exist? Two different entities (God and that which is not God) cannot occupy the same space. The kabbalistic answer is that the very act of creation involved a self-limitation on the part of God. God, as it were, contracted His presence so that finitude – space and time and the things that occupy them – could emerge.

The Hebrew word for space and time, *olam*, which means both "universe", i.e., the totality of space, and "eternity," i.e., the totality of time, also means "hidden" as in the word *ne'elam*. Thus, embedded in the Hebrew language is the idea that space and time are dimensions of the hiddenness of God, who is beyond space and time.

Yet were God entirely hidden from the universe it would be, experientially and functionally, as if He did not exist. At best, Deism would be true – the idea, widespread during the scientific Enlightenment of the seventeenth and eighteenth centuries, that God created the universe but thereafter played no part in it, neither intervening in history in the form of miracles, nor disclosing Himself through revelation. God would be a *Deus absconditus*, a creator who deserted humanity.

---

3. Shabbat is the first thing declared holy in the Torah: Genesis 2:3 (this is the only occurrence of the word in Genesis). Overwhelmingly in Exodus, "holy" occurs either in the context of Shabbat or the Sanctuary. The phrase "holy of holies" appears in Exodus 26:33–34; 29:37; 30:10, 29, 36; 40:10. It appears 20 times in Leviticus, four in Numbers.

4. The classic study is Gershom Scholem, *Major Trends in Jewish Mysticism* (London: Thames and Hudson, 1955), 244–286. See also Lawrence Fine, *Physician of the Soul, Healer of the Cosmos: Isaac Luria and His Kabbalistic Fellowship* (Stanford University Press, 2003).

Thus the very terms of creation involve a paradox. Without God the universe would not exist; but the presence of God threatens the existence of anything apart from Him. "No man," says God, "can see Me and live" (Exodus 33:20).

To this the Torah has an answer at once simple and profound. The universe was created in six days; yet creation itself involved seven days. The seventh day is declared by God Himself to be holy – meaning, henceforth it will become the window in time through which we see the presence of God.

How do we do so? By renouncing our own status as creators. On Shabbat, all *melakha*, which is defined as "creative work," is forbidden. On Shabbat we are passive rather than active. We become creations, not creators. We renounce making in order to experience ourselves as made. Shabbat is the room we make for God within time.

Likewise the Tabernacle. Essentially this was a large portable tent, a framework and its hangings. Wherever it was erected, it defined a certain space as holy, meaning, set aside for God. Within that space nothing was to intervene between the worshipper and God. In particular, priests had to avoid contact with death or anything resembling it, since death is peculiarly human – as in the term "mortal" – while God represents life.[5] The Tabernacle is the room we make for God within space.

The immensely detailed instructions for the construction of the Tabernacle and its service (like the equally detailed laws of Shabbat) are there to signal that nothing in holiness is the result of human initiative. To occupy holy space or time is to renounce human creativity so as to be existentially open to divine creativity. That is why Nadav and Avihu died because they brought an offering "that was not commanded" (Leviticus 10: 1). The holy is space / time as defined by divine, not human will. We

---

5. That too is why worshippers had to purify themselves from contact with death, through the rite of the Red Heifer (Numbers 19), before entering the Sanctuary. God in Judaism is seen as the Author of life; death is the antithesis of the Divine Presence. See Judah Halevi, *The Kuzari*, 11, 60. Maimonides in *The Guide for the Perplexed*, III:10, explains that all evil, including death, is a form of negation and is not brought about by God. When we say that God creates evil, or causes death, this is a metaphorical way of speaking.

enter God's domain on his terms, not ours. That is not a consequence of holiness but its very meaning.

Thus, not every time or space is holy. That is essential for us as humans. A world in which all time was Sabbatical, or in which all space had the sanctity of the Tabernacle, would be one in which human beings could not exist *as* human beings. There would be neither time nor space for human endeavour or achievement. That is precisely what God does not want to happen. He welcomes human work. That is what the Torah means when it says that we are created in God's image, meaning that we, like God, are creative. We, like God, are capable of imagining a world that is not yet and bringing it into being.

However, if no time or space were holy, the opposite danger would exist, namely, that a world in which God is hidden would be one in which, for many people, God does not exist. This would be a world with no limits on human self-assertion – always the prelude to political, military, economic or environmental disaster. Therefore there must be some window – some point of transparency – in the screen between the infinite and the finite. That is what holiness is.

Holiness is the space we make for God. In the simplest and most elegant way, holiness is to humanity what *tzimtzum* is to God. Just as God effaces Himself to make space for mankind, so we efface ourselves to make space for God. We do this by a temporary renunciation of creativity. Holiness is that bounded emptiness filled by the Divine Presence.

This idea was utterly incomprehensible to the Hellenistic mind. When the Greeks and Romans first encountered Jews, they could not understand Shabbat. They knew the concept of a holy day – every religion has such days. What they had never before encountered was a day made holy by rest, a day of being rather than doing. Many of them expressed their candid opinion that Jews observed the Shabbat because they were lazy.[6] That was the only explanation they could give.

---

6. Seneca was particularly critical of the Sabbath which, he wrote, condemned its practitioners to one day in seven of idleness. Plutarch saw it as a form of superstition, which caused Jews to lose wars because they were forbidden to fight on that day. Tacitus maintained that, having become accustomed, through indolence, to rest every seventh day, they extended the principle to the seventh year also. See Allan Gould, ed., *What Did They Think of the Jews?* (Jason Aronson: 1991), 5–13.

Likewise, an ancient tradition states that when the Roman General Pompey invaded Jerusalem and entered the Temple he was amazed to find that the holy of holies was empty.[7] He expected to find in it the Israelites' holiest idol. The idea that empty space – like empty time – might be holy, was beyond him.

Holiness is the space we make for the Otherness of God – by listening, not speaking; by being, not doing; by allowing ourselves to be acted on rather than acting. It means disengaging from that flow of activity whereby we impose our human purposes on the world, thereby allowing space for the divine purpose to emerge. All holiness is a form of renunciation, but since God desires the existence of human beings as responsible and creative beings, He does not ask for total renunciation. Thus some times are holy, not all; some spaces are holy, not all; some people are holy, not all. All nations contain holy individuals. What makes Israel unique is that it is a holy nation, meaning, a nation all of whose members are summoned to holiness. It was the first faith to see holiness as a property not of a sacred elite, but of national life itself.

The concept of a nation is fundamental to Judaism, because the nation is a basic unit of culture. As a socio-political entity, it constructs its own form of order through law, ritual, and custom. It is where many smaller groupings, families and communities, come together to construct the basic terms of their common life. And God wants his presence to inform public life – otherwise he would have limited his concerns to the individual and the soul.

Judaism knows the faith of individuals. That is what Genesis is about, and the book of Psalms, which is the eternal lexicon of the soul in dialogue with God. Judaism also knows the faith of humanity. That is the meaning of the first eleven chapters of Genesis and their culmination in the Noahide covenant, the covenant God makes with all mankind. But Judaism's great concerns are with the life we construct together and the terms on which we do so: justice, compassion, human dignity, peace, the limited and proper conduct of war, care for the dependent, welfare for the poor, concern for the long-term viability of the environment,

7. Heinrich Graetz, *History of the Jews* (Jewish Publication Society of America, 1956), 2:66.

and above all, the rule of law, in which strong and weak, powerful and powerless, are subject to the same code of conduct applied equally to all. These institutions and ideals are essentially political; hence they require the constitution of a nation as a political entity. That is the meaning of the phrase *goy kadosh*, a holy nation. At Sinai the Jewish people, until then a mere aggregate of individuals, linked by family, memory and the experience of exodus, became a body politic, with the Torah as its written constitution. The word *goy* – like its cognate term *geviya* – means "a body." It is a metaphor for a group of individuals whose relationship to one another is as of limbs to a body. Sinai creates the terms of collective existence. Henceforth the Israelites are implicated in one another's fate.

The word *kadosh* in this context therefore designates a third emptiness, not time (Shabbat), nor space (the Tabernacle) but the empty throne (*cathedra*, the seat of authority). The place occupied in other nations by the monarch, ruler or Pharaoh, is, in the case of Israel, to be left empty for God. Israel is to become a republic of faith under His direct sovereignty. He is the author of its constitution, the framer of its rules, the one who guides it through its long journeys, sustains it in hours of need, and gives it hope in times of crisis. The essence of the Sinai revelation is that the Israelites become the first – indeed the only – nation formed on the basis of a covenant with God.

Hence the significance of the setting: the wilderness. All other nations become nations because they have lived together for a long time in the territory they see as home. Whether through war, assassination, coup d'état, plebiscite or general acclaim, they elect an individual or group to be their leader, and create a political structure which determines relationships between rulers and ruled.

Israel becomes a nation prior to all these things. It has not yet reached its land. It does not yet have a king. These things lie far ahead in the future. Sinai constitutes the creation of a nation long in advance of those things that normally lead to the birth of a nation, because it is not a normal nation but a holy one.

What then does it mean to be a holy nation? At least the following:

Jewish history will continually point to something beyond itself, something that cannot be explained by the usual laws of history. That is what Moses means when he says:

"Ask now about the former days, long before your time, from the day God created man on the earth; ask from one end of the heavens to the other. Has anything so great as this ever happened, or has anything like it ever been heard of? ... Has any god ever tried to take for himself one nation out of another nation, by testings, by miraculous signs and wonders, by war, by a mighty hand and an outstretched arm, or by great and awesome deeds, like all the things the Lord your God did for you in Egypt before your very eyes?" (Deuteronomy 4:32–34)

This too is the meaning of Isaiah's remarkable statement: "You are My witnesses," declares the Lord, "that I am God" (Isaiah 43:12). In its collective fate and destiny, Israel will constitute the most compelling evidence of divine involvement in human history. It will reach heights of achievement, and sometimes depths of degradation, that have no counterpart in the fate of other nations. As Tolstoy once wrote, "The Jew is the emblem of eternity."[8]

Further, Jewish law – the eternal structure of its collective existence – will bear witness to its more-than-human character. Hence Moses' statement:

"See, I have taught you decrees and laws as the Lord my God commanded me, so that you may follow them in the land you are entering to take possession of it. Observe them carefully, for this will show your wisdom and understanding to the nations, who will hear about all these decrees and say, 'Surely this great nation is a wise and understanding people'... What other nation is so great as to have such righteous decrees and laws as this body of laws I am setting before you today?" (Deuteronomy 4:5–8)

The graciousness of its welfare legislation, and the lucidity of its (unremittingly anti-mythological) faith will bespeak a social order more than human in its sheer humanity. As Matthew Arnold wrote: "As long

8. Letter found in the archives of the Bulgarian statesman F. Gabai. Text in Allan Gould, ed., *What Did They Think of the Jews?* (Jason Aronson, 1991), 180–181.

as the world lasts, all who want to make progress in righteousness will come to Israel for inspiration, as to the people who have had the sense for righteousness most glowing and strongest."[9]

Israel will be a nation that recognises in all its laws the existence of something beyond itself. Thus the very land it inhabits will not be its own, but God's: "The land shall not be sold in perpetuity because the land is Mine"(Leviticus 25:23). All forms of rulership, whether of judges, elders or monarchs, will be limited by the overarching sovereignty of God. Israel will know no absolutes – not the state nor the individual nor the status quo – for there is only one absolute, namely God Himself. This single fact will save it, in the course of history, from tyranny on the one hand, and anarchy on the other. It will always be the enemy of tyrants, because it will always refuse to worship anything less than God Himself.

Israel's governance will always rest on consent rather than obedience to power. This fact is implicit at Sinai, where God Himself had to secure the assent of the people before giving it its laws.[10]

Historically, the most remarkable outcome of the Sinai covenant was that even when they lost their land and sovereignty, Jews did not cease to be a nation – because they had already become a nation prior to attaining those elements of nationhood. In exile they became the world's first global people, the first virtual nation, defined not by shared territory, fate, culture, political system or even spoken language, but purely by a covenant enacted by their ancestors more than a thousand years earlier.

Kadosh therefore means: *that which in itself points beyond itself*. It means the time which signals eternity (Shabbat), the space which intimates being-beyond-space (the Tabernacle), and the nation whose history and way of life bespeak something outside the normal parameters of history and ways of life.

Encapsulating this idea in contemporary terms, the American writer, Milton Himmelfarb, once wrote:

9. Matthew Arnold, *Literature and Dogma* (Nelson, 1873), chap. 1.
10. In Exodus 19:3–6, God commands Moses to seek the assent of the people to the general terms of the covenant. Only when they have given their consent (19:8) does God proceed with the revelation.

Each Jew knows how thoroughly ordinary he is; yet taken together, we seem caught up in the things great and inexplicable…The number of Jews in the world is smaller than a small statistical error in the Chinese census. Yet we remain bigger than our numbers. Big things seemed to happen around us and to us.[11]

That is as good a way as any of saying what it means to be a holy nation.

---

11. "In the Light of Israel's Victory," an essay written shortly after the Six Day War in 1967; reprinted in Milton Himmelfarb, *Jews and Gentiles* (New York: Encounter Books, 2007), 141–42.

Mount Sinai and the Birth of Freedom

T he revelation at Mount Sinai – the central episode not only of the *parasha* of Yitro, but of Judaism as a whole – was unique in the religious history of mankind. Other faiths (Christianity and Islam) have claimed to be religions of revelation, but in both cases the revelation of which they spoke was to an individual ("the son of God," "the prophet of God"). Only in Judaism was God's self-disclosure not to an individual (a prophet) or a group (the elders) but to an entire nation, young and old, men, women and children, the righteous and not-yet-righteous alike.

From the very outset, the people of Israel knew something unprecedented had happened at Sinai. Moses had no doubt that it was an event without parallel:

> "Ask now about the former days, long before your time, from the day God created man on earth; ask from one end of the heavens to the other. Has anything so great as this ever happened, or has anything like it ever been heard of? Has any other people heard the voice of God speaking out of fire, as you have, and lived?" (Deuteronomy 4:32–33).

For the great Jewish thinkers of the Middle Ages, its significance was primarily epistemological. It created certainty and removed doubt. The authenticity of a revelation experienced by one person could be questioned. One witnessed by millions could not. God disclosed His presence in public to remove any possible suspicion that the presence felt, and the voice heard, were not genuine.

Looking, however, at the history of mankind since those days, it is clear that there was another significance also – one that had to do not with religious knowledge, but with politics. At Sinai a new kind of nation was being formed, and a new kind of society – one that would be an antithesis of Egypt, in which the few had power and the many were enslaved. It was to be, in Abraham Lincoln's words in the Gettysburg Address, "a new nation, conceived in Liberty, and dedicated to the proposition that *all men are created equal.*" Indeed without the covenant at Mount Sinai, Lincoln's words might have been inconceivable. For nowhere else do we find anything like the politics of Mount Sinai, with its radical vision of a society held together not by power but by the free consent of its citizens to be bound, individually and collectively, by a moral code and by a covenant with God.[1]

Standard works on the history of the politics of freedom trace it back through Marx, Rousseau and Hobbes to Plato's *Republic*, Aristotle's *Politics*, and the Greek city states (Athens in particular) of the fifth century BCE. This is a serious error. To be sure, words like "democracy" (rule by the people) are Greek in origin. The Greeks were gifted at abstract nouns and systematic thought. However, if we look at the "birth of the modern" – at figures like Milton, Hobbes and Locke in England, and the founding fathers of America – the book with which they were in dialogue was not Plato or Aristotle but the Hebrew Bible. Hobbes quotes it 657 times in *The Leviathan* alone. Long before the Greek philosophers, and far more profoundly, at Mount Sinai the concept of a free society was born.

---

1. "The government of the Israelites was a Federation, held together by no political authority, but by the unity of race and faith, and founded, not on physical force, but on a voluntary covenant." Lord Acton, *Essays in the History of Liberty* (Liberty Press, 1985), 7.

Three things about that moment were to prove crucial. The first is that long before Israel entered the land and acquired their own system of government (first by judges, later by kings), they had entered into an overarching covenant with God. That covenant (*brit Sinai*) set moral limits to the exercise of power. The code we call Torah established for the first time the primacy of right over might. Any king who behaved contrarily to Torah was acting *ultra vires* (beyond legitimate authority), and could be challenged. This is the single most important fact about biblical politics.

Democracy on the Greek model always had one fatal weakness. Alexis de Tocqueville and John Stuart Mill called it "the tyranny of the majority."[2] J.L. Talmon called it "totalitarian democracy."[3] The rule of the majority contains no guarantee of the rights of minorities. As Lord Acton rightly noted, it was this that led to the downfall of Athens: "There was no law superior to that of the state. The lawgiver was above the law."[4] In Judaism, by contrast, prophets were mandated to challenge the authority of the king if he acted against the terms of the Torah. The classic example is the accusation God tells Elijah to make to King Ahab for seizing Naboth's vineyard: "Thus says the Lord: Would you murder and take possession?" (1 Kings 21:19).

Individuals were empowered to disobey illegal or immoral orders. The first example, as we noted in the essay "Civil Disobedience," (p. 21), was the Hebrew midwives who "feared God and did not do what the Egyptian king had commanded" (Exodus 1:17). Another key moment was when King Saul ordered his servants to kill the priests of Nob, who had given shelter to David, "But the king's servants would not raise a hand to strike down the priests of the Lord" (1 Samuel 22:17).[5] It was on this tradition that Calvin – inspiration of the seventeenth-century

---

2. Alexis de Tocqueville, *Democracy in America*, bk. 1, chap. 15; John Stuart Mill, introduction to *On Liberty*.
3. J.L. Talmon, *The Origins of Totalitarian Democracy* (Secker and Warburg, 1955).
4. Lord Acton, *Essays in the History of Liberty*, 13.
5. On civil disobedience in Judaism, see the essays by Moshe Greenberg, Maurice Lamm and Milton Konvitz in *Contemporary Jewish Ethics*, ed. Menachem Kellner (Sanhedrin Press, 1978), 211–254; and Harold Schulweis, *Conscience: The Duty to Obey and the Duty to Disobey* (Jewish Lights, 2008).

Puritan radicals in England and America – drew, when he said "prophets and teachers may take courage and thus boldly set themselves against kings and nations."[6] It was on the same tradition that Thomas Paine based his pamphlet *Common Sense* (1776), widely credited at the time as the inspiration that led to the American revolution.[7] Historically, it was the covenant at Sinai and all that flowed from it, not the Greek political tradition, that inspired the birth of freedom in Britain and America, the first people to take that road in the modern age.

The second key element lies in the prologue to the covenant. God tells Moses:

> "This is what you are to say to the house of Jacob and tell the people of Israel. 'You yourselves have seen what I did to Egypt and how I carried you on eagles' wings and brought you to Me. Now, if you obey Me fully and keep My covenant, you will be My treasured possession, for the whole earth is Mine. You will be for Me a kingdom of priests and a holy nation…'" (Exodus 19:3–6)

Moses tells this to the people, who reply: "We will do everything the Lord has said" (19:8). Until the people had signified their consent, the revelation could not proceed. The principle at stake was that there is no legitimate government without the consent of the governed,[8] even if the governor is Creator of heaven and earth. I know of few more radical ideas anywhere.

To be sure, there were sages in the Talmudic period who questioned whether the acceptance of the covenant at Sinai was completely free. There is a famous statement in the Talmud:

> "And they stood under [normally translated as, "at the foot of"]

---

6. Calvin, *Jeremiah*, lecture 2: 1.44. Cited in Michael Walzer, *The Revolution of the Saints: A Study in the Origins of Radical Politics* (New York: Atheneum, 1972), 63.
7. Reprinted in Thomas Paine, *Political Writings* (Cambridge University Press, 1989), 3–38. The pamphlet sold 100,000 copies in 1776 alone. Paine drew entirely on the anti-monarchical passages in the Hebrew Bible.
8. The phrase comes from the American Declaration of Independence.

the mountain" (Exodus 19:17) – this teaches that the Holy One, blessed be He, overturned the mountain above them like a cask and said to them, "If you accept the Torah, it is well, but if not, this will be your burial place."[9]

What the sages are doing here is to question whether the Israelites really had a free choice at Sinai. They had not yet entered the land. They were dependent on God for their food, water and protection. Where could they go, and to whom could they turn, if they said no to God?

The Talmud itself says that "Nonetheless, they re-accepted it in the days of Ahasuerus,"[10] that is, at the time described in the book of Esther – one of the only two books in the Bible that does not contain the name of God.[11] In that context there could be no question of divine coercion. However, at the simplest level, this is the significance of the two covenant renewal ceremonies, one at the end of Moses' life, as the Israelites were about to enter the land (Deuteronomy 29–31), the other at the end of Joshua's life, when the people had conquered the land (Joshua 24). The covenant was renewed precisely so that no one could say that it had been entered into coercively when there was no alternative.

At the heart of Judaism is the idea – way ahead of its time, and not always fully realised – that the free God desires the free worship of free human beings. God, said the rabbis, does not act tyrannically with His creatures.[12]

The third, equally ahead of its time, was that the partners to the covenant were to be "all the people" – men, women and children. This fact is emphasised later on in the Torah in the mitzva of *Hak-hel*, the septennial covenant renewal ceremony. The Torah states specifically that the entire people is to be gathered together for this ceremony, "men, women and children" (Deuteronomy 31:10–13). A thousand years later, when Athens experimented with democracy, only a limited section of

9. *Shabbat* 88a.
10. *Shabbat* 88a.
11. The other is Shir HaShirim, the Song of Songs.
12. *Avoda Zara* 3a.

society had political rights. Women, children, slaves and foreigners were excluded. In many respects this held true until very recently. In Britain, women did not get the vote until 1918. In America, women's suffrage was complete only in 1920, though some states had enacted it earlier.

According to the sages, when God was about to give the Torah at Sinai, He told Moses to consult first with the women and only then with the men. This is the meaning of the verse "This is what you are to say to the house of Jacob and tell the people of Israel" (Exodus 19:3). The house of Jacob, our sages tell us, refers to the women.[13] The Torah, Israel's "constitution of liberty," includes everyone. It is the first moment, by thousands of years, that citizenship is conceived as being universal.

Perhaps the greatest testimony to the politics of the Hebrew Bible was given by Jean-Jacques Rousseau, in an unpublished manuscript discovered after his death:

> The Jews provide us with an astonishing spectacle: the laws of Numa, Lycurgus, Solon are dead; the very much older laws of Moses are still alive. Athens, Sparta, Rome have perished and no longer have children left on earth; Zion, destroyed, has not lost its children…. What must be the strength of legislation capable of working such wonders, capable of braving conquests, dispersions, revolutions, exiles, capable of surviving the customs, laws, empire of all the nations, and which finally promises them, by these trials, that it is going to continue to sustain them all, to conquer the vicissitudes of things human, and to last as long as the world? … any man whosoever he is, must acknowledge this as a unique marvel, the causes of which, divine or human, certainly deserve the study and admiration of the sages, in preference to all that Greece and Rome offer of what is admirable in the way of political institutions and human settlements.[14]

---

13. *Mekhilta*, ad loc.
14. These unpublished notes are preserved in the public library at Neuchatel. Cited in Leon Poliakov, *The History of Anti-Semitism* (Routledge and Kegan Paul, 1975), vol. 3:104–5.

With the revelation at Sinai, something unprecedented entered the human horizon, though it would take centuries, millennia, before its full implications were understood. At Sinai, the politics of freedom was born.

Mishpatim
מִשְׁפָּטִים

Following the revelation at Mount Sinai, *Mishpatim* fleshes out the details of the predominantly civil law that was to govern the Israelites: laws relating to slaves and their release, personal injuries and property laws, laws of social responsibility, justice and compassion, and laws relating to Shabbat and the festivals. It ends with a ratification of the covenant, and Moses ascending the mountain for forty days.

In the essays that follow, the first examines the law about helping an enemy, and the social psychology that underlies it. The second looks at two interpretations of a passage that would eventually lead to divergent Jewish and Christian approaches to abortion. The third is about the contrast between the simplicity of the Ten Commandments and the complexity and detail of the laws of *Mishpatim*. Why does the Torah use both methodologies? The fourth is about one of the most challenging and distinctive of all biblical imperatives: the command to love the stranger.

Helping an Enemy

Alarge part of the *parasha* of *Mishpatim* is taken up with a code of laws giving detailed expression to the just society the Israelites were commanded to create, in line with the idea already stated in connection with Abraham: "For I have chosen him, so that he will direct his children and his household after him to keep the way of the Lord by doing what is right [*tzedaka*] and just [*mishpat*]" (Genesis 18:19). *Mishpatim* are thus laws that promote the rule of justice.

Maimonides, in the *Guide for the Perplexed*, notes that *mishpat* is a complex idea. It denotes "the act of deciding upon a certain action in accordance with justice which may demand either mercy or punishment."[1] Justice in Judaism is rarely "strict justice," known in rabbinic Hebrew as *middat hadin*. There are times when it must be tempered with compassion and humanity. One notable example is contained in this week's *parasha*. It is stated briefly and unemphatically, yet it has far-reaching implications, as well as subtlety and moral beauty:

---

1. *Guide*: III, 53.

If you see your enemy's ass sagging under its burden, you shall not pass by. You shall surely release it with him. (Exodus 23:5)

There are two principles at stake here. One is concern for the animal. Jewish law forbids *tza'ar ba'alei ḥayim*, the needless infliction of pain on animals.[2] It is as if the Torah is here saying: a conflict between two human beings should not lead either of them to ignore the fact that the ass is labouring under its load. It is innocent. Why then should it suffer? That in itself is a powerful moral lesson.

The second is stronger still. It says, in effect: your enemy is also a human being. Hostility may divide you, but there is something deeper that connects you: the covenant of human solidarity. Distress, difficulty – these things transcend the language of difference. A decent society will be one in which enemies do not allow their rancour or animosity to prevent them from coming to one another's assistance when they need help.

If someone is in trouble, help. Don't stop to ask whether they are friend or foe. Get involved – as Moses got involved when he saw shepherds roughly handling the daughters of Jethro (Exodus 2:16–19); as Abraham did when he prayed for the people of the cities of the plain (Genesis 18:23–33). There are several significant nuances here. The first arises out of a parallel command in Deuteronomy:

You shall not see your brother's ass or his ox falling [under its load] in the road, and hide yourself from them. You shall lift it [the load] up with him. (22:4)

Exodus talks about enemies; Deuteronomy, about friends. On these two commands the Talmud states:

If [the animal of] a friend requires unloading, and an enemy's

---

2. Other examples in the Torah – all in Deuteronomy – include "sending the mother bird away" (22:6), letting animals rest on Shabbat (5:14), not muzzling an ox when it is treading grain (25:4), and not ploughing with an ox and an ass yoked together (22:10).

loading, you should first help your enemy – in order to suppress the evil inclination.[3]

Both equally need help. In the case of an enemy, however, there is more at stake than merely helping someone in distress. There is also the challenge of overcoming estrangement, distance, and ill-feeling. Therefore, it takes precedence. The sages were reading a nuance in the text. The phrase, "you shall not pass by" seems superfluous, but it is not. What it highlights is that when we see our enemy suffering, our first instinct is to pass by. Hence part of the logic of the command is "to suppress the evil inclination."

More striking still are the Aramaic translations (*Targum Onkelos*, and more explicitly *Targum Yonatan*[4]). They take the phrase "You shall surely release" to mean not just the physical burden, but also the psychological burden: "You shall surely let go of the hate you have in your heart towards him."

There is, however, one proviso. Note that the text says, "You shall surely release it [the burden] *with him*." From this the sages deduced the following:

If [the owner of the animal] sits down and says to the passer-by: "The obligation is yours. If you wish to unload [the animal], do so," the passer-by is exempt because it is said, "with him" [meaning: they must share the work]. If however the owner [is unable to help because he] is old or infirm, then one must [unload the animal on one's own].[5]

Why should this be so? After all, the beast is still suffering under its burden. Why should the enemy's refusal to help excuse you from the duty of help?

3. *Bava Metzia* 32b.
4. *Targum Onkelos*, commentary to Exodus 23:5 translates the passage as "You shall surely let go of what is in your heart against him." *Targum Yonatan* reads it as "You shall surely let go at that moment of the hatred that is in your heart."
5. Mishna, *Bava Metzia* 32a.

A fundamental principle of biblical morality is involved here: reciprocity. We owe duties to those who recognise the concept of duty. We have a responsibility to those who acknowledge responsibility. If, however, the person concerned refuses to exercise his duty to his own overloaded animal, then we do not make things better by coming to his aid. On the contrary, we may make it worse, by allowing him to escape responsibility. We become – in the language of addiction-therapy – co-dependents. We reinforce the very problem we are trying to help solve by allowing the individual to believe that there will always be someone else to do what is morally necessary. We create what the psychologist Martin Seligman calls "learned helplessness."[6] In strictly personal terms, it may be righteous to help someone who refuses to help himself. But there is a risk that we are thereby making ourselves better at the cost of making society worse – and biblical morality is not a code of personal perfection, but of social grace.

There is something distinctive about the Torah's approach to hatred and enemies. It is realistic rather than utopian. It does not say, "Love your enemy." It says, help him. Saints apart, we cannot love our enemies, and if we try to, we may eventually pay a high psychological price: we will eventually hate those who ought to be our friends.[7] Instead the Torah says, when your enemy is in trouble, come to his assistance. That way, part of the hatred will be dissipated. Who knows whether help given may not turn hostility to gratitude and from there to friendship? That is a practical way of moving beyond hate.

To be sure, Judaism has strong things to say against hate. Moses commanded the people: "Do not hate an Edomite, because he is your brother. Do not hate an Egyptian, for you were strangers in his land." (Deuteronomy 23:8). These were the paradigm cases of enemies. Edom was Esau, Jacob's rival. The Egyptians were the people who had enslaved the Israelites. Yet Moses commands that it is forbidden to hate them.

6. Martin Seligman, *Learned Optimism* (New York: Vintage, 2006), esp. 17–30.
7. The price, historically, has often taken the form of demonizing the enemy, so that he (or she) no longer comes within the category of the human at all. A classic text is Joshua Trachtenberg, *The Devil and the Jews*, 2nd ed. (Jewish Publication Society of America, 1983). See also Richard Kearney, *Strangers, Gods and Monsters: Interpreting Otherness* (London: Routledge, 2002).

A more general prohibition against hating enemies occurs in the very passage that commands the love of neighbours:

> Do not hate your brother in your heart. Rebuke your neighbour frankly so you will not share in his guilt. Do not seek revenge or bear a grudge against one of your people, but love your neighbour as yourself. I am the Lord. (Leviticus 19:17–18)

On this, Maimonides writes:

> You shall blot [any offences against you] out of your mind and not bear a grudge. For as long as one nurses a grievance and keeps it in mind, one may come to take vengeance. The Torah therefore emphatically warns us not to bear a grudge, so that the impression of the wrong should be completely obliterated and no longer remembered. This is the right principle. It alone makes civilized life and social interaction possible. [8]

What makes the law of the over-laden donkey significant, however, is the creative way in which it uses an occasion of distress to heal wounds and overcome animosities. And it works. For this, we now have the evidence of the most fascinating research exercises in social science, the study carried out in 1954 by Muzafer Sherif, known as "The Robbers Cave Experiment."[9]

Sherif wanted to understand the dynamics of group conflict and prejudice. To do so, he and his fellow researchers selected a group of twenty-two white, eleven-year-old boys, none of whom had met one another before. They were taken to a remote summer camp in Robbers Cave State Park, Oklahoma. They were randomly allocated into two groups. Initially neither group knew of the existence of the other. They were staying in cabins far apart. The first week was dedicated to team-building. The boys hiked and swam together. Each group chose a name

8. *Mishneh Torah*, Hilkhot De'ot 7:8.
9. Muzafer Sherif et al., *Intergroup Conflict and Cooperation: The Robbers Cave Experiment* (1954/1961). Full text available at: http://psychclassics.yorku.ca/Sherif/

for itself – they became the Eagles and the Rattlers. They stencilled the names on their shirts and flags.

Then, for four days the two teams were introduced to one another through a series of competitions. There were trophies, medals and prizes for the winners, and nothing for the losers. Almost immediately there was tension between them: name-calling, teasing, and derogatory songs. It got worse. Each burned the other's flag and raided their cabins. They objected to eating together with the others in the same dining hall.

Stage three was called the "integration phase." Meetings were arranged. The two groups watched films together. They lit Fourth-of-July firecrackers together. The hope was that these face-to-face encounters would lessen tensions and lead to reconciliation. They didn't. Several broke up with the children throwing food at one another.

In stage four, the researchers arranged situations in which a problem arose that threatened both groups simultaneously. The first was a blockage in the supply of drinking water to the camp. The two groups identified the problem separately and gathered at the point where the blockage had occurred. They worked together to remove it, and celebrated together when they succeeded. In another, both groups voted to watch some films. The researchers explained that the films would cost money to hire, and there was not enough in camp funds to do so. Both groups agreed to contribute an equal share to the cost. In a third, the coach on which they were travelling stalled, and the boys had to work together to push it. By the time the trials were over, the boys had stopped having negative images of the other side. On the final bus ride home, the members of one team used their prize money to buy drinks for everyone.

What Sherif had done in stage four was essentially to replicate the situation of the over-laden donkey by creating problems that neither group could solve alone, but could be resolved by both groups working together. The conclusion is nothing short of revolutionary. The fault-lines between enemies are not, as it has often been thought, an inexorable fact of human nature, hardwired into our genes. We do indeed feel hostile to the outsider, the other, the stranger, the alien. That is written into our evolutionary psychology, and it will surface whenever it is given the chance to.

But the boundaries can be redrawn so that erstwhile enemies are on the same, not opposite, side of the table. All it takes is a shared task that both can achieve together but neither can do alone. That is the situation exemplified in the law of the over-laden donkey. It does not require us to perform the almost superhuman task of loving our enemies. In the Robbers Cave experiment, what broke down the walls of estrangement and intergroup hostility was simply the necessity of working together to solve a shared problem.[10]

Tanakh, the Hebrew Bible, is not a code for Utopia. That is a prophetic dream, not a present-tense reality. In the here-and-now, however, the Torah tells us something not without moral grandeur: that small gestures of mutual assistance can in the long run transform the human situation. At the heart of the law of the over-laden ass is one of Judaism's most beautiful axioms: "Who is a hero? One who turns an enemy into a friend."[11]

---

10. For more on the subject, see Jonathan Sacks, *The Home We Build Together* (Continuum, 2007), 173–182.
11. *Avot deRabbi Natan*, 23.

Text and Interpretation: The Case of Abortion

Behind Jewish belief in *Torah shebe'al Peh*, the "Oral Law," lies a fundamental truth. The meaning of a text is not given by the text itself. Between a text and its meaning lies the act of interpretation – and this depends on who is interpreting, in what context, and with what beliefs.

Without an authoritative tradition of interpretation – in Judaism, the Oral Law – there would be chaos. There have been sectarian groups within Judaism – Sadducees, Karaites and others – who accepted the Written Torah but not the Oral Law, but in reality such a doctrine is untenable.

The Babylonian Talmud demonstrates this elegantly and with humour. It tells of a certain non-Jew who sought to convert to Judaism, and went to the great sage Hillel to do so.[1] He made one proviso: "Convert me on condition that I accept the Written but not the Oral Law." He was willing to be a Jew, but only a heretical one.

Hillel made no protest, and told the man to come to him for

---

1. *Shabbat* 31a.

instruction. The first day, Hillel taught him the first four letters of the Hebrew alphabet: aleph, bet, gimmel, daled. The next day he taught him the same letters in reverse order: daled, gimmel, bet, aleph. "But yesterday," protested the man, "you taught me the opposite." "You see," said Hillel, "you have to rely on me even to learn the alphabet. Rely on me also when it comes to the Oral Law." Without agreed principles, there can be no teaching, no learning, no authority, no genuine communication.

There is a passage in this week's *parasha* that shows how differences in interpretation can lead to, or flow from, profound differences in culture. Ironically, the subject – abortion – remains deeply contentious to this day.[2]

The text deals not with abortion per se, but with a fight between two people in which a bystander, a pregnant woman, is hit, with the result that she miscarries. What is the punishment in such a case? Here is the text:

> If men who are fighting hit a pregnant woman and she has a miscarriage, but there is no other fatal damage [*ason*], the offender must be fined whatever the woman's husband demands and the court allows. But if there is fatal damage [*ason*], you are to take life for life... (Exodus 21:22–23)

The word *ason* means "mischief, evil, harm, calamity, disaster." Jacob uses it when his sons tell him that the viceroy of Egypt (Joseph) insists that they bring their youngest brother Benjamin with them when they return, if they are to be cleared of the charge of spying. With Joseph missing, Benjamin is the only son left of Jacob's beloved wife Rachel, who died giving birth to him. Jacob initially refuses to give permission for Benjamin to leave home, saying: "If you take this one from me, too,

---

2. The best presentation of the historical development summarised in this chapter is David M. Feldman, *Marital Relations, Birth Control and Abortion in Jewish Law* (New York: Schocken, 1974), 251–294. See also J. David Bleich, *Judaism and Healing* (Ktav, 1981), 96–102; Fred Rosner, *Modern Medicine and Jewish Ethics* (Ktav, 1986), 139–160; Basil Herring, *Jewish Ethics and Halakhah for Our Time* (Ktav, 1984), 25–46.

and he meets with disaster (*ason*), you will send my white head down to the grave in sorrow" (Genesis 44:29).[3]

Ason apparently means a fatal accident. The law under consideration is about collateral damage – harm to an innocent third party – when people are engaged in a public and potentially murderous fight. If the third party is a pregnant woman, and as a result of being hit she miscarries but suffers no other injury, the person responsible must pay compensation for the loss of the unborn child, but suffers no other penalty. If, however, the woman dies, he is guilty of a much more serious offence (the sages disagreed as to whether this means that he is liable to capital punishment or not[4]).

One thing, however, is clear on this interpretation. Causing a woman to miscarry – being responsible for the death of a foetus – is not a capital offence. Until birth, the foetus does not have the legal status of a person. Such was the view of the sages in the land of Israel.

There was, however, a significant Jewish community in Alexandria, Egypt, during the late Second Temple period and the age of the teachers of the Mishna (the first two centuries of the Common Era). A passage in the Talmud[5] describes the great splendour of the synagogue there. The Alexandrian Jewish community – whose most famous member was the first-century philosopher Philo – was highly Hellenized. It developed its own traditions, at times quite different from those of the rabbinic mainstream. In one of his works, Philo, explaining the main principles of Jewish law to a non–Hebrew-reading public, turns to the biblical passage under review, and paraphrases it in these words:

> But if anyone has a contest with a woman who is pregnant, and

---

3. The word appears three times in the Jacob-Joseph-Benjamin story (Genesis 42:4, 42:38, 44:29) and twice in the present context (Exodus 21:22, 23). These are the only occurrences in the Hebrew Bible.
4. *Sanhedrin* 79a. The argument turns on the question as to whether, if X intends to kill Y but instead kills Z, X is guilty of murder. This affects the meaning of the phrase describing the punishment: "you are to take life for life." If the case is judged to be murder, "life for life" means capital punishment. If it is not considered murder, then "life for life" means – as in the case of "an eye for an eye" – monetary compensation.
5. *Sukka* 51b.

strike her a blow on her belly, and she miscarry, if the child which was conceived within her is still unfashioned and unformed, he shall be punished by a fine, both for the assault which he has committed and also because he has prevented nature, who was fashioning and preparing that most excellent of all creatures, a human being, from bringing him into existence. But if the child which was conceived had assumed a distinct shape in all its parts, having received all its proper connective and distinctive qualities, he shall die; for such a creature as that, is a man, whom he has slain while still in the workshop of nature, who had not thought it as yet a proper time to produce him to the light, but had kept him like a statue lying in a sculptor's workshop, requiring nothing more than to be released and sent out into the world.[6]

Philo is here following the Septuagint, the Greek translation of the Bible made in the third century BCE during the reign of Ptolemy II. There are numerous divergences between the Septuagint and the Hebrew text, and this is one of them. The Greek version translates *ason* not as "calamity," but rather "form."[7] The meaning of the two verses is now completely different. Now, according to Philo, they are talking about damage to the foetus only. In the first case, "there is no *ason*" means the foetus was "unformed" – i.e., the woman miscarries, but the foetus was at an early stage of development. The second verse speaks of a foetus "that has form," i.e., the woman was at a later stage of pregnancy. Philo puts this rather finely when he compares the developed foetus to a sculpture that has been finished but has not yet left the sculptor's workshop. In this view, foeticide – and hence abortion – can be a capital crime, an act of murder.

Philo's interpretation – and the views of the Alexandrian Jewish community generally – were to play a significant part in the religious history of the West. This was not because they had an impact on Jews: they did not. Rather, they had an impact on Christianity. The first Chris-

6. Philo, *The Special Laws*, III:XIX, ed. Leopold Cohn, vol. 5:180–182.
7. On this passage in the Septuagint, see Viktor Aptowitzer, "Observations on the Criminal Law of the Jews," *Jewish Quarterly Review* 15 (1924).

tian texts were written in Greek rather than Hebrew. They were, at the same time, intensely dependent on the Hebrew Bible. In fact, the one serious attempt to divorce Christianity completely from the Hebrew Bible – made by the second-century Gnostic Marcion – was deemed to be a heresy.[8]

Christians were therefore dependent on Greek translations of and commentaries to Tanakh, and these – especially the Septuagint – were to be found among Alexandrian Jewry. The result was that early Christian teaching on abortion followed Philo rather than the sages. The key distinction was, as Augustine put it, between *embryo informatus* and *embryo formatus* – an unformed or formed foetus.[9] If the foetus was formed (i.e., more than forty or eighty days had passed since conception: there was argument over the precise period), then causing its death was murder. So taught Tertullian in the second century.[10] So the law remained until 1588, when Pope Sixtus V ordained that abortion at any stage was murder. This ruling was overturned three years later by Pope Gregory XIV, but reintroduced by Pope Pius IX in 1869.

This is not to say that Jewish and Catholic views on abortion are completely different. In practice, they are quite close, especially when compared to the cultures of ancient Greece and Rome, or the secular West today, where abortion is widespread and not seen as a moral evil at all. Judaism permits abortion only to save the life of the mother or to protect her from life-threatening illness. A foetus may not be a person in Jewish law, but it is a potential person, and must therefore be protected. However, the theoretical difference is real. In Judaism, abortion is not murder. In Catholicism, it is.

8. Marcion of Sinope (85–160) was a Christian theologian who advocated a complete break with Judaism and its Scriptures. He believed that Christianity was a new religion, owing nothing to Judaism. Like the Gnostics, he held that the creator of the physical universe – the God of the Jews – was a lesser deity, and that the true God, the God of heaven, was purely spiritual and had nothing to do with laws regulating life on earth.
9. Augustine *Questiones in Exodum* 80.
10. Tertullian *Treatise on the Soul* XXXVII: "On the Formation and State of the Embryo." On the history of Christian attitudes to abortion, see E. Westermarck, *The Origin and Development of the Moral Ideas* (London: Macmillan, 1906).

It is fascinating to see how this difference arose – over a difference in interpretation of a single word, *ason*. Without tradition, and all the sages meant by "the Oral Law," we would simply not know what a verse means. Between a text and its meaning stands the act of interpretation. Without rules to guide us – rules handed down across the generations – we would be in the same position as Hillel's student, unable even to begin.

God Is in the Details

The contrast between the *parasha* of *Yitro* and that of *Mishpatim* is immense. In the former, the Torah takes us to the greatest encounter ever between human beings and God, the revelation at Mount Sinai, with its broad statement of principles popularly known as the Ten Commandments.[1] In the latter, we are suddenly plunged into a plethora of detail: laws about the release of slaves, liability for personal injury, the protection of property and so on. We seem to move from the sublime to the prosaic, from an all-encompassing moral and spiritual vision to the small print of a law code. Yet there is a profound connection between them, and it is Rashi, the greatest of the Torah commentators, who gives us an understanding of what is at stake.

On the opening phrase of *Mishpatim*, "And these are the laws you are to set before them" (Exodus 21:1), Rashi comments:

> "And these are the laws" – Wherever [the Torah only] uses the word "these" it signals a discontinuity with what has been stated

---

1. *Aseret HaDibrot*, commonly translated as "ten commandments" is more accurately translated as ten "utterances" or "overarching principles."

previously. Wherever it uses the term "and these" it signals a continuity. [So it is here, to teach that] just as the former commands [the Ten Commandments] were given at Sinai, so these [the civil laws] were given at Sinai. Why then are the civil laws placed in juxtaposition to the laws concerning the altar [at the end of the previous chapter]? To tell you to place the Sanhedrin [the Supreme Court] near to the Sanctuary. "Which you shall set before them" – God said to Moses: You should not think, I will teach them a category and a law two or three times until they know the words verbatim but I will not take the trouble to make them understand the reason [behind the law] and its significance. Therefore the Torah states "which you shall set before them" like a fully laid table with everything ready for eating.

Three remarkable propositions are being set out here, which have shaped the contours of Judaism ever since.

The first is that just as the general principles of Judaism set forth in the Decalogue at Sinai are divine, so too are the details – the minutiae of the civil laws. In the 1960s the Danish architect Arne Jacobson designed a new college campus in Oxford. Not content with designing the building, he went on to design the cutlery and crockery to be used in the dining hall, and supervised the planting of every shrub in the college garden. When asked why, he replied in the words of another architect, Mies van der Rohe: "God is in the details."

That is a Jewish sentiment. There are those who believe that what is holy in Judaism is its broad vision, never so compellingly expressed as in the Decalogue at Sinai. The truth however is that God is in the details: "Just as the former were given at Sinai, so these [the civil laws] were given at Sinai." The greatness of Judaism is not simply in its noble vision of a free, just and compassionate society, but in the way it brings this vision down to earth in detailed legislation.

Throughout history there have been philosophers – Plato, Aristotle, Locke, Hume, Kant, Bentham, Mill – who have attempted to reduce the moral life to a few broad principles: rationality, sympathy, duty or the greatest happiness for the greatest number. But though these are important, morality, if it is to become the text and texture of a society, must be translated into a code of conduct. We are made moral by what we do on a day-to-day basis, and by what others do likewise. Morality is like a language, and just as we cannot invent our own language and hope thereby to communicate with others, so we cannot invent our own morality and hope to live graciously with others in a society of shared ideals.

That is why, in *Mishpatim* specifically and the Torah generally, God reveals Himself in the form of laws, for it is law that gives colour and specificity to a social order. Here is a simple example:

> If you take your neighbour's cloak as a pledge, return it to him by sunset, because his cloak is the only covering he has for his body. What else will he sleep in? When he cries out to Me, I will hear, for I am compassionate. (Exodus 22:26–27)

This is law with a human face. Superficially, we are dealing with a simple economic transaction. Someone borrows money and gives the lender an item of clothing as security for the repayment of the loan, an everyday occurrence in ancient times. Yet the Torah insists that we must not forget the existential human situation. The borrower may be poor. The cloak may be the only one he has. The lender must not forget this fact. In strict legal terms he may be within his rights simply to hold on to the pledge, but a decent society depends on more than legal rights.

The Torah adds a detail by way of justification. God Himself says about the poor borrower, "When he cries out to Me, I will hear, for I am compassionate." God, the lawgiver, is not a remote abstraction. He is a direct personal presence in the lives of those who keep His law. And just as God tempers justice with compassion, so must His people do likewise.

Note how the Torah teaches this principle. It does it by specific example. It does not say, "Be compassionate." It gives us one example of what this might mean in daily life, and there are many others. Deuteronomy provides us with a different scenario: "Do not take a pair of millstones – not even the upper one – as security for a debt, because that would be taking a man's livelihood as security" (24:6). Here the concern is that someone in need of a loan might have nothing of sufficient value to offer as security except that by which he earns his living.

Were he to pledge this, he would be caught in a debt-trap, unable to repay what he has borrowed.

Here as elsewhere the Torah builds up the picture of a moral life by way of concrete illustrations. As Nahmanides explains in his comment on the command in Deuteronomy (6:18), "Do what is right and good in the Lord's sight," it is impossible to specify in detail the moral response to every human interaction. Life is simply too complex and unpredictable. Therefore the Torah gives us general rules on the one hand, and examples on the other, so that we are able to see both the broad picture and some of the brushstrokes out of which it is made.[2] God is not only in the generalities; he is also in the details.[3]

The second principle, no less fundamental, is that civil law is not secular. We do not believe in the idea "render to Caesar what is Caeser's and to God what belongs to God." We believe in the separation of powers[4] but not in the secularisation of law or the spiritualisation of faith. The Sanhedrin or Supreme Court must be placed near the Temple, to teach that law itself must be driven by a religious vision.

There is a famous rabbinic tradition that states that when Moses ascended to heaven to receive the Torah, the ministering angels protested to God: "Will You give Your most precious possession to mere mortals?" God told Moses to reply. Moses turned to the angels and said, "It says in the Torah, 'Remember the seventh day to keep it holy?' Do you angels work so that you need a day of rest? It says in the Torah, 'Honour your father and mother.' Do you have parents whom you need to honour?

---

2. Ramban, commentary to Deuteronomy 6:18.
3. Avishai Margalit, in *The Ethics of Memory* (Harvard University Press, 2002), makes a distinction between what he calls "i.e. philosophers" (explicators) and "e.g. philosophers" (illustrators). The former specialize in definitions and general principles, the latter in "striking examples." Ramban is making the point that the Torah uses both methodologies.
4. During the biblical era this was achieved through the separation of authority into three distinct domains, those of king, priest, and prophet. This is elegantly stated in a verse in Isaiah (33:22): "The Lord is our *judge*, the Lord is our *lawgiver*, the Lord is our *king*; he will save us." Though not identical with, it is strikingly close to, the principle of the separation of powers set out by Montesquieu in *L'Esprit des Lois* (1748), who divided them into the legislature, the judiciary and the executive. See Stuart Cohen, *The Three Crowns* (Cambridge University Press, 2007).

It says in the Torah, 'Do not commit adultery.' Do you angels have an impulse to adultery that needs to be kept in check by such a prohibition?" The angels thereupon ceased to object.[5]

God is in heaven, but we honour Him here on earth: that is what Torah – the word that means "law, teaching, ethical instruction" – is about. It is precisely through the instrumentality of law that we enact spiritual truths in physical circumstances, creating fragments of heaven in our interactions on earth.

It is not simply that, in Judaism, God is our lawgiver. It is that the law itself is thereby transformed, etched throughout with signals of transcendence. This is already foreshadowed in the first chapter of the Torah, with its statement of the equal and absolute dignity of the human person as the image of God (Genesis 1:26–27). Law and justice are primary vehicles of equality. That is why society must be based on the rule of law, impartially administered, treating all alike: "Do not follow the crowd in doing wrong. When you give testimony in a lawsuit, do not pervert justice by siding with the crowd, and do not show favouritism to a poor man in his lawsuit" (Exodus 23:2–3).

To be sure, at the highest levels of mysticism, God is to be found in the innermost depths of the human soul, but God is equally to be found in the public square and in the structures of society: the marketplace, the corridors of power, and the courts of law. There must be no gap, no dissociation of sensibilities, between the court of justice (the meeting-place of man and man) and the Temple (the meeting-place of man and God).

The third principle, and the most remarkable of all, is the idea that law does not belong to lawyers. It is the heritage of every Jew: "Do not think, I will teach them a category and a law two or three times until they know the words verbatim but I will not take the trouble to make them understand the reason [behind the law] and its significance. Therefore Torah states 'which you shall set before them' like a fully laid table [*shulkhan arukh*] with everything ready for eating." This is the origin of the name of the most famous of all Jewish codes of law, Rabbi Joseph Karo's *Shulkhan Arukh*.

---

5.   *Shabbat* 88b–89a.

From the earliest times, Judaism expected everyone to know and understand the law. Legal knowledge was never the closely guarded property of an elite. Instead, we have the famous phrase, "Torah is the heritage of the congregation of Jacob" (Deuteronomy 33:4). Already in the first century CE Josephus could write that "should any one of our nation be asked about our laws, he will repeat them as readily as his own name. The result of our thorough education in our laws from the very dawn of intelligence is that they are, as it were, engraved on our souls. Hence to break them is rare, and no one can evade punishment by the excuse of ignorance."[6] That may be why there are so many Jewish lawyers. Judaism is a religion of law – not because it does not believe in love ("You shall love the Lord your God," "You shall love your neighbour as yourself,") but because, without justice, neither love nor liberty nor human life itself can flourish.

The *parasha* of *Mishpatim*, with its detailed rules and regulations, can sometimes seem an anticlimax after the breathtaking grandeur of the revelation at Sinai. It should not be. *Parashat Yitro* contains the vision, but God is in the details. Without the vision, law is blind, but without the details, the vision floats in heaven. With them, the Divine Presence is brought down to earth, where we need it most.

6. Josephus *Contra Apionem* ii. 177–8.

Loving the Stranger

There are commands that leap off the page by their sheer moral power. So it is in the case of the social legislation in *Mishpatim*. Amid the complex laws relating to the treatment of slaves, personal injury and property, one command in particular stands out, by virtue of its repetition (it appears twice in our *parasha*), and the historical-psychological reasoning that lies behind it:

> Do not ill-treat a stranger or oppress him, for you were strangers in Egypt. (Exodus 22:20)

> Do not oppress a stranger; you yourselves know how it feels to be a stranger [literally, "you know the soul of a stranger"], because you were strangers in Egypt. (23:9)

Mishpatim contains many laws of social justice – against taking advantage of a widow or orphan, for example, or taking interest on a loan to a fellow member of the covenantal community, against bribery and injustice, and so on. The first and last of these laws, however, is the repeated command against harming a *ger*, a "stranger." Clearly something fundamental is at stake in the Torah's vision of a just and gracious social order.

The term *ger* itself is undefined in the Torah. There are other words for stranger, namely *zar* and *nokhri*, both of which have a stronger sense of "alien" or "foreigner," a visitor from elsewhere. The word *ger*, by contrast, signifies one who is not an Israelite by birth but who has come to live, on a long-term basis, within Israelite society. The oral tradition accordingly identified two forms of the *ger*: the *ger tzedek*, or convert (Ruth is the classic example), and the *ger toshav*, a "resident alien" who has chosen to live in Israel without converting to Judaism but instead agreeing to keep the seven Noahide laws mandatory on all mankind. *Ger toshav* legislation represents the biblical form of minority rights.

One of the questions the sages asked when they examined this law was about the difference between "ill-treatment" and "oppression." "Oppression," they concluded, meant monetary wrongdoing, taking financial advantage by robbery or overcharging. "Ill-treatment" referred to verbal abuse – reminding the stranger of his or her origins:

> Just as there is overreaching in buying and selling, so there is wrong done by words ... If a person was a son of proselytes, one must not taunt him by saying, "Remember the deeds of your ancestors," because it is written "Do not ill-treat a stranger or oppress him."
>
> Rabbi Yoḥanan said in the name of Rabbi Shimon bar Yoḥai: verbal wrongdoing is worse than monetary wrongdoing, because of the first it is written, "And you shall fear your God" but not of the second. Rabbi Eleazar said: one affects the person, the other only his money. Rabbi Shmuel bar Naḥmani said: for one restoration is possible, but not for the other.[1]

This emphasis on verbal abuse is typical of the sages in their sensitivity to language as the creator or destroyer of social bonds. As Rabbi Eleazar notes, harsh or derogatory speech touches on self-image and self-respect in a way that other wrongs do not. What is more, as

1. *Bava Metzia* 58b.

Rabbi Samuel bar Naḥmani makes clear, financial wrongdoing can be rectified in a way that wounding speech cannot. Even after apology, the pain (and the damage to reputation) remains. A stranger, in particular, is sensitive to his or her status within society. He or she is an outsider. Strangers do not share with the native-born a memory, a past, a sense of belonging. They are conscious of their vulnerability. Therefore we must be especially careful not to wound them by reminding them that they are not "one of us."

The second thing the sages noted was the repeated emphasis on the stranger in biblical law. According to Rabbi Eliezer, the Torah "warns against the wronging of a *ger* in thirty-six places; others say, in forty-six places."[2]

Whatever the precise number, the repetition throughout the Mosaic books is remarkable. Sometimes the stranger is mentioned along with the poor; at others, with the widow and orphan. On several occasions the Torah specifies: "You shall have the same law for the stranger as for the native-born."[3] Not only must the stranger not be wronged; he or she must be included in the positive welfare provisions of Israelite/Jewish society. But the law goes beyond this; the stranger must be loved:

> When a stranger lives with you in your land, do not mistreat him. The stranger living with you must be treated as one of your native-born. Love him as yourself, for you were strangers in Egypt. I am the Lord your God. (Leviticus 19:33–34)

This provision appears in the same chapter as the command, "You shall love your neighbour as yourself" (Leviticus 19:18). Later, in the book of Deuteronomy, Moses makes it clear that this is the attribute of God Himself:

> "For the Lord your God is God of gods and Lord of lords, the great God, mighty and awesome, who shows no partiality and accepts no bribes. He defends the cause of the fatherless and the

2. *Bava Metzia* 59b.
3. Exodus 12:49; Leviticus 24:22; Numbers 15:16, 29.

widow, and loves the stranger, giving him food and clothing. And you are to love those who are strangers, for you yourselves were strangers in Egypt." (Deuteronomy 10:17–19)

What is the logic of the command? The most profound commentary is that given by Nahmanides:

> The correct interpretation appears to me to be that He is saying: do not wrong a stranger or oppress him, thinking as you might that none can deliver him out of your hand; for you know that you were strangers in the land of Egypt and I saw the oppression with which the Egyptian oppressed you, and I avenged your cause on them, because I behold the tears of such who are oppressed and have no comforter, and on the side of their oppressors there is power, and I deliver each one from him that is too strong for him. Likewise you shall not afflict the widow and the orphan for I will hear their cry, for all these people do not rely upon themselves but trust in Me.
>
> And in another verse He added this reason: for you know what it feels like to be a stranger, because you were strangers in the land of Egypt. That is to say, you know that every stranger feels depressed, and is always sighing and crying, and his eyes are always directed towards God, therefore He will have mercy upon him even as He showed mercy to you, as it is written, and the children of Israel sighed by reason of the bondage, and they cried, and their cry came up to God by reason of the bondage, meaning that He had mercy on them, not because of their merits but only on account of the bondage [and likewise He has mercy on all who are oppressed].[4]

According to Nahmanides the command has two dimensions. The first is the relative powerlessness of the stranger. He or she is not surrounded by family, friends, neighbours, a community of those ready to come to their defence. Therefore the Torah warns against wronging

4. Ramban, commentary to Exodus 22:22.

them because God has made Himself protector of those who have no one else to protect them. This is the political dimension of the command.

The second reason, as we have already noted, is the psychological vulnerability of the stranger (we recall Moses' own words at the birth of his first son, while he was living among the Midianites: "I am a stranger in a strange land," Exodus 2:22). The stranger is one who lives outside the normal securities of home and belonging. He or she is, or feels, alone – and, throughout the Torah, God is especially sensitive to the sigh of the oppressed, the feelings of the rejected, the cry of the unheard. That is the emotive dimension of the command.

Rabbi Ḥayim ibn Attar (Ohr HaḤayim) adds a further fascinating insight. It may be, he says, that the very sanctity that Israelites feel as children of the covenant may lead them to look down on those who lack a similar lineage. Therefore they are commanded not to feel superior to the *ger*, but instead to remember the degradation their ancestors experienced in Egypt.[5] As such, it becomes a command of humility in the face of strangers.

Whichever way we look at it, there is something striking about this almost endlessly iterated concern for the stranger – together with the historical reminder that "you yourselves were slaves in Egypt." It is as if, in this series of laws, we are nearing the core of the mystery of Jewish existence itself. What is the Torah implying?

Concern for social justice was not unique to Israel.[6] What we sense, however, throughout the early biblical narrative, is the lack of basic rights to which outsiders could appeal. Not by accident is the fate of Sodom and the cities of the plain sealed when they attempt to assault Lot's two visitors. Nor can we fail to feel the risk to which Abraham and Isaac believe they are exposed when they are forced to leave home and take refuge in Egypt or the land of the Philistines. In each of the three episodes (Genesis chapters 12, 20, 26) they are convinced that their lives are at stake; that they may be murdered so that their wives can be taken into the royal harem.

---

5. Ohr HaḤayim, commentary to Exodus 22:20.
6. See Moshe Weinfeld, *Social Justice in Ancient Israel and in the Ancient Near East* (Jerusalem: Magnes Press, 1995).

Jacob's daughter Dina is raped and abducted when she wanders into the territory of Sheḥem. There are repeated implications, in the course of the Joseph story, that in Egypt, Israelites are regarded as pariahs (the word "Hebrew," like the term *hapiru* found in the non-Israelite literature of the period, seems to have a strong negative connotation). One verse in particular – when the brothers visit Joseph a second time – indicates the distaste with which they were regarded:

> They served him [Joseph] by himself, the brothers by themselves, and the Egyptians who ate with him by themselves, because Egyptians could not eat with Hebrews, for that is detestable to Egyptians. (Genesis 43:32)

So it was, in the ancient world. Hatred of the foreigner is the oldest of passions, going back to tribalism and the prehistory of civilization. The Greeks called strangers "barbarians" because of their (as it seemed to them) outlandish speech that sounded like the bleating of sheep.[7] The Romans were equally dismissive of non-Hellenistic races. The pages of history are stained with blood spilled in the name of racial or ethnic conflict. It was precisely this to which the Enlightenment, the new "age of reason," promised an end. It did not happen. In 1789, in revolutionary France, as the Rights of Man were being pronounced, riots broke out against the Jewish community in Alsace. Hatred against English and German immigrant workers persisted throughout the nineteenth century. In 1881 in Marseilles a crowd of ten thousand went on a rampage attacking Italians and their property. Dislike of the unlike is as old as mankind.

This fact lies at the very heart of the Jewish experience. It is no coincidence that Judaism was born in two journeys *away* from the two greatest civilizations of the ancient world: Abraham's from Mesopotamia, Moses' and the Israelites' from Pharaonic Egypt. The Torah is the world's great protest against empires and imperialism. There are many dimensions to this protest. One dimension is the protest against the attempt to justify social hierarchy and the absolute power of rulers in the name

---

7. The verb *barbarízein* in ancient Greek meant imitating the linguistic sounds non-Greeks made, or making grammatical errors in Greek.

of religion. Another is the subordination of the masses to the state – epitomized by the vast building projects, first of Babel, then of Egypt, and the enslavement they entailed. A third is the brutality of nations in the course of war (the subject of Amos' oracles against the nations). Undoubtedly, though, the most serious offence – for the prophets as well as the Mosaic books – was the use of power against the powerless: the widow, the orphan and, above all, the stranger.

To be a Jew is to be a stranger. It is hard to avoid the conclusion that this was why Abraham was commanded to leave his land, home and father's house; why, long before Joseph was born, Abraham was already told that his descendants would be strangers in a land not their own; why Moses had to suffer personal exile before assuming leadership of the people; why the Israelites underwent persecution before inheriting their own land; and why the Torah is so insistent that this experience – the retelling of the story on Passover, along with the never-forgotten taste of the bread of affliction and the bitter herbs of slavery – should become a permanent part of their collective memory.

Enlightenment thought was marked by two great attempts to ground ethics in something other than tradition. One belonged to the Scottish enlightenment – David Hume and Adam Smith – who sought it in emotion: the natural sympathy of human beings for one another.[8] The other was constructed by Immanuel Kant on the basis of reason. It was illogical to prescribe one ethical rule for some people and another for others. Reason is universal, argued Kant; therefore an ethic of reason would provide for universal respect ("Treat each person as an end in himself").[9]

Neither succeeded. In the twentieth century, villages and townships where Jews had lived for almost a thousand years witnessed their mass murder or deportation to the extermination camps with little or no protest. Neither Kantian reason nor Humean emotion were strong enough to inoculate Europe against genocide. Centuries of religiously inspired hate came together with pseudo-scientific theories of race and

8. David Hume, *A Treatise of Human Nature* (Oxford University Press, 1978); Adam Smith, *The Theory of Moral Sentiments* (Cambridge University Press, 2002).
9. Immanuel Kant, *The Moral Law* (Routledge, 2005).

social Darwinism ("the survival of the fittest" as Herbert Spencer put it) to relegate whole populations – above all, the Jews – to the category of the subhuman.

It is terrifying in retrospect to grasp how seriously the Torah took the phenomenon of xenophobia, hatred of the stranger. It is as if the Torah were saying with the utmost clarity: reason is insufficient. Sympathy is inadequate. Only the force of history and memory is strong enough to form a counterweight to hate.

The Torah asks, why should you not hate the stranger? Because you once stood where he stands now. You know the heart of the stranger because you were once a stranger in the land of Egypt. If you are human, so is he. If he is less than human, so are you. You must fight the hatred in your heart as I once fought the greatest ruler and the strongest empire in the ancient world on your behalf. I made you into the world's archetypal strangers so that you would fight for the rights of strangers – for your own and those of others, wherever they are, whoever they are, whatever the colour of their skin or the nature of their culture, because though they are not in your image, says God, they are nonetheless in Mine. There is only one reply strong enough to answer the question: Why should I not hate the stranger? Because the stranger is me.

Teruma
תרומה

With *Teruma* begins the longest single passage in the book of Exodus, continuing to the end of the book and interrupted only by the episode of the Golden Calf. Its subject is the *Mishkan*, the Tabernacle or Sanctuary the Israelites were commanded to make as a centre of worship and as a visible sign of the presence of God in their midst. The sheer length and detail of the narrative signal its central significance to the Israelites, yet it demands a considerable effort of interpretation to translate this into the language and thought of today.

In the first of the following essays, we examine the connection between the Tabernacle and the later institution of the synagogue. In the second we look at why it was important for it to be made out of the voluntary contributions of the Israelites. In the third we explore the connection between the Israelites' creation of the Tabernacle and God's creation of the universe. In the fourth we ask why it was important that everyone had a share in the ark, in which the tablets of stone, representing the Torah, were carried.

A Portable Home

The *parasha* of *Teruma* describes the construction of the Tabernacle, the first collective house of worship in the history of Israel. The first but not the last; it was eventually succeeded by the Temple in Jerusalem. I want to focus on one moment in Jewish history which represents Jewish spirituality at its lowest ebb and highest flight: the moment the Temple was destroyed.

It is hard to understand the depth of the crisis into which the destruction of the First Temple plunged the Jewish people. Their very existence was predicated on a relationship with God symbolised by the worship that took place daily in Jerusalem. With the Babylonian conquest in 586 BCE, Jews lost not only their land and sovereignty. In losing the Temple, it was as if they had lost hope itself. For their hope lay in God, and how could they turn to God if the very place where they served Him was in ruins? One document has left a vivid record of the mood of Jews at that time, one of the most famous of the psalms:

> By the waters of Babylon we sat and wept as we remembered Zion ... How can we sing the songs of the Lord in a strange land? (Psalm 137)

It was then that an answer began to take shape. The Temple no longer stood, but its memory remained, and this memory was strong enough to bring Jews together in collective worship. In exile, in Babylon, Jews began to gather to expound Torah, articulate a collective hope of return, and recall the Temple and its service.

The prophet Ezekiel was one of those who shaped a vision of return and restoration, and it is to him we owe the first oblique reference to a radically new institution that eventually became known as the *Beit Knesset*, the synagogue: "This is what the sovereign Lord says: although I sent them far away among the nations and scattered them among the countries, yet I have become to them a small Sanctuary [*Mikdash me'at*] in the countries where they have gone" (Ezekiel 11:16). The central Sanctuary had been destroyed, but a small echo, a miniature, remained.

The synagogue is one of the most remarkable examples of an *itaruta de'letata*, "an awakening from below." It came into being not through words spoken by God to Israel, but by words spoken by Israel to God. There is no synagogue in Tanakh, no command to build local houses of prayer. On the contrary, insofar as the Torah speaks of a "house of God" it refers to a central Sanctuary, a collective focus for the worship of the people as a whole.[1]

We tend to forget how profound the concept of a synagogue was. Professor M. Stern has written that "in establishing the synagogue, Judaism created one of the greatest revolutions in the history of religion and society, for the synagogue was an entirely new environment for divine service, of a type unknown anywhere before."[2] It became, according to Salo Baron, the institution through which the exilic community "completely shifted the emphasis from the place of worship, the Sanctuary, to the gathering of worshippers, the congregation, assembled at any time and any place in God's wide world."[3] The synagogue became Jerusalem in exile, the home of the Jewish heart. It is the ultimate expression

1. II Samuel 7:27; I Kings 6:1ff, 8:27; I Chronicles 22:1, etc.
2. H.H. Ben-Sasson, ed., *A History of the Jewish People* (Harvard University Press, 1976), 285.
3. Salo Baron, *The Jewish Community* (Jewish Publication Society of America, 1945), 1:62.

of monotheism – that wherever we gather to turn our hearts towards heaven, there the Divine Presence can be found, for God is everywhere.

Where did it come from, this world-changing idea? It did not come from the Temple, but rather from the much earlier institution described in this week's *parasha*: the Tabernacle. Its essence was that it was portable, made up of beams and hangings that could be dismantled and carried by the Levites as the Israelites journeyed through the wilderness. The Tabernacle, a temporary structure, turned out to have permanent influence, whereas the Temple, intended to be permanent, proved to be temporary – until, as we pray daily, it is rebuilt.

More significant than the physical structure of the Tabernacle was its metaphysical structure. The very idea that one can build a home for God seems absurd. It was all too easy to understand the concept of sacred space in a polytheistic worldview. The gods were half-human. They had places where they could be encountered. Monotheism tore this idea up at its roots, nowhere more eloquently than in Psalm 139:

> Where can I go from Your Spirit?
> Where can I flee from Your presence?
> If I go up to the heavens, You are there;
> If I make my bed in the depths, You are there.

Hence the question asked by Israel's wisest King, Solomon: "But will God really dwell on earth? The heavens, even the highest heaven, cannot contain You. How much less this temple I have built!" (1 Kings 8:27).

The same question is posed in the name of God by one of Israel's greatest prophets, Isaiah:

> Heaven is My throne,
> and the earth is My footstool.
> Where is the house you will build for Me?
> Where will My resting place be? (Isaiah 66:1)

The very concept of making a home in finite space for an infinite presence seems a contradiction in terms.

The answer, still astonishing in its profundity, is contained at the beginning of this week's *parasha*: "They shall make a Sanctuary for Me, and I will dwell in them [*betokham*]" (Exodus 25:8). The Jewish mystics pointed out the linguistic strangeness of this sentence. It should have said, "I will dwell in it," not " "I will dwell in them." The answer is that the Divine Presence lives not in a building but in its builders; not in a physical place but in the human heart. The Sanctuary was not a place in which the objective existence of God was somehow more concentrated than elsewhere. Rather, it was a place whose holiness had the effect of opening hearts to the One worshipped there. God exists everywhere, but not everywhere do we feel the presence of God in the same way. The essence of "the holy" is that it is a place where we set aside all human devices and desires and enter a domain wholly set aside for God.

If the concept of the *Mishkan*, the Tabernacle, is that God lives in the human heart whenever it opens itself unreservedly to heaven, then its physical location is irrelevant. Thus the way was open, seven centuries later, to the synagogue: the supreme statement of the idea that if God is everywhere, He can be reached anywhere. I find it moving that the frail structure described in this week's *parasha* became the inspiration of an institution that, more than any other, kept the Jewish people alive through almost two thousand years of dispersion – the longest of all journeys through the wilderness.

Voluntary Contribution

This week's *parasha* and those that follow it for the remainder of the book of Exodus, describe the great collective project of the Israelites in the desert: building a *Mishkan*, a portable Sanctuary, that would serve as the visible home of the Divine Presence. It was the first collective house of worship in the history of Israel.

The opening command, however, emphasizes an unusual dimension of the project:

> God spoke to Moses saying: "Speak to the Israelites and have them bring Me an offering. Take My offering from everyone whose heart impels him to give…They shall make Me a Sanctuary, and I will dwell among them." (Exodus 25:1–2, 8)

The emphasis is on the voluntary nature of the gifts. Why so? The Sanctuary and its service were overwhelmingly compulsory, not voluntary. The regular offerings were minutely prescribed. So too were the contributions. Everyone had to give a half-shekel for the silver sockets needed for the building, and another half-shekel annually for the sacrifices. The Sanctuary itself was the pre-eminent domain of the holy, and the holy is where God's will rules, not ours. Why then was the Sanctuary specifically to be built through voluntary donations?

There are some biblical passages whose meaning becomes clear only in hindsight, and this is one. To understand this week's *parasha* we have to move forwards almost five hundred years, to the time when King Solomon built the Temple. The story is one of the most ironic in Tanakh.

Our initial impression of Solomon is that he was a supremely wise king. He had asked God for wisdom, and was granted it in abundance:

> God gave Solomon wisdom and very great insight, and the breadth of his understanding was measureless as is the sand on the seashore. (1 Kings 4:29)

During Solomon's reign, Israel reached its greatest heights, economic and politically. The building of the Temple was itself seen by the Bible as the completion of the exodus from Egypt. Unusually, the text tells us the date of the project, not only in terms of years of the king's reign, but specifically also in terms of the exodus:

> In the four hundred and eightieth year after the Israelites had come out of Egypt, in the fourth year of Solomon's reign…he began to build the Temple of the Lord. (1 Kings 6:1)

The reference to the exodus is striking and deliberate. It reminds us of the phrase Moses used to the Israelites as they were about to enter the land: "Now you have not yet come to the resting place and the inheritance that the Lord your God is giving you" (Deuteronomy 12:9). The classic commentators take this to be a reference to Jerusalem and the Temple.[1] Thus Solomon's project brought the narrative of the exodus to closure. It was the last chapter in a long story.

Yet ultimately, and significantly, Solomon failed as a king. The initial impression we get from the biblical text is that his primary fail-

---

1. Rashi, ad loc., on the basis of *Zevaḥim* 119a. The text continues (12:11), "Then to the place the Lord your God will choose as a dwelling for His Name – there you are to

ing was in marrying foreign wives who led him astray into idolatry (1 Kings 11:4). However, a close reading shows that it had more to do with the way he set about building the Temple. This made immense demands on the people and led, as we will see, to fateful consequences. After Solomon's death, the kingdom divided. The ten northern tribes seceded from his son Rehoboam, and formed their own kingdom under the rebel Jeroboam. This was a critical turning point in biblical history. Weakened by division, it could only be a matter of time before both kingdoms eventually fell to neighbouring empires, and so it came to pass.

The real question is not, why did Jeroboam rebel? Politics is full of such events. The real question is: how was he able to do so and succeed? Coups d'état do not happen when a nation is flourishing, successful and at peace. Israel was all these things in Solomon's reign. How then was Jeroboam able to mount a coup, with real expectation of success?

The answer lies in the impact the building of the Temple had on the people. We are told:

> King Solomon conscripted labourers from all Israel – thirty thousand men. He sent them off to Lebanon in shifts of ten thousand a month, so that they spent one month in Lebanon and two months at home. Adoniram was in charge of the forced labour. Solomon had seventy thousand carriers and eighty thousand stonecutters in the hills, as well as thirty-three hundred foremen who supervised the project and directed the workmen. (1 Kings 5:27–30)

The Tanakh tells us that it was this burden that made the people restive after Solomon's death:

> So they [the people] sent for Jeroboam, and he and the whole assembly of Israel went to Rehoboam and said to him: "Your father put a heavy yoke on us, but now lighten the harsh labour

bring everything I command you: your burnt offerings and sacrifices, your tithes and special gifts, and all the choice possessions you have vowed to the Lord" – a reference to the Temple.

and the heavy yoke he put on us, and we will serve you." (I Kings 12:3–4)

The elders who had been Solomon's advisors told Rehoboam to accede to the people's request: "If today you will be a servant to this people and serve them and give them a favourable answer, they will always be your servants" (12:7). Rehoboam, influenced by his own young, impetuous advisors, ignored their advice. He told the people he would increase, not reduce, the burden. From then on, his fate was sealed.

Something strange is happening in this narrative. On several occasions we hear words that appear in the Mosaic books either in the context of Egyptian slavery or in laws forbidding the Israelites to act harshly towards slaves. The phrase "harsh labour," spoken by the people to Rehoboam, is used at the beginning of Exodus to describe the enslavement of the Israelites.[2] The description of Solomon's "carriers," *nosei saval*, reminds us of the sentence, "Moses grew up, and went out to his brothers and saw their burdens (*sivlotam*)."[3] After Solomon's death, the people use the word yoke: "Your father put a heavy yoke on us."[4] This is yet another term that recalls slavery in Egypt: "Therefore, say to the Israelites: I am the Lord, and I will bring you out from under the yoke of the Egyptians."[5]

Solomon's supervisors are described as *harodim ba'am*, the verb used in Leviticus 25 to describe how a master should not treat a slave: "Do not rule over (*tirdeh*) them ruthlessly."[6] Solomon built "store cities," *miskenot*, the same word used to describe the cities built by the Israelite slaves for Pharaoh.[7] Like Pharaoh, Solomon had chariots and riders – *rekhev* and *parashim*.[8]

Without saying so explicitly, and indeed, at one point denying it:

---

2. Exodus 1:14.
3. Ibid. 2:11.
4. I Kings 12:4.
5. Exodus 6:6.
6. Leviticus 25:43, 46, 53.
7. I Kings 9:19; Exodus 1:11.
8. I Kings 9:19; Exodus 14–15.

"But Solomon did not make slaves of any of the Israelites,"[9] the Tanakh is hinting that the building of the Temple turned Israel into a second Egypt. Solomon was altogether too close to being an Israelite Pharaoh.

The irony is overwhelming. Solomon was Israel's wisest king. The nation stood at the apex of its power and prosperity. Momentarily, it was at peace. The king was engaged in the holiest of tasks, the one that brought the exodus narrative to completion. Yet at that precise moment, the fault line developed that was eventually to bring centuries of tragedy. Why? Because Solomon in effect turned the Israelites into a conscripted labour force: the very thing they had left Egypt to avoid.

No sooner do we understand this than we realize in retrospect the significance of God's command in the making of the Tabernacle: "Speak to the Israelites and have them bring Me an offering. Take My offering *from everyone whose heart impels him to give*" (Exodus 25:2). As we said in the previous essay: God lives not in buildings but in builders, not in monuments of stone but in the minds and souls of human beings when they dedicate themselves to Him.

The Temple was intended to stand at the heart, geographical and spiritual, of a nation that had been taken by God from slavery to freedom. The faith of Israel therefore had to be an expression of liberty. Its Temple should have been built out of voluntary contributions, just as was the Tabernacle. This was no minor detail. It lay at the very heart of the project itself. Faith, coerced, is not faith. Worship, forced, is not true worship. A Temple built by conscripted labour conflicts with the very nature of God to whom it is dedicated. For a moment Solomon acted as if he were an Egyptian pharaoh, not a king of Israel, and the pent-up frustration and anger of the people eventually exploded after his death, splitting the nation into two.

It was thus not accidental, but of the essence, that the first house of God – small, fragile, portable; the opposite of the grandeur of the Temple – was built through free, uncoerced, voluntary contributions. For God lives not in houses of wood and stone, but in the minds and souls of free human beings. He is to be found not in monumental architecture, but in the willing heart.

9.   1 Kings 9:22.

The Home We Make for God

The Torah describes two acts of creation: God's creation of the universe, and the Israelites' creation of the *Mikdash* or *Mishkan*, the Sanctuary that travelled with them in the desert, the prototype of the Temple in Jerusalem.

The connection between them is not accidental or incidental. As a number of commentators have noted, the Torah invokes a series of verbal parallels between them.

The universe (Genesis)	The Mishkan (Exodus)
"And God made the sky"	"They shall make Me a Sanctuary"
"And God made the two large lights"	"They shall make an ark"
"And God made the beasts of the earth" (1:7, 16, 25)	"Make a table" (25:8, 9, 23)

"And God saw all that He had made, and behold it was very good." (1:31)	"Moses saw all the skilled work and behold they had done it; as God commanded it, they had done it." (39:43)
"The heavens and earth and all of their array were completed." (2:1)	"All the work of the Tabernacle of the tent of meeting was completed" (39:32)
"And God completed all the work that He had done" (2:2)	"And Moses completed the work" (40:33)
"And God blessed" (2:3)	"And Moses blessed" (39:43)
"And sanctified it" (2:3)	"And you shall sanctify it and all its vessels (40:9)

The effect is unmistakable. The latter mirrors the former. As God made the universe so He instructed the Israelites to make the *Mishkan*. It is their first great constructive and collaborative act after crossing the Reed Sea, leaving the domain of Egypt and entering their new domain as the people of God.

Just as the universe began with an act of creation, so Jewish history (the history of a redeemed people) begins with an act of creation. The key words – *make, see, complete, bless, sanctify, work, behold* – are the same in both narratives. The effect is to suggest that making the *Mishkan* was, for the Israelites, what creating the universe was for God.

The sages sensed the connection and linked the two events. So for example we find the following midrash:

> It has been taught that on the day [the Tabernacle was inaugurated] there was joy before the Holy One blessed be He, as on the day when heaven and earth were created.[1]

Here is an explicit comparison between the making of the *Mishkan* and the creation of the universe. Not only that: the passage makes the

---

1. *Sifra*, commentary to Leviticus 9:1; *Megilla* 10b.

extraordinary assertion that God rejoices in human creation as much as in His own.

There are other connections. The *Mishkan* was inaugurated on 1 Nisan.[2] According to Rabbi Yehoshua this was the date on which the universe was created.[3] Again, it is suggestive that the two events occur on the same calendrical date.

Another rabbinic tradition asserts that Betzalel, who made the appurtenances of the Tabernacle, knew the secret of combining letters – the mystical secret of how God created the universe.[4]

One of the most striking parallels lies in the figures who appear only twice in the Torah, once in the Garden of Eden, a second time in the Tabernacle, namely the cherubim.[5] These were guardian angels who, after Adam and Eve were exiled from Eden, barred the way to the tree of life. In the Tabernacle, the cherubim were figures placed above the ark that contained the Torah – described in the book of Proverbs (3:18) as "a tree of life to those who grasp her."

These connections suggest two things. First, the Tabernacle was conceived as a micro-cosmos, a symbolic representation of the universe as a whole. More profoundly, however, the construction of the Tabernacle was a kind of *tikkun*, a repair of something broken long before. What had been broken was, of course, the harmony between humanity and God, and between humanity and nature, after the sin of Adam and Eve. Before then, God had been an intimate presence. He had fashioned man, and then woman, with His own hands – a metaphorical expression of closeness and love. As a result of sin, paradise was lost. Now, however, with the construction of the Tabernacle, God was again to be close: "Make Me a Tabernacle and I will dwell among them" (Exodus 25:8). In some sense, the Tabernacle represented paradise regained.

One midrash describes the ten stages by which the Divine Presence was further and further distanced from earth as a result of humanity's sins. But then, beginning with Abraham, the Divine Presence came

2. Exodus 40:2, 17.
3. *Rosh HaShana* 11a.
4. *Berakhot* 55a.
5. Genesis 3:24; Exodus 25:20–21, 26:1, 31.

closer and closer, until, with the making of the *Mishkan*, it came as close as it had at the beginning:

> Then came Moses and brought the Divine Presence down to earth. When? When the Tabernacle was erected. Then the Holy One, blessed be He, said: "I have come into My garden, My sister, My bride" – I have come to that which I desired [from the outset]. This is the meaning of "It came to pass on the day that Moses finished erecting the Tabernacle" – the source of Rabbi Shimon bar Yohai's statement that "Wherever it says 'and it came to pass' it refers to something that existed in the past, and was then interrupted, and then returned to its original situation."[6]

The making of the *Mishkan* was therefore a cosmic event; a return to Eden and a mending of the exile between humanity and God. God would once again have a home, a habitation, among human beings. It would be sited in the centre of the Israelites' camp, travelling when they travelled, resting when they rested. No longer would the Israelites sense the presence and proximity of God only in miracles or moments of crisis. It would be a daily event, a constant epiphany. Only thus can we understand the parallels between the Tabernacle and creation. Yet obvious questions remain.

First is the sheer disparity between the lengths of the two narratives. The creation of the universe takes a mere thirty-four verses (Genesis 1 together with the first three verses of 2). The making of the *Mishkan* takes hundreds of verses (the *parashot* of *Teruma*, *Tetzaveh*, part of *Ki Tissa*, *Vayak-hel* and *Pekudei*) – considerably more than ten times as long. Why so? The universe is vast. The Sanctuary was small, a modest construction of poles and drapes that could be dismantled and carried from place to place as the Israelites journeyed through the wilderness. Given that the length of any passage in the Torah is a guide to the significance it attaches to an episode or law, why devote so much time and space to the Tabernacle?

Second, why the apparent repetition in the story of the Taber-

6. Solomon Buber, comp., *Tanḥuma, Naso*, 24.

nacle? The story is told two times, once before, the other after, the sin of the Golden Calf. The first account (Exodus 25–30) consists of God's instructions. The second (Exodus 35:4–40) is a description of how those instructions were carried out. Why tell the story twice?

Third, when all is said and done, what sense are we to make of the idea that God is found in a building, a place? God is vaster than the universe with its hundred billion galaxies, each with billions of stars. Does it not verge on blasphemy to build an earthly home for God?

The answer, it seems to me, lies in the last two chapters of Exodus. In chapter 39, about the making of the priestly garments, we find, repeated seven times, the phrase, "as the Lord had commanded Moses." The same phrase appears seven times in chapter 40, describing how Moses erected the Tabernacle. In both cases, the sevenfold repetition recalls the seven days of creation and the seven times God calls creation "good."

What is radical about the Torah's account of creation is the concept of the divine will. God speaks and the world comes into being. There is no cosmic struggle, as there is in every mythological account of the origin of things. God's will reigns supreme.

All is well until God creates the first humans and grants them freedom. They are the first and to this day the only life-form endowed with the capacity to undo the work of creation, because humans, alone apart from God, have the gift of free will. All the good that humans do comes from this capacity of will – to choose to help others, for example. But so too comes all the evil. When two wills clash, the result is often violence. All conflict comes from a collision of wills.

The only *tikkun*, the only repair, is to subordinate our will to the will of God. When we do God's will, we choose to act, as it were, from the vantage point, and for the benefit of, the universe as a whole. Other people's interests matter, not just my own. Long-term consequences matter, not just the immediate satisfaction of my desires. The will of God is what connects me to the rest of the universe by way of its Creator. I become one with infinity when I renounce my will in favour of the will of the Infinite.

But this is a deep, metaphysical idea. And much of Judaism is about how to take deep ideas and make them real in human lives.

Somehow it needs to be symbolized in a vivid and concrete way at the centre of the collective life of the people of the covenant. That is what the *Mishkan* was. It was a microcosm of the universe, created by human beings in total obedience to the will of God.

Hence the sevenfold repetitions of the phrase, "as the Lord had commanded Moses." God spoke and the Israelites did, just as in creation, God spoke and the elements obeyed. Hence the twofold telling of the story, the first as divine command, the second as the human response to the command. Now too we understand the significance of the fact that the two halves of the narratives are interrupted by the story of the Golden Calf, as if to say: this is what happens when people do not obey God's command. They invent a god of their own making. Yet the command remains. The very fact that the Israelites make the Tabernacle in obedience to God heals the wound opened up by the Golden Calf, just as it heals the earlier and deeper wound of Adam and Eve's sin in the Garden of Eden.

Now, too, we understand why the making of the Tabernacle is recounted in such detail. It is to tell us that nothing was made by human initiative. Every measurement, every item, every feature of every vessel, represented God's will made actual by the freely assenting human will. The Tabernacle mirrored the universe to tell us that we too can be creators of universes, but only if we heed the will of God. Without that, we will eventually become destroyers of the universe.

We now know, thanks to recent discoveries in cosmology, that the universe was only able to come into existence through the most extraordinary precision of the mathematical constants that govern the forces unleashed in the Big Bang – constants like the strength of the electrical forces holding atoms together, or the ratio of gravity to the amount of energy necessary to overcome it on a galactic scale.[7] Had they been even slightly different, the universe would simply not have coalesced into stars, planets, and on earth, into life. The precision of the Tabernacle in some unmistakable way evokes a sense of the exactitude of the cosmic order which, in miniature, it symbolized.

The meaning of the Tabernacle was not that God lives there but

7. The story is well told in Martin Rees, *Just Six Numbers* (Basic Books, 2001).

not elsewhere. It is that God lives wherever we subordinate our will to His. The Tabernacle symbolized, in space, the place where God's will reigns supreme.

This explains an otherwise inexplicable saying of the sages. They said, "Whoever prays on the night of Shabbat and says, 'Now the heavens and the earth were finished' (Genesis 2:1) is regarded as if he had become a partner with the Holy One, blessed be He, in the work of creation."[8] We would have expected just the opposite, namely that we become God's partners in creation when we create, not when, as on Shabbat, we refrain from creating.

However, what the sages are saying is that it is precisely when we renounce our will in favour of the will of God, as we do on Shabbat, that we become God's partners in creation. That is what we do, in time, on Shabbat, and what the Israelites did, in space, by making the Tabernacle exactly as God commanded. At the heart of the Jewish enterprise – symbolized by the Tabernacle at the centre of the camp – is an act of sacrifice. We sacrifice our will to the will of God, not abstractly and in general, but precisely and practically, following the most detailed instructions.

The universe is the space God made for humanity. The *Mishkan* is the space human beings made for God. James Kugel puts this idea simply and elegantly. The point of the construction of the Tabernacle was, he says,

> for them to open up a space in order to allow Him to fill it. And this is the most basic principle of our way, to open up such a space in our lives and in our hearts. Then such a space will have the capacity to radiate outward. So the holiness of the *Mishkan* radiated out to fill the whole camp of the Israelites during their wanderings, and the camp itself became changed as a result. And it was quite proper that the people be the ones to build God's dwelling, because this is the way it always must be: the people create the space and then God can fill it.[9]

8. *Shabbat* 119b.
9. James Kugel, *On Being a Jew* (Harper San Francisco, 1990), 36.

God fills the space we make for Him, and that is no small thing. It is the way, the only way, we heal the wounds brought about by human self-assertion, and create a universe worthy of His presence.

The Making of an Ark

s I have written elsewhere in these essays, the Torah was meant to be listened to, not read. The eye can scan many lines at once; but listening is always a sequential, word-by-word process. The result is that the ear can sometimes hear a discrepancy that the eye misses. A discrepancy is always significant when it comes to Torah. Like a discord in a work by Mozart, or the asymmetrical background to Leonardo's Mona Lisa, it is meant to draw attention to something, to launch reverberations of complexity, to add depth to an otherwise superficial response. So it is in the apparently prosaic details of the construction of the Tabernacle. Though it is a matter of only two letters in the text, there is an important incongruity.

God instructs Moses in the making of the Sanctuary and its appurtenances, detail by detail. In each case the verb is in the second person singular: *vetzipita, ve'asita, veyatzakta, venatata, veheveta,* "you shall cover…you shall make…you shall pour…you shall place…you shall bring."[1] However, there is one exception to this rule; the ark. There the verb is in the third person plural: *ve'asu aron atzei shittim,* "They shall

1. Exodus 25:11, 12, 14, 15.

make an ark of acacia wood."² Why "they," not "you"? Why the shift from the singular to the plural?

The ark was made to hold the tablets of stone given to Moses by God at Mount Sinai:

> There was nothing in the ark except the two stone tablets that Moses had placed in it at Horeb,³ where the Lord made a covenant with the Israelites after they came out of Egypt. (1 Kings 8:9)

The Torah calls the tablets "the testimony" ("And you shall put into the ark the testimony which I will give you," Exodus 25:16) since they were the physical symbol of the Sinai covenant. According to the sages, "both the [complete second set of] tablets and the fragments of the [first] tablets [which Moses broke after the Golden Calf] were in the ark."⁴ The ark, in short, symbolized and represented Torah.

The reason, therefore, that the construction of the ark was commanded in the plural is that everyone was to have a share in it:

> Rabbi Judah son of R. Shalom said: The Holy One blessed be He, said, "Let them all come and occupy themselves with the ark in order that they may all merit the Torah."⁵

Unlike other aspects of service in the Sanctuary or Temple, Torah was the heritage of everyone. All Israel were parties to the covenant. All were expected to know and study its terms. Judaism might know other hierarchies, but when it came to knowledge, study and the dignity conferred by scholarship, everyone stood on equal footing.

Judaism is a profoundly egalitarian faith. As the historian Norman Gottwald puts it:

> "The Chosen People" is the distinctive self-consciousness of a soci-

---

2. Exodus 25:10.
3. Horeb is another name for Sinai. See Exodus 3:1, 17:6, 33:6; Deuteronomy 1:6, etc.
4. *Berakhot* 8b, *Bava Batra* 14b.
5. *Shemot Raba* 34:2.

ety of equals created in the intertribal order and demarcated from a primarily centralised and stratified surrounding world. "Covenant" is the bonding of de-centralised social groups in a larger society of equals committed to co-operation without authoritarian leadership and a way of symbolising the locus of sovereignty in such a society of equals... Israel *thought* it was different because it *was* different: it constituted an egalitarian social system in the midst of stratified societies...[6]

Gottwald's point is that ancient Israel was the first attempt we know of to create a society of equal dignity under the sovereignty of God. Since God had created all in His image, all were equal. This was an idea so far in advance of its age that we do not find it elsewhere until relatively recent times. All the great civilizations of the ancient world were highly stratified and governed by rigid hierarchies, a human counterpart of the hierarchy people saw in heaven itself, with its sun, moon and stars. The idea that things might be otherwise would have struck them as absurd.

In the American Declaration of Independence, Thomas Jefferson translated this idea into the famous words: "We hold these truths to be self-evident, that all men are created equal, that they are endowed by their Creator with certain unalienable Rights, that among these are Life, Liberty and the pursuit of Happiness..." What is interesting about this sentence is that "these truths" are anything but self-evident. They would have been regarded as subversive by Plato, who held that humanity is divided into people of gold, silver and bronze and that hierarchy is written into the structure of society.[7] They would have been incomprehensible to Aristotle who believed that some were born to rule and others to be ruled.[8] They are "self-evident" only to one steeped in the Bible.

Any attempt at creating an egalitarian society runs up against the perennial difficulty that people are born unequal in talents, endowments and natural abilities, as well as in their early environment. Communism, like every other attempt to enforce equality, ends up by demanding an

---

6. Norman K. Gottwald, *The Tribes of Yahweh* (Continuum, 1999), 692–3.
7. Plato *Republic* bk. 3, 415a–c.
8. Aristotle *Politics* 1254b10–26.

unacceptable price in terms of liberty. How then can a society be free and equal at the same time?

To put more fully the idea I noted in the essay, "A Kingdom of Priests": no civilization has ever come closer to creating such a society than the people of the covenant – and it did so in a way still unrivalled in its insight and depth. Physical goods – wealth and with it, power – always represent, at least in the short term, zero-sum games. The more I give away, the less I have. For that reason these are always arenas of conflict, in which there are winners and losers. Political and economic systems play the important function of mediating conflict by the imposition of rules (such as elections in the case of democracy, exchange in the case of market economies). In this way, competition does not degenerate into anarchy. That is the necessity for, and the glory, of politics and economics. But they do not create equality.

Spiritual (sometimes called social or public) goods, however, have a different logic. They are non-zero-sum games. The more love or influence or trust I give away, the more I have. That is because they are goods the existence of which depends on being shared. They give rise to structures of co-operation, not competition. It has been one of the great discoveries of sociobiology on the one hand, and "civil society" or "communitarian" political thought on the other, that the survival of any group depends at least as much on co-operation as competition. No individual, however strong or gifted, can rival the achievements of a group in which each contributes his or her talents to an orchestrated, collective endeavour. On this, Aristotle and Maimonides agreed: Homo sapiens is, above all, a social animal whose very existence depends on specialization, co-operation and trust.[9]

It was the genius of Judaism to see that the primary social good is knowledge. The simplest and most effective way of creating a society of equal dignity is to make knowledge equally accessible to all. The symbol of this was the ark, the container of the most important of all bodies of knowledge, namely the Torah: the written constitution of Israel as a nation under the sovereignty of God. If everyone has knowledge of the law, then everyone is, in the fullest sense, a citizen (one could almost say

9. See Jonathan Sacks, *The Politics of Hope* (London: Vintage, 2000).

that Israel is defined as a nation of constitutional lawyers). Knowledge is power; and if knowledge is distributed equally, so too is power. That is why, here alone in its list of the component parts of the Sanctuary, the Torah shifts from the second person singular to the third person plural. When it comes to the ark, home and symbol of the most significant form of knowledge, everyone must have an equal share.

On no other subject were the sages more eloquent. The midrashic passage quoted above goes on to state in the name of Rabbi Shimon bar Yohai:

> There are three crowns: the crown of kingship, the crown of priest-hood, and the crown of Torah. The crown of kingship – this is the table…the crown of priesthood – this is the altar…the crown of Torah – this is the ark…Why does it say of the rest [of the items of the Tabernacle] "And you shall make" whereas of the ark it says, "And they shall make"? To teach you that the crown of Torah stands above all. When one has acquired the Torah it is as if he has acquired all the rest.[10]

In a striking statement, the sages ruled:

> A bastard who is a scholar takes precedence over an ignorant high priest, for it is said, "More precious is it than rubies (*peninim*)" – meaning that [one who is wise] is more precious than the High Priest who enters the innermost Sanctuary (*lifnei velifnim*).[11]

These are intensely political statements. They reflect the fact that biblical Israel was not a *wholly* egalitarian society. Initially, the firstborn in each family was to have become a priest, but after the Golden Calf that role was transferred to a single tribe, Levi, and a single family within the tribe, namely the sons of Aaron.

Initially, Israel did not have a monarchy. Throughout the long

---

10. *Shemot Raba* 34:2.
11. *Horayot* 13a; Talmud Yerushalmi *Horayot* 3:5; Rambam, *Mishneh Torah*, Talmud Torah 3:2.

period covered by the Book of Judges it existed as a confederation of tribes without a political leader. At times of crisis individuals would emerge, known as "judges," who would lead the people in battle, but they had no formal office or succession. Eventually in the days of Samuel the people asked for, and were given, a king.

So hierarchy existed as of necessity in the case of both the "crown" (domain) of priesthood and kingship. In a vaulting leap of imagination, however, the sages saw that the political threat to Israel under Roman rule could be countered, spiritually and educationally, by a full implementation of the biblical ideal, a society of equals. Even if there should come a time when there would be no more kings or (functioning) priests, still the "crown of Torah" would remain. By creating the world's first system of universal compulsory education, they were able to lay the foundations of a national identity built on literacy, study and the life of the mind. Here is how the Talmud describes the process, culminating in the work of Yehoshua ben Gamla, a high priest in the last days of the Second Temple:

> Truly the name of that man is to be blessed, namely Yehoshua ben Gamla, for but for him the Torah would have been forgotten from Israel. For at first if a child had a father, his father taught him, and if he had no father he did not learn at all ... They then made an ordinance that teachers of children should be appointed in Jerusalem ... Even so, however, if a child had a father, the father would take him up to Jerusalem and have him taught there, and if not, he would not go up to learn there. They therefore ordained that teachers should be appointed in each prefecture, and that boys should enter school at the age of sixteen or seventeen. [They did so] and if the teacher punished them they used to rebel and leave the school. At length Yehoshua b. Gamla came and ordained that teachers of young children should be appointed in each district and each town and that children should enter school at the age of six or seven.[12]

12. *Bava Batra* 21a.

That was when the "ark" became indeed the property of all. To be sure, even then there were temptations (when are there not?) for those well versed in Torah to hold themselves superior to others, the *ammei ha'aretz* (the ignorant, those who had not mastered the texts). Yet this sense of superiority was always answerable to the fact that the sages knew, in their heart of hearts, that learning was not the preserve of an elite. Two stories from the Talmud illustrate this with great poignancy:

> Once Rabbi Yannai was walking along the way, when he met a man who was handsomely attired. He said to him, "Would the master mind being my guest?" He replied, "As you please." He then took him home and questioned him on Bible, but he knew nothing; on Mishna, but he knew nothing; on Talmud, but he knew nothing; on *aggada*, but he knew nothing. Finally he asked him to say grace. He replied, however, "Let Yannai say grace in his house." He then asked him, "Can you repeat what I tell you?" He answered, "Yes." He then exclaimed, "Say, a dog has eaten Yannai's bread." At this point the guest rose and seized him, demanding, "What of my inheritance with you, that you are cheating me?" "What inheritance of yours do I have?" asked R. Yannai. He replied, "The children recite, 'Moses commanded us the Torah, an inheritance of the congregation of Jacob.' It is not written here 'congregation of Yannai' but 'congregation of Jacob.'" At this, they became reconciled.[13]

Rabbi Yannai mistakenly assumed that from the man's impressive appearance, he was a scholar. On finding that he was ignorant, he treated him with contempt. However, the stranger defeated the rabbi on a simple point of Jewish principle. The Torah is the inheritance of the entire congregation, not of an aristocracy of scholars. The fact that Rabbi Jannai was forced to concede the point demonstrates its power.

The second story concerns the temporary removal from office of the Nasi (religious head of the community) Rabban Gamliel. As leader, Rabban Gamliel had adopted an exclusive approach to the house

13. *Vayikra Raba* 9:3.

of study. He insisted that only those whose "inside was like their outside" – whose integrity was unchallengeable – were permitted to enter. The Talmud states that when he was deposed, the doors of the houses of study were opened to all.

> On that day, many benches were added…Rabban Gamliel became alarmed and said, "Perhaps, God forbid, I withheld Torah from Israel." He was shown in a dream, white casks full of ashes [suggesting that those to whom he refused entry were in fact unworthy of a place in the house of study]. This however was not so. He was only shown the dream to set his mind at ease.[14]

Rabban Gamliel's exclusivism was wrong. The doors of the house of study should be open to everyone.

At roughly the same time, in the first century CE, Josephus could write:

> Should any one of our nation be asked about our laws, he will repeat them as readily as his own name. The result of our thorough education in our laws from the very dawn of intelligence is that they are, as it were, engraved on our souls.[15]

A twelfth-century monk wrote in one of his commentaries, "A Jew, however poor, if he had ten sons, would put them all to letters, not for gain, as the Christians do, but for the understanding of God's Law; and not only his sons but his daughters too."[16] With a touch of exaggeration, the historian Paul Johnson calls Judaism an "ancient and highly efficient social machine for the production of intellectuals."[17] It was, of course, not the production of intellectuals that motivated the Judaic love of learning, but rather the idea that a society structured around divine law should be one in which everyone had equal access to knowledge and

---

14. *Berakhot* 28a.
15. *Contra Apionem* 2:177–78.
16. B. Smalley, *The Study of the Bible in the Middle Ages* (Oxford, 1952), 78.
17. Paul Johnson, *A History of the Jews* (Weidenfeld and Nicolson, 1987), 341.

therefore equal dignity as citizens in the republic of faith. It was, and remains, a beautiful idea, hinted at for the first time in the simple, yet resonant detail that though all else in the Tabernacle was constructed by individuals ("you"), the Ark belonged to everyone ("they"). Seldom has so slight a nuance signalled so high an ethical and intellectual ideal.

Tetzaveh
תצוה

In *Tetzaveh*, the role of the priests in the service of the Tabernacle takes centre stage. For once the limelight is no longer turned on Moses, but on his brother Aaron, the High Priest. We read about the tasks of the priesthood, their robes of office and their consecration, as well as further details about the Tabernacle itself.

Because this is the first time priesthood is given such attention in the Torah, the essays that follow look at what made priests different from other kinds of religious leader, especially the prophet. The first looks at the priest as a symbol of constancy and continuity in Jewish life. The second looks at the parts priest and prophet played in the development of Jewish prayer. The third analyzes the relationship between Moses the prophet and Aaron the priest, the last act in the five-part story about brothers that began in Genesis. The fourth essay looks at the idea of robes of office and their place in Judaism and other cultures.

Priests and Prophets

*T*etzaveh is, as commentators have noted, the only *parasha*, from the birth of Moses at the beginning of the book of Exodus, to the end of the book of Numbers, that does not contain Moses' name. For most of the narrative he is centre-stage. Here, he is in the background. Why? Several interpretations have been offered.

The Vilna Gaon suggests that it is related to the fact that in most years, *Tetzaveh* is read during the week in which the seventh day of the month of Adar falls: the day of Moses' death. During this week we sense the loss of the greatest leader in Jewish history – and his absence from *Tetzaveh* expresses that loss.[1]

The Ba'al HaTurim (Rabbi Jacob ben Asher, 1270–1340) relates it to Moses' plea, in the following *parasha*, for God to forgive Israel. "If not," says Moses, "blot me out of the book you have written" (Exodus 32:32). There is a principle that "The curse of a sage comes true, even if

---

1.   Dov Eliach, ed., *Peninim MiShulḥan HaGra al HaTorah* (Jerusalem: 1997), 129.

it was conditional [and the condition has not been satisfied]."[2] Thus for one week his name was "blotted out" from the Torah.[3]

The *Paneaḥ Raza*[4] relates it to another principle: "There is no anger that does not leave an impression."[5] The last time Moses declined God's invitation to lead the Jewish people out of Egypt, saying, "Please send someone else," God "became angry with Moses" (4:13–14), and told him that his brother Aaron would accompany him. For that reason Moses forfeited the role he might otherwise have had, of becoming the first of Israel's priests, a role that went instead to Aaron. That is why he is missing from the *parasha* of *Tetzaveh*, which is dedicated to the role of the priests.

All three explanations focus on an absence. However, perhaps the simplest explanation is that *Tetzaveh* is dedicated to a presence, one that had a decisive influence on Judaism and Jewish history.

Judaism is unusual in that it recognises not one form of religious leadership but two: the *navi* and the kohen, the prophet and the priest. The figure of the prophet has always captured the imagination. He (or she) is a person of drama, "speaking truth to power," unafraid to challenge kings and courts, or society as a whole, in the name of high, even utopian ideals. No other type of religious personality has had the impact as the prophets of Israel, of whom the greatest was Moses. The priests, by contrast, were for the most part quieter figures, apolitical, serving in the Sanctuary rather than in the spotlight of political debate. Yet they, no less than the prophets, sustained Israel as a holy nation. Indeed, though the people of Israel were summoned to become "a kingdom of priests" (Exodus 19:6) they were never called on to be a people of prophets (Moses did say, "Would that all God's people were prophets," [Numbers 11:29] but this was a wish, not a reality).

Let us therefore consider some of the differences between a prophet and a priest.

2. *Makkot* 11a.
3. Commentary of Ba'al HaTurim to Exodus 27:20.
4. *Paneaḥ Raza* was compiled by R. Isaac ben Judah Halevi. Much of the material is based on the comments of R. Isaac ben Samson Katz, son-in-law of R. Judah Loewe (Maharal) of Prague (1525–1609).
5. *Zevaḥim* 102a.

The role of priest was dynastic. It passed from father to son. The role of prophet was not dynastic. Moses' own sons did not succeed him; Joshua, his disciple did.

The task of the priest was related to his office. It was not inherently personal or charismatic. The prophets, by contrast, each imparted their own personality. "No two prophets had the same style."[6]

The priests wore a special uniform; the prophets did not.

There are rules of *kavod* (honour) due to a kohen. There are no corresponding rules for the honour due to a prophet. A prophet is honoured by being listened to, not by formal protocols of respect.

The priests were removed from the people. They served in the Temple. They were not allowed to become defiled. There were restrictions on whom they might marry. The prophets, by contrast, were usually part of the people. They might be shepherds like Moses or Amos, or farmers like Elisha. Until the word or vision came, there was nothing special in their work or social class.

The priest offered up sacrifices in silence. The prophet served God through the spoken word.

They lived in two different modes of time. The priest functioned in cyclical time – the day (or week or month) that is like yesterday or tomorrow. The prophet lived in covenantal (sometimes inaccurately called linear) time – the today that is radically unlike yesterday or tomorrow. The service of the priest never changed; that of the prophet was constantly changing. Another way of putting this is to say that the priest worked to sanctify nature, the prophet to respond to history. Thus the priest represents the principle of structure in Jewish life, while the prophet represents spontaneity.

The key words in the vocabulary of the kohen are *kodesh* and *hol*, *tahor* and *tamei*; sacred and secular, pure and impure. The key words in the vocabulary of the prophets are *tzedek* and *mishpat*, *hesed* and *rahamim*; righteousness and justice, kindness and compassion.

---

6. *Sanhedrin* 89a. This, incidentally, is why there were prophetesses but no priestesses: this corresponds to the difference between formal office and personal authority. See R. Eliyahu Bakshi-Doron, *Responsa Binyan Av* 1:65.

The key verbs of priesthood are *lehorot*[7] and *lehavdil*,[8] to instruct and distinguish. The key activity of the prophet is to proclaim "the word of the Lord."[9] The distinction between priestly and prophetic conscious-ness (*torat kohanim* and *torat nevi'im*) is fundamental to Judaism, and is reflected in the differences between law and narrative, *halakha* and *aggada*, creation and redemption. The priest speaks the word of God for all time; the prophet, the word of God for his time.

There is an extraordinary aggadic passage that casts light on this idea. Its subject is the "great principle" on which Judaism depends – in the spirit of Hillel's famous dictum, "What is hateful to you do not do to others. The rest is commentary: go and learn."[10] As we will see, this particular text takes the subject in an unexpected direction:

> Ben Zoma said, "We find a more all-embracing verse, namely, 'Hear O Israel' (Deuteronomy 6:4). Ben Nannas said, "There is a yet more all-embracing verse, 'You shall love your neighbour as yourself'" (Leviticus 19:18). Ben Pazzi said, "there is a more embracing verse still: 'Prepare one lamb in the morning and the other towards evening'" (Numbers 28:4). A certain rabbi stood up and declared: "the law is in accordance with Ben Pazzi."[11]

The first two views are predictable. "Hear O Israel" is the greatest one-verse summary of Jewish faith. "Love your neighbour as yourself" is the briefest summary of Jewish ethics. But "Prepare one lamb in the morning and the other towards evening" – the verse specifying the daily morning and evening sacrifices – is not a text many would choose as epitomizing the whole of Judaism. Ben Pazzi, though, is making the fundamental assertion that without the daily service of God, there would be neither Jewish faith nor Jewish ethics. The foundation on which all else was built was the daily, undramatic yet essential service of the priests, offering

7. See, e.g., Leviticus 14:57; Deuteronomy 24:8, 33:10; Ezekiel 44:23.
8. Leviticus 11:47; Ezekiel 42:20.
9. Isaiah 1:10; Jeremiah 1:2; Ezekiel 1:3, etc.
10. *Shabbat* 31a.
11. This passage appears in the preface of *HaKotev* to *Ein Yaakov*, Vb (R. Jacob ben Solomon ibn Habib, 1445–1516).

sacrifices in the Sanctuary and the Temple while they stood. That was the Jewish people's living connection with God.

At its heart, Judaism is a priestly religion. We can see this through the very organization of the Mosaic books. They are organized as a chiastic or mirror-image structure, of the form ABCBA. Here is the simplest way of describing it:

A. Genesis: prehistory of Israel
B. Exodus: the journey to Sinai
C. Leviticus: priesthood, sacrifice and holiness
B1. Numbers: the journey from Sinai
A1. Deuteronomy: the future of Israel

In a chiasmus, the key term is the middle one. The middle book of the Pentateuch, Leviticus, is about priests and the service of the Sanctuary. So too are the last third of Exodus (25–40) and the first third of Numbers (1–10). We tend to forget this, because the narrative drama lies elsewhere, and besides, we have not had a Temple and sacrifices for almost two thousand years.

Judaism is a religion of ritual, of repeated daily deeds. It is a religion of holiness whose focus is the house of worship, successor institution to the *Mishkan*. It is a religion of education, and the priests were the first educators.[12] All the great achievements of Israel's kings and the incandescent moral passion of Israel's prophets would not have been possible without the continuity and devotion of the priests.

Without the prophet, Judaism would not be a religion of history and destiny. But without the priest, the children of Israel would not have become the people of eternity. This is beautifully summed up in the opening verses of *Tetzaveh*:

> Command the Israelites to bring you clear oil of pressed olives, to keep the lamp constantly burning [*leha'alot ner tamid*, literally, "to raise an eternal light"]. In the tent of meeting, outside the curtain that is in front of the Testimony, Aaron and his sons

12. See Deuteronomy 30:10; Malachi 2:4–7.

shall keep the lamps burning before the Lord from evening to morning. This is to be a lasting ordinance among the Israelites for the generations to come. (Exodus 27:20–21)

Moses the prophet dominates four of the five books that bear his name. But in the *parasha* of *Tetzaveh*, for once it is Aaron, the first of the priests, who holds centre stage, undiminished by the rival presence of his brother. For whereas Moses lit the fire in the souls of the Jewish people, Aaron tended the flame and turned it into "an eternal light."

Whose Footsteps Do We Follow When We Pray?

In the previous essay I discussed the difference between priests and prophets. They represent not just two different roles, but two different ways of being, two distinct modes of consciousness. I want, in this essay, to focus on one specific dimension of this difference. How did they relate to God? As we will see, they did so in completely different ways. This has more than historical significance. It affects us now, for we are their heirs.

The story we will uncover is a fascinating one, and far too little known. But I want to begin in the middle, as it were, with an apparently unrelated question, namely: what is the nature of worship in Judaism? On this there was a fundamental disagreement between two of the greatest sages of the Middle Ages, Maimonides and Nahmanides. This will turn out to be the clue that allows us to solve a key question about the nature of Jewish spirituality, both in the distant past and the living present.

Our starting point is the ruling of Maimonides on the nature of the duty to pray.[1] He writes as follows:

> To pray daily is a positive duty, as it is said, "And you shall serve the Lord your God" (Exodus 23:25). The service here referred to, according to the teaching of tradition, is prayer, as it is said, "And to serve Him with all your heart" (Deuteronomy 11:13), on which the sages commented, "What is the service of the heart? Prayer." The number of prayers is not prescribed in the Torah. No form of prayer is prescribed in the Torah. Nor does the Torah prescribe a fixed time for prayer...The obligation in this precept is that every person should daily, according to his ability, offer up supplication and prayer...[2]

Maimonides regards prayer as a biblical command, even though the details (texts, times and so on) were formulated much later by the rabbis. Nahmanides fundamentally disagrees.

His dissent appears in his critical glosses to *Sefer HaMitzvot*, the book in which Maimonides listed the 613 biblical commands. Maimonides argued there[3] that though phrases like "to serve Him with all your heart" were often meant as general directives rather than specific commands, in this case the sages explicitly said[4] that "service of the heart" includes prayer. For that reason he included prayer as one of the 613 commands.

Nahmanides disagrees.[5] First, he brings a string of citations from the Talmud to show that for the sages, prayer – unlike reciting the Shema or saying Grace after meals – is regarded as a rabbinic, not a biblical imperative. To be sure, people prayed during the biblical era, but that was not because they had a duty to do so. On the contrary, they did so because they knew that God, in His kindness, listens to prayer. Prayer

1. Prayer, throughout this essay, refers to the *Amida*, the "standing prayer," said three times daily.
2. Rambam, *Mishneh Torah*, Hilkhot Tefila 1:1–2.
3. *Sefer HaMitzvot*, positive commands, 5.
4. In *Sifrei*, commentary to Deuteronomy 11:13.
5. Ramban, glosses to *Sefer HaMitzvot*, positive command 5.

was a privilege, not an obligation. At most, Nahmanides is prepared to accept that there is a biblical obligation to cry out to God at times of national distress (derived from a quite different source, "When you go into battle in your own land against an enemy who is oppressing you, sound a blast on the trumpets," [Numbers 10:9]).

As for the command, "to serve him with all your heart," it means what it says, no more, no less: that we should be wholehearted in our service to God. And the primary service of God during the biblical era was the offering of sacrifices at the altar. That is what the word *avoda*, "service," means: the service of the priests in the Temple.[6] It seems that for Nahmanides, the whole institution of prayer as a religious obligation is post-biblical. This is a massive disagreement. How are we to understand it?

There is a key passage in the Talmud which sets us thinking in the right direction:

> It has been stated: R. Yose son of R. Ḥanina said: The prayers [morning, afternoon and evening] were instituted by the patriarchs. R. Yehoshua b. Levi said: The prayers were instituted to replace the daily sacrifices.[7]

According to R. Yose son of R. Ḥanina, the patriarchs set the precedent for prayer. Abraham established the morning prayer, as it is said "And Abraham got up early in the morning to the place where he had stood" (Genesis 19:27). Isaac instituted the afternoon prayer, as it is said, "and Isaac went out to meditate in the field towards evening" (24:63). Jacob instituted the evening prayer when he received his vision, at night, of a ladder stretching from earth to have heaven with angels ascending and descending (28:11–12). The sages cited proof texts to show that each of these was an occasion of prayer.

According to R. Yehoshua b. Levi, however, the prayers correspond to the daily sacrifices: the morning and afternoon prayers

---

6. This is one of the views expressed in *Sifrei* and *Midrash Tanaim* to Deuteronomy 11:13.
7. *Berakhot* 26b.

represent the morning and afternoon offerings. The evening prayer mirrors the completion of the sacrificial process (the burning of the limbs) which was done at night.

This is a fascinating dispute because it reminds us of the very different ways in which priest and prophet approached God.

The prophets prayed. They used words. They addressed God directly in speech. Prophetic prayer in the Bible is spontaneous. It arises out of the situation and the moment. We think of Abraham's prayer on behalf of Sodom and Gomorrah; Jacob's prayer before his encounter with Esau; Moses' prayer to God to forgive the Israelites after the Golden Calf; Hannah's prayer for a child. No two such prayers are alike.

Quite different was the service of the priests. Here, what was primary was the sacrifice, not the words – in fact, though the Levites sang songs at the Temple, and though the priests had a fixed formula of blessing, for the most part the priestly worship took place in silence. The actions of the priests were precisely regulated; moreover, any deviation, such as the spontaneous offering of Aaron's two sons, Nadav and Avihu, was fraught with danger. The priests did the same thing, in the same place, at the same time, following a daily, weekly, monthly and yearly cycle. R. Yose son of R. Ḥanina and R. Yehoshua b. Levi do not disagree on the facts: the patriarchs prayed, the priests offered sacrifice. The question on which they differ is: to which tradition do our prayers belong?

Another passage, this time in the Mishna, suggests a similar disagreement. Rabban Gamliel states that at each prayer a person should say the "eighteen blessings."[8] Rabbi Yehoshua says that one should say an "abbreviated eighteen." Rabbi Eliezer says: if a person makes his prayer "fixed" (*keva*) then it is not a genuine "supplication."[9]

Later sages, in both the Babylonian and Jerusalem Talmuds, argue over what exactly Rabbi Eliezer meant.[10] Some suggest he was talking not about the words we say, but the way we say them: we should not regard prayer as "a burden" or read it "like one who reads a letter." Others say that he meant that we should say a new prayer every day, or at least

8. The original form of the *Amida*, the "standing prayer."
9. *Berakhot* 4:4.
10. *Berakhot* 29b; Talmud Yerushalmi, *Berakhot* 4:4.

introduce something new into the eighteen blessings. This is a disagreement about the respective places of structure and spontaneity in prayer.

Another argument in the Mishna focuses on the role of the individual as against the community in prayer. The anonymous view in the
Mishna states that "just as the leader of prayer (*shaliah tzibbur*) is obligated [to recite the prayer] so each individual is obligated." Rabban Gamliel, however, holds that "The leader of prayer exempts the individual
members" of the congregation. [11]

What connects these disagreements is a profound difference of
opinion as to which tradition of prayer is primary: the priestly or the
prophetic. The priest offered sacrifices on behalf of the whole people.
His acts were essentially communal and followed a precisely ordered,
invariable pattern. However, the patriarchs and prophets spoke as individuals, spontaneously, as the circumstance required.

All the arguments now fall into place. Rabbi Eliezer, with his
opposition to *keva*, "fixed" prayer, favours the prophetic tradition, with
its spontaneity and absence of fixed forms. So does the view that each
individual is obliged to pray. In the opposite direction, Rabban Gamliel,
with his insistence on a fixed text and his belief that "the leader of prayer"
exempts the individual members of the congregation, sees prayer from a
priestly perspective. The "leader of prayer" is like a priest, prayer is like
a sacrifice, and worship an essentially communal act. There are other
ways of interpreting these passages, but this is the simplest.

We are now in a position to understand the disagreement between
Maimonides and Nahmanides. For Maimonides, prayer goes back to the
dawn of Jewish history. The patriarchs and prophets spoke directly to
God, each in their own way, and we, by praying, follow in their footsteps.
When it comes to prayer, there is an unbroken continuity between the
era of the Bible and us. Therefore, for Maimonides, prayer is a biblical
obligation.

Nahmanides sees things quite differently. To be sure, the patriarchs prayed, but they did not set a binding precedent. They spoke to
God because they felt moved to do so, not because there was an obligation to pray. Throughout the biblical era, the primary form of worship

---

11. *Rosh HaShana* 4:9.

was the sacrifices offered by the priests, first in the Tabernacle, later in the Temple, on behalf of the whole people. Only when the Temple was destroyed did prayer replace sacrifice. That is why prayer is only a rabbinic, not a biblical, obligation. It was established by the rabbis in the wake of the destruction.

Not only do they disagree about the nature of the obligation. They disagree about the nature of prayer itself. For Maimonides, at the heart of prayer is the prophetic experience of the individual in conversation with God. For Nahmanides, by contrast, prayer is the collective worship of the Jewish people, a continuation of the pattern set by the Temple service.

We see, therefore, that running through the whole of Jewish history have been two distinct modes of worship, two forms of *avoda*, the "service" of God. Prophets and priests made contact with God, each in their own way, prophets by "the service of the heart," priests by the service of the Sanctuary and its sacrifices. During the biblical era, they existed side by side. It was only after the Hebrew Bible reached closure, the Temple was destroyed, and there were no more actively functioning priests and prophets, that prayer became the single channel of communication between heaven and earth. The question that divided the rabbis was: what is the genealogy of prayer? Is it like a sacrifice? Or is it like the heartfelt pleas of the prophets? Even by the twelfth and thirteenth centuries, the age of Maimonides and Nahmanides, the question had not been resolved.

But the story does not end there, and it has an unexpected denouement. For we can now see the reason for the strange custom which is so familiar that we take it for granted without stopping to ask why, namely that we say each prayer (with the exception of the evening prayer) twice. We pray once silently as individuals; then out loud (the "reader's repetition") as a community.

The explanation is simple. The first recitation is prophetic, the second priestly. Jewish prayer as it has existed for almost two thousand years is a brilliant synthesis of two modes of biblical spirituality, supremely exemplified by two brothers: Moses the prophet and Aaron the High Priest. Without the prophetic tradition, we would have no spontaneity. Without the priestly tradition, we would have no continuity. The rabbis brought together what, for more than a thousand years, had existed apart: the prophetic and priestly traditions, one with its emphasis on the heart, the other with its fixed forms, one focused on the individual and his or her relationship with God, the other essentially communal.[12]

The *parasha* of *Tetzaveh*, in which the name of Moses is missing and the focus is on Aaron, reminds us that our heritage derives from both. Moses was the lonely man of faith, wrestling with God. Aaron was closer to the community, ministering to God on their behalf. His role, though less dramatic than that of Moses, was no less consequential. The priestly dimension of worship – collective, structured, never changing – is the other hemisphere of the Jewish mind, the voice of eternity in the midst of time.

---

12. We now understand why there is no reader's repetition in the evening service: there was no sacrifice at night. We now also understand why the reader's repetition needs a quorum, but the silent prayer does not. The daily sacrifices were communal; the prayers of the prophets were individual.

Brothers: A Drama in Five Acts

In the previous essays we noted the absence of Moses from the parasha of *Tetzaveh*. For once Moses, the hero, the leader, the liberator, the lawgiver, is offstage. Instead our focus is on his elder brother Aaron who, elsewhere, is often in the background. Indeed, virtually the whole *parasha* is devoted to the role Moses did not occupy, except briefly – that of priest in general, high priest in particular.

In the previous essays I discussed the importance of focusing a *parasha* on the legacy of the priestly role for Judaism. However, need this focus have removed Moses from the passage entirely? Is there any larger significance to his absence? The commentators offered various suggestions.[1]

One given in the Talmud refers to an event at the beginning of Moses' leadership: his encounter with God at the burning bush. Moses repeatedly expressed reluctance to undertake the mission of leading the people out of Egypt. Finally we read:

But Moses said, "O Lord, please send someone else to do it."

1. See earlier essay, "Priests and Prophets," p. 219.

233

Then the Lord's anger burned against Moses and He said, "What about your brother, Aaron the Levite? I know he can speak well. He is already on his way to meet you, and his heart will be glad when he sees you. You shall speak to him and put words in his mouth; I will help both of you speak and will teach you what to do." (Exodus 4:13–15)

The Talmud records a debate about the lasting consequences of that moment when Moses, as it were, refused one time too many. To decline a leadership challenge once or twice is a sign of humility. To continue to do so when it is God himself issuing the challenge risks provoking divine anger, as happened here. The Talmud comments:

"Then the Lord's anger burned against Moses" – Rabbi Yehoshua ben Karḥa said: every instance of [divine] anger in the Torah leaves a lasting effect, except in this instance. Rabbi Shimon bar Yoḥai said: here too it left a lasting effect, for it goes on to say, "What about your brother, Aaron the Levite?" Surely Aaron was a priest [not just a Levite]. Rather, what God meant was: I originally intended that you [Moses] would be a priest and he [Aaron] would merely be a Levite. But now [because of your refusal], he will eventually become a priest and you will only be a Levite.[2]

According to Rabbi Shimon bar Yoḥai, the lasting effect of Moses' reluctance to lead was that one leadership role – priesthood – would eventually go to Aaron rather than to Moses himself.

Basing himself on this passage, Rabbi Jacob ben Asher (1270–1340) suggests that Moses' name is missing from *Tetzaveh*, which deals with the priestly garments, "to spare him distress" on seeing Aaron acquire the insignia of priesthood that might have been Moses' own.[3]

Without negating this or other explanations, there is also a more fundamental message. One of the recurring themes of Genesis is sibling rivalry, hostility between brothers. This story is told, at ever-increasing

2. *Zevaḥim* 102a.
3. R. Jacob ben Asher, commentary of Baal HaTurim to Exodus 27: 20.

length, four times: between Cain and Abel, Isaac and Ishmael, Jacob and Esau, and Joseph and his brothers.

There is an identifiable pattern to this set of narratives, best seen in the way each ends. The story of Cain and Abel ends with murder – fratricide. Isaac and Ishmael, though they grow up apart, are seen together at Abraham's funeral. Evidently there had been a reconciliation between them, though this can only be read between the lines (and spelled out in midrash), not directly in the text. Jacob and Esau meet, embrace and go their separate ways. Joseph and his brothers are reconciled and live together in peace, Joseph providing them with food, land, and protection.

Genesis is telling us a story of great consequence. Fraternity – one of the key words of the French revolution – is not simple or straightforward. It is often fraught with conflict and contention. Yet slowly, brothers can learn that there is another way. On this note Genesis ends. But it is not the end of the story.

The drama has a fifth act: the relationship between Moses and Aaron. Here, for the first time, there is no hint of sibling rivalry.[4] The brothers work together from the very outset of the mission to lead the Israelites to freedom. They address the people together. They stand together when confronting Pharaoh. They perform signs and wonders together. They share leadership of the people in the wilderness together. For the first time, brothers function as a team, with different gifts, different talents, different roles, but without hostility, each complementing the other.

Their partnership is a constant feature of the narrative. But there are certain moments where it is highlighted. The first occurs in the passage already cited above. God tells Moses that Aaron "is already on his way to meet you, and *his heart will be glad when he sees you.*" How different this is from the tense encounters between brothers in Genesis!

Aaron, we may have thought, might have many reasons not to rejoice on seeing Moses return. The brothers had not grown up together. Moses had been adopted by Pharaoh's daughter and raised in an Egyptian palace, while Aaron remained with the Israelites. Nor had they been

---

4. Some developed later – see Numbers, chap. 12 – but was resolved by Moses' humility.

together during the Israelites' sufferings. Moses, fearing for his life after his assault on an Egyptian taskmaster, had fled to Midian.

Besides this, Moses was Aaron's younger brother, and yet it was he who was about to become the leader of the people. Always in the past, when the younger had taken something the elder might have believed belonged naturally to him, there was jealousy, animosity. Yet God assures Moses: "when Aaron sees you, he will rejoice." And so he did:

> And the Lord said to Aaron, Go to the wilderness to meet Moses. And he went, and met him in the mount of God, and kissed him. (Exodus 4:27)

The second fascinating clue is contained in a strange passage that traces the descent of Moses and Aaron:

> Amram married his father's sister Yocheved, who bore him Aaron and Moses. Amram lived 137 years ... *It was this same Aaron and Moses* to whom the Lord said, "Bring the Israelites out of Egypt by their divisions." They were the ones who spoke to Pharaoh king of Egypt about bringing the Israelites out of Egypt. *It was this same Moses and Aaron.* (Exodus 6:20, 26–27)

The repeated phrase, "It was this same," is emphatic even in translation. It is all the more so when we note two peculiarities of the text. The first is that the phrases, though at first they sound identical, in fact place the names of the brothers in a different order: the first says "Aaron and Moses," the second, "Moses and Aaron."[5] Even more striking is the grammatical oddity of the phrase. Both times, the third person singular is used. Literally, they read: "He was Aaron and Moses," "He was Moses and Aaron." The text should have said, "They" – all the more so since the pronoun "they" is used in the middle of the passage: "They were the ones who spoke to Pharaoh."

The unmistakable implication is that they were like a single individual; they were as one. There was no hierarchy between them:

---

5. "This teaches that they were equals" (Tosefta, *Keritot*, end).

sometimes Aaron's name appears first, sometimes Moses'. There is a wonderful midrash that bears out this idea, based on the verse in Psalms (85:11) "Loving-kindness and truth meet together; righteousness and peace kiss each other."

> Loving-kindness – this refers to Aaron. Truth – this refers to Moses. Righteousness – this refers to Moses. Peace – this refers to Aaron.[6]

The midrash brings prooftexts for each of these identifications, but we understand them immediately. Moses and Aaron were quite different in temperament and role. Moses was the man of truth, Aaron of peace. Without truth, there can be no vision to inspire a nation. But without internal peace, there is no nation to inspire. Aaron and Moses were both necessary. Their roles were in creative tension. Yet they worked side by side, each respecting the distinctive gift of the other. As the midrash goes on to say:

> "And he kissed him" [the brothers kissed when they met] – This means: each rejoiced at the other's greatness.[7]

A final midrash completes the picture by referring to this week's *parasha* and the vestments of the High Priest, especially the breastplate with its *Urim* and *Tumim*:

> "His heart will be glad when he sees you" – Let the heart that rejoiced in the greatness of his brother be vested with the *Urim* and *Tumim*.[8]

The *Urim* and *Tumim* were a form of oracle, carried by the High Priest in his breastplate. They conveyed divine inspiration and guidance, a kind of priestly equivalent of the divine word that came to the

6. *Shemot Raba* 5:10.
7. Ibid., ad loc.
8. Ibid. 3:17.

prophet.[9] It was precisely the fact that Aaron did not envy his younger brother but instead rejoiced in his greatness that made him worthy to be High Priest. So it came to pass – measure for measure – that just as Aaron made space for his younger brother to lead, so the Torah makes space for Aaron to lead. That is why Aaron is the hero of *Tetzaveh*: for once, not overshadowed by Moses.

"Who is honoured?" asked ben Zoma. "One who honours others."[10] Aaron honoured his younger brother. That is why Moses (not mentioned by name but by implication) is told in this week's *parasha*, "Make sacred garments for your brother Aaron, to give him honour and splendour" (Exodus 28:2). To this day a kohen is honoured by being the first to be called up to the Torah – the Torah that Aaron's younger brother Moses gave to the Jewish people.

The story of Aaron and Moses, the fifth act in the biblical drama of brotherhood, is where, finally, fraternity reaches the heights. And that surely is the meaning of Psalm 133, with its explicit reference to Aaron and his sacred garments: "How good and pleasant it is when brothers live together in unity! It is like precious oil poured on the head, running down on the beard, running down on Aaron's beard, down upon the collar of his robes." It was thanks to Aaron, and the honour he showed Moses, that at last brothers learned to live together in unity.

9. According to Ramban, they consisted of letters spelling out the divine name or names, some of which would light up at key moments, spelling out a message to be deciphered by the High Priest.
10. *Avot* 4:1.

Do Clothes Make the Man?

> *"You shall bring forward your brother Aaron, with his sons from among the Israelites to serve me as priests: Aaron, Nadav and Avihu, Eleazar and Ithamar, the sons of Aaron. You shall make only clothes for Aaron your brother, for glory and for beauty." (Exodus 28:1–2)*

With these words a new phenomenon makes its appearance in Jewish life. Never before have we encountered robes of office, formal insignia marking off their wearers as holy people charged with a particular function in religious life.

Indeed this whole section of the biblical narrative strikes us as strange, given all we know of what has come before. Abraham, Isaac and Jacob did not wear special clothes. Nor did Moses. They were shepherds. They dressed simply. In any event, what they wore is utterly irrelevant to the biblical message. As Erich Auerbach noted in his classic study,

"Odysseus' Scar,"[1] the great difference between Homer and the Torah is that Homer constantly describes appearances; the Torah rarely does.

Homer is fascinated by the play of light on surfaces. The Torah is deeply disinterested in surfaces: landscapes, portraits, physical descriptions. With few exceptions – only when it is necessary to understand what happens – the Torah does not tell us what its heroes and heroines looked like or what they wore. The biblical text is, in Auerbach's phrase, "fraught with background,"[2] meaning that the physical setting of its narratives is unspecified in the text, inviting us, the listeners, to supply it from our own imagination. If Homer is like television, the Torah is like radio. It focuses not on the image but the voice.

It does so for a deeply serious reason. There is a definitive moment in Samuel I when the prophet is commanded by God to anoint a new king. Saul has failed. He is too temperamental, insecure and concerned with popularity. He fails to fulfil the divine command. And it should be noted that this is a classic case where the Bible *does* emphasise appearances, precisely to show that they are misleading. Saul, when we first encounter him, is described as "a young man in his prime; no one among the Israelites was handsomer than he; he was a head taller than any of the people."[3] He had physical stature but not moral stature. That is the message the text seeks to convey.

Samuel is told to go to the home of Jesse (Yishai) because one of his sons is the man chosen to be king:

When he arrived and he saw Eliav, he thought: "Surely the Lord's anointed stands before Him."[4] But the Lord said to Samuel, "Pay no attention to his appearance or his stature, for I have rejected him. For not as man sees [does the Lord see]; man sees only what is visible, but the Lord sees into the heart."[5]

Judaism – the religion of inwardness, not appearances; of ethics,

---

1. Erich Auerbach, *Mimesis: The Representation of Reality in Western Literature* (Princeton University Press, 1953), chap. 1.
2. Ibid., 12.
3. 1 Samuel 9:2.
4. Ibid., 16:6.
5. Ibid., 16:17.

not power; of character, not the formal dress of office – is not the place we usually turn to, to find the specification of official uniforms.

On at least two famous occasions we find biblical heroes donning robes of majesty. There is Joseph in Egypt:

> So Pharaoh said to Joseph, "I hereby put you in charge of the whole land of Egypt." Then Pharaoh took his signet ring from his finger and put it on Joseph's finger. He dressed him in robes of fine linen and put a gold chain around his neck. He had him ride in a chariot as his second-in-command, and men shouted before him, "Make way!" Thus he put him in charge of the whole land of Egypt. (Genesis 41:41–43)

And there is Mordechai in Persia:

> [Haman] answered the king, "For the man the king delights to honor, have them bring a royal robe the king has worn and a horse the king has ridden, one with a royal crest placed on its head. Then let the robe and horse be entrusted to one of the king's most noble princes. Let them robe the man the king delights to honour, and lead him on the horse through the city streets, proclaiming before him, 'This is what is done for the man the king delights to honour!'"
>
> "Go at once," the king commanded Haman. "Get the robe and the horse and do just as you have suggested for Mordecai the Jew, who sits at the king's gate. Do not neglect anything you have recommended." So Haman got the robe and the horse. He robed Mordechai, and led him on horseback through the city streets, proclaiming before him, "This is what is done for the man the king delights to honour!" (Esther 6:7–11)

The non-Jewish, non-Israelite setting of these passages is obvious. That – Tanakh seems to imply – is how others do these things; not us. Robes, rings, chains of office, chariots, horses: these are external signs of glory, unworthy of a people who judge authority by humility, and majesty by obedience. It is hardly coincidental from the Torah's perspective that it is precisely Pharaonic Egypt and Xerxes' (Ahasuerus') Persia, that celebrate the visual trappings of official dress, who also issue the first decrees of genocide against the Jewish people. A culture that worships external symbols of power will in the end lack the inwardness and humanity to respect the dignity of the powerless.

Nor is this all. At least five episodes in the book of Genesis turn on the subject of clothes.[6] There are Esau's *bigdei ḥamudot*, "best clothes" (27:15), that Jacob puts on to take Isaac's blessing. There is the *ketonet pasim*, the "richly embroidered cloak" or "coat of many colours" (37:3) that Jacob has made for his favourite son, Joseph. There are the clothes of a [temple] prostitute that Tamar puts on when she removes her "widow's garments" [*bigdei almenuta*] in order to attract Judah (38:14). There is the *beged*, cloak or robe, that Joseph leaves in the hand of Potiphar's wife when he flees from her attempt to seduce him (39:12). And there are, as mentioned above, the special robes [*bigdei shesh*] and insignia of office that Joseph wears as second-in-command to Pharaoh (41:42).

One fact links all these episodes. Garments are used to deceive. Jacob wears Esau's clothes to deceive his blind father Isaac when he puts out his hand to feel him. The brothers stain Joseph's cloak with goat's blood to persuade their father Jacob that he has been killed by a wild animal. Tamar changes her clothes and puts on a veil to hide her identity from Judah. Potiphar's wife uses the robe Joseph has abandoned to bolster her claim that he tried to rape her. And Joseph uses his newfound appearance as a senior Egyptian ruler to hide his identity from his brothers ("Joseph recognized his brothers but they did not recognize him" [42:8]).

It comes therefore as both a shock and a confirmation when we discover that the Hebrew word for "garment," *beged*, also means "betrayal" (as in the Yom Kippur confession, *Ashamnu, bagadnu*). That is precisely what garments are in Genesis – instruments of deception and betrayal. Indeed that is the message conveyed by the very first reference to gar-

---

6. The nineteenth-century English writer Thomas Carlyle wrote a book, *Sartor Resartus*, dedicated to a "philosophy of clothes." In a certain sense Genesis is an anti-philosophy of clothes.

ments in the Torah, when Adam and Eve, against God's instruction, eat from the fruit of the tree in the midst of the garden:

> Then the eyes of both of them were opened, and they realized they were naked; so they sewed fig leaves together and made coverings for themselves.
>
> Then the man and his wife heard the sound of the Lord God as He was walking in the garden in the cool of the day, and they hid from the Lord God among the trees of the garden. But the Lord God called to the man, "Where are you?"
>
> He answered, "I heard you in the garden, and I was afraid because I was naked; so I hid."
>
> And He said, "Who told you that you were naked? Have you eaten from the tree that I commanded you not to eat from?" (Genesis 3:7–11)

Clothes were the sign of the first great betrayal, the first breaking of a divine command.

Clothes are what separates nature from culture. Desmond Morris once called man "the naked ape."[7] Of course, that is precisely wrong. Homo sapiens is the non-naked animal, the only being in creation whose external appearance is fabricated, made, a detachable second-skin. Hence the gap in human affairs between appearance and reality, the appearance we make by (among other things) the clothes we wear and the reality of what we think, plan and feel. Shakespeare has Hamlet deliver to his mother the queen a remarkable speech, the thrust of which is that not only is he dressed like a mourner; in addition, he actually does mourn:

> Seems, madam! Nay, it is; I know not seems.
> 'Tis not alone my inky cloak, good mother,
> Nor customary suits of solemn black,
> Nor windy suspiration of forc'd breath,
> No, nor the fruitful river in the eye,
> Nor the dejected 'haviour of the visage,

---

7. Desmond Morris, *The Naked Ape* (Cape, 1967).

Together with all forms, moods, shows of grief,
That can denote me truly: these, indeed, seem;
For they are actions that a man might play;
But I have that within which passeth show;
These but the trappings and the suits of woe.[8]

The Torah's point is Hamlet's also: there is a difference between "is" and "seems" – between what we really feel and "the trappings and the suits" of what we wear.

If we are to understand Judaism we must never forget that it represents a specific moment in – as well as an eternal truth about – the history of mankind. Neither Moses, nor even Abraham, are primeval figures (as they would be if the Torah were myth). They are "latecomers." The great symbol of ancient civilization, the Tower of Babel, precedes the call of God to Abraham. Judaism does not represent the birth of civilization; it represents a critique of civilization. It is precisely when human beings discover technology, build cities, construct advanced methods of warfare (the Egyptian horse-drawn chariot is the key biblical example) and erect self-serving monuments that the human potential for evil becomes seriously destructive. Empires elevate rulers by degrading the mass of mankind.

One of the most visible symbols of empire is the robe of office. They exalt the few at the cost of the many. They represent a thoroughly hierarchical society of a kind to which Judaism is essentially opposed. The English language lacks a word like the Hebrew *beged*, which links "garments" and "betrayal." But it has another one that covers roughly the same territory, namely, "sophisticated." On the one hand it has a positive connotation – it means "refined, cultured." On the other it has an ancient and disreputable history deriving from the pre-Socratic philosophers (the Sophists) who used to teach for money and were known (and criticised by Plato) for their persuasive but fallacious arguments. Thus "sophisticate" also means "to spoil, adulterate, corrupt, pervert, mislead."

Civilization always runs the risk of substituting "seems" for "is." Those who dress like kings may have the hearts of slaves, fearful, resent-

8. *Hamlet*, act 1, sc. 2.

ful and vindictive. Those who wear the robes of holy people may (like the sons of Samuel) be corrupt. That is why Jewish sensibility is, on the whole, sceptical of official uniforms. God sees, and teaches us to see, the inward person, what Hamlet called, "that within which passeth show."[9]

Why then, given this focus away from clothes and superficial appearance, did God command Moses to set in motion the making of special garments for the priests, "for glory and for beauty" (28:2)? The answer lies in the analysis given by the nineteenth-century sociologist Max Weber. Weber was fascinated by the question of leadership. What is it that gives some individuals authority over others? His most famous insight – it has become part of the language of everyday speech – is that certain rare figures have what he called charisma.[10] Charismatic leaders, by the force of their personality, are able to exercise influence over others. They speak to their fears, their concerns, hopes and dreams. They articulate a narrative that explains them to themselves. They construct (or, in the case of prophets, receive) a vision that motivates and moves. They are transformational. They do not leave a group or nation as it was before. They do not (as some leaders do) merely "keep the show on the road" or "keep the ship from sinking." They change the people with whom they come into contact. They are the midwives of something new.

But charisma begins to die almost as soon as it is born. Charismatic authority is strictly personal. It is unique to the individual who wields it, and it can never be replicated over time. Indeed, it is essential to the survival of the group that it is *not* replicated over time. A charismatic leader is an agent of change, but a group, in order to survive, needs a form of leadership that is resistant to change; that is, instead, a vehicle of continuity, tradition and stability. Without this, the group will not persist long into the future. That is why, after the appearance in

9. Ibid.
10. Weber defines it as "a certain quality of an individual personality, by virtue of which one is 'set apart' from ordinary people and treated as endowed with supernatural, superhuman, or at least specifically exceptional powers or qualities. These as such are not accessible to the ordinary person, but are regarded as divine in origin or as exemplary, and on the basis of them the individual concerned is treated as a leader." Max Weber, *Theory of Social and Economic Organization*, trans. A.R. Anderson and Talcott Parsons (William Hodge, 1947), 358–59.

its midst of a charismatic leader, the group must undergo what Weber called the routinization of charisma.[11] This is the process whereby a certain form of authority is vested, not in an individual-as-individual but in an individual (or group) as bearers-of-an-office. Thus charisma is handed down from generation to generation in an orderly and predictable way, through laws of succession, together with rules regulating the behaviour of the holders of the office and their relationship to the group as a whole.

The prime example of the routinization of charisma is contained in *Tetzaveh*, in the process through which Moses invests priestly authority in Aaron and his sons. The *bigdei kehuna*, the "priestly vestments" are its visible symbol. The kohanim are – by virtue of birth and descent, not personal qualities – the carriers of sacred office. Their work is holy. Their domain is the Tabernacle, the physical embodiment of sacred space. They are charged with mediating between the people and God. Their clothes mark their office and role.

Not accidentally, therefore, is *Tetzaveh* the only *parasha* between the beginning of Exodus and the end of Deuteronomy in which the name of Moses does not appear. The most important fact about routinized charisma is that it exists when the charismatic leader (i.e., Moses) is no longer there. We now understand precisely the connection between the *parasha* of *Tetzaveh* and the episode of the Golden Calf (later in the book of Exodus but, according to most commentators, taking place earlier in time). The Golden Calf was a response to the crisis posed by Moses' absence: "This Moses, the man who brought us up from the land of Egypt – we don't know what has become of him" (Exodus 32:1). It illustrated the weakness of charismatic authority: powerful in its presence but debilitating in its absence. The Israelites had to become the people who would continue to serve God after Moses had left them. That is what the Tabernacle, the sacrifices and the priesthood represent: continuity, the ability to sustain long into the future the experience of Sinai and the presence, in the midst of the people, of God.

A prophet needs no official vestments. His or her authority is charismatic, personal, spontaneous, unrepeatable. But a priest needs *bigdei kehuna*, "priestly vestments," to show that in his case the office

---

11. Ibid., chap.: "The Nature of Charismatic Authority and its Routinization."

is greater than the person; it continues from generation to generation; it represents stability and "the persistence of faith"[12] through time. The greatness of biblical Israel is that it never completely routinized charisma. From Moses to Malachi prophets arose to challenge the abuse of power and prevent the service of God from becoming merely routine. But had there been only prophets, and no priests, Israel would have disappeared long ago. It would have lacked the essential ability to sustain its mission over time.

Partly because of the prophets, biblical Israel was able to correct the dangers of the routinization of charisma. As the commentators point out in their remarks on the phrase *mamlekhet kohanim*, "a kingdom of priests," the word kohen itself means both "a prince" and "a servant." The sons of Aaron may have been aristocrats of the spirit, but they were also servants, of both the people and God. The last of the prophets, Malachi, has a wonderful description of the role of a priest:

> True instruction was in his mouth
> And nothing false was on his lips.
> He walked with me in peace and uprightness,
> And turned many from sin.
> For the lips of a priest preserve knowledge,
> And from his mouth men should seek instruction
> For he is a messenger of the Almighty Lord. (Malachi 2:6–7)

In a famous phrase, the book of Psalms contains the prayer, "May your priests be clothed in righteousness." It is clear then that the phrase in *Tetzaveh*, "for glory and for beauty" does not mean "for the glory and beauty of the priest." It means "for the glory of God and the beauty of His presence."[13] The task of the kohen – and the message of his clothes – was to be a "signal of transcendence,"[14] to point *in* himself to something *beyond* himself, to be a living symbol of the Divine Presence in the midst of the nation.

12. Jonathan Sacks, *The Persistence of Faith* (Weidenfeld and Nicolson, 1991).
13. Sforno, commentary to Exodus 28:2.
14. The phrase comes from Peter Berger, *A Rumor of Angels* (Doubleday, 1969).

The last chapter in this story of the priestly class, however, is the most remarkable. It happened after the destruction of the Second Temple and the end of a functioning priesthood. It was then that *kehuna* was essentially universalized and democratized. In prayer, everyone became a priest. Each synagogue throughout the world was a miniature Temple. Through the *teshuva* (repentance) of Yom Kippur, each Jew was like a High Priest atoning for sins. "From the day the Temple was destroyed," said the sages in one of their most haunting aphorisms, "the Holy One blessed be He has nothing in this world apart from the four cubits of halakha."[15]

There was always halakha. But after the Temple's destruction, it became the vehicle through which the priestly task was spread throughout the people. Halakha invested, and invests, every detail of daily life with the charisma of holiness. No longer did anyone need a special uniform to single them out as priests or holy people, because the Jewish people as a whole had become, individually and collectively, "a kingdom of priests and a holy nation" (Exodus 19:6). If the kohen represented the routinization of charisma, Judaism – through its halakhic sanctification of everyday life – eventually became the charismatization of routine.

---

15. *Berakhot* 8a.

Ki Tissa
כִּי תִשָּׂא

Ki Tissa begins with the final details about the Sanctuary, including a collection of money from the people that was to serve as a census. The *parasha* then moves into high drama with one of the most gripping narratives in Jewish history. The people, panicking in the absence of Moses (who is up the mountain, receiving the tablets from God), make a Golden Calf and dance before it. God tells Moses to go down. Moses does, and in his anger smashes the tablets. He censures the people, then returns to the mountain to plead with God to forgive them. Eventually God does, and Moses returns, with a second set of tablets, unaware that his face is now radiant.

     The first of the following essays looks at Moses' prayer to God to forgive the people "because they are stiff-necked." Is there a positive side to Jewish obstinacy? The second essay, prompted by a contemporary Golden Calf, looks at the command Moses gives immediately before and after the people's sin: Shabbat. Why is this command the antidote to false worship? The third is about the strange way the people was to be counted. Does this tell us something significant about Jewish demography? The fourth poses the question: why did the second tablets, in which Moses had a share, survive, while the first – the work of God alone – did not?

A Stiff-Necked People

It is a moment of the very highest drama. The Israelites, a mere forty days after the greatest revelation in history, have made an idol: a Golden Calf. God threatens to destroy them. Moses, exemplifying to the fullest degree the character of Israel as one who "wrestles with God and man," confronts both in turn. To God, he prays for mercy for the people. Coming down the mountain and facing Israel, he smashes the tablets, symbol of the covenant. He grinds the calf to dust, mixes it with water, and makes the Israelites drink it. He commands the Levites to punish the wrongdoers. Then he re-ascends the mountain in a prolonged attempt to re-establish the shattered relationship between God and the people.

God allows Himself to be entreated. In an extraordinary epiphany, He causes His "glory" to pass by Moses saying, "You will see My back, but My face may not be seen" (Exodus 33:23). He instructs Moses to carve two new tablets of stone, and proclaims His attributes of mercy. At this point, however, Moses makes a strange appeal:

> And Moses hurried and knelt to the ground and bowed, and he said, "If I have found favour in your eyes, my Lord, may my Lord go among us, because [*ki*] it is a stiff-necked people, and

forgive our wickedness and our sin, and take us as your inheritance." (34:8–9)

The difficulty in the verse is self-evident. Moses cites as a reason for God remaining with the Israelites the very attribute that God had previously given for wishing to abandon them:

"I have seen these people," the Lord said to Moses, "and they are a stiff-necked people. Now leave Me alone so that My anger may burn against them and that I may destroy them. Then I will make you into a great nation." (32:9)

And again:

"Go up to the land flowing with milk and honey. But I will not go with you, because you are a stiff-necked people and I might destroy you on the way." When the people heard these distressing words, they began to mourn and no one put on any ornaments. For the Lord had said to Moses, "Tell the Israelites, 'You are a stiff-necked people. If I were to go with you even for a moment, I might destroy you. Now take off your ornaments and I will decide what to do with you.'" So the Israelites stripped off their ornaments at Mount Horeb. (33:3–5)

How can Moses invoke the people's obstinacy as the very reason for God to maintain His presence among them? What is the meaning of Moses' "because" – "may my Lord go among us, *because* it is a stiff-necked people"?

The commentators offer a variety of interpretations. Rashi reads the word *ki* as "if" – "If they are stiff-necked, then forgive them."[1] Ibn

---

1. Rashi, commentary to Exodus 34:9.

Ezra[2] and Chizkuni[3] read it as "although" or "despite the fact that" (*af al pi*). Alternatively, suggests Ibn Ezra, the verse might be read, "[I admit that] it is a stiff-necked people – therefore forgive our wickedness and our sin, and take us as Your inheritance."[4] These are straightforward readings, though they assign to the word *ki* a meaning it does not normally have.

Nahmanides takes a different approach:

> This is to be understood in its literal sense. God is to go in their midst because they are a stiff-necked people, for now that the Holy One, blessed be He, has become reconciled with them, His presence amongst those who are stiff-necked would be better than that of the angel. For He will want to increase their blessings more, since they are His people and His inheritance... At a time of goodwill it is better for them that the divine glory go with them, because they are a stiff-necked people, and He would more readily show grace and mercy upon His servants.[5]

For Nahmanides it is precisely the waywardness of Israel that requires the close attention of a forgiving God – like a rebellious child for whom the kindest cure is the attentive concern of a loving parent. His comment anticipates the famous and audacious prayer of the Hassidic master Rabbi Levi Yitzchak of Berditchev: "Lord of the universe, I want to propose a deal. We have many sins. You have much forgiveness. Let us exchange our sins for Your forgiveness. And if You should say that this is not a fair exchange, then my reply is: If we had no sins, what would You do with Your forgiveness?"[6]

There is, however, another and far more striking line of interpretation that can be traced across the centuries. In the twentieth century

---

2. In his "short" commentary to Exodus 34:9. In his long commentary he quotes this view in the name of R. Yonah ibn Yanah (R. Marinus, 990–1050).
3. Hezekiah ben Manoah, a French rabbi and exegete who lived during the thirteenth century.
4. Ibn Ezra, "long" commentary ad loc.
5. Ramban, commentary to Exodus 34:9.
6. See Elie Wiesel, *Souls on Fire* (London: Weidenfeld and Nicolson, 1972), 108.

it was given expression by Rabbi Yitzchak Nissenbaum. The argument he attributed to Moses was this:

> Almighty God, look upon this people with favour, because what is now their greatest vice will one day be their most heroic virtue. They are indeed an obstinate people. When they have everything to thank You for, they complain. Mere weeks after hearing Your voice they make a Golden Calf. But just as now they are stiff-necked in their disobedience, so one day they will be equally stiff-necked in their loyalty. Nations will call on them to assimilate, but they will refuse. Mightier religions will urge them to convert, but they will resist. They will suffer humiliation, persecution, even torture and death because of the name they bear and the faith they profess, but they will stay true to the covenant their ancestors made with You. They will go to their deaths saying *Ani ma'amin*, "I believe." This is a people awesome in its obstinacy – and though now it is their failing, there will be times far into the future when it will be their noblest strength.[7]

The fact that Rabbi Nissenbaum lived and died in the Warsaw ghetto gives added poignancy to his words.[8]

Many centuries earlier, a midrash made essentially the same point:

> There are three things which are undaunted: the dog among beasts, the cock among birds, and Israel among the nations. R. Isaac ben Redifa said in the name of R. Ami: You might think that this is a negative attribute, but in fact it is praiseworthy, for it means: "Either be a Jew or prepare to be hanged."[9]

Jews were stiff-necked, says Rabbi Ami, in the sense that they were ready

---

7. This is my paraphrase of the commentary cited in the name of R. Yitzhak Nissenbaum in Aaron Yaakov Greenberg, ed., *Itturei Torah*, Shemot (Tel Aviv, 1976), 269–70.
8. For R. Nissenbaum's remarkable speech in the Warsaw Ghetto, see Emil Fackenheim, *To Mend the World* (New York: Schocken, 1982), 223.
9. *Beitza* 25b; *Shemot Raba* 42:9.

to die for their faith. As Gersonides (Ralbag) explained in the fourteenth century, a stubborn people may be slow to acquire a faith, but once it has done so it never relinquishes it.[10]

We catch a glimpse of this extraordinary obstinacy in an episode narrated by Josephus, one of the first recorded incidents of mass non-violent civil disobedience. It took place during the reign of the Roman emperor Caligula (37–41 CE). He had proposed placing a statue of himself in the precincts of the Temple in Jerusalem, and had sent the military leader Petronius to carry out the task, if necessary by force. This is how Josephus describes the encounter between Petronius and the Jewish population at Ptolemais (Acre):

> But there came ten thousand of the Jews to Petronius at Ptolemais to offer their petitions to him that he would not compel them to violate the law of their forefathers. "But if," they said, "you are wholly resolved to bring the statue and install it, then you must first kill us, and then do what you have resolved on. For while we are alive we cannot permit such things as are forbidden by our law..."
>
> Petronius, however, was angry at them and said: "...Caesar has sent me. I am compelled to observe his decrees..." Then the Jews replied, "Since, therefore, you are so disposed, O Petronius, that you will not disobey Caesar's orders, neither will we transgress the commands of our law..."
>
> When Petronius saw by their words that their determination was hard to be removed, and that...he would not be able to be obedient to Caligula in the dedication of his statue, and that there must be a great deal of bloodshed, he took his friends and servants and hastened to Tiberius, to see how the Jews there felt about the affair; but many tens of thousands of Jews met Petronius again when he came to Tiberius...
>
> Then Petronius came to them (at Tiberius): "Will you then make war with Caesar, regardless of his great preparations for war and your own weakness?" They replied, "We will not by

---

10. Ralbag, commentary to Exodus 34:9.

any means make war with Caesar, but we will die before we see our laws transgressed." Then they threw themselves down on their faces and stretched out their throats and said that they were ready to be slain. And this they did for forty days, neglecting to till their soil, though this was the season of sowing. Thus they continued firm in their resolution and proposed themselves to die willingly rather than see the statue dedicated."[11]

Faced with such heroic defiance on so large a scale, Petronius gave way and wrote to Caligula urging him, in Josephus' words, "not to drive so many ten thousands of these men to distraction; that if he were to slay these men, he would be publicly cursed for all future ages." Nor was this a unique episode. The rabbinic literature, together with the chronicles of the Middle Ages, are full of stories of martyrdom, of Jews willing to die rather than convert. Indeed the very concept of *kiddush Hashem*, sanctification of God's name, came to be associated in the halakhic literature with the willingness "to die rather than transgress." The rabbinic conclave at Lod (Lydda) in the second century CE, which laid down the laws of martyrdom (including the three sins about which it was said that "one must die rather than transgress")[12] may have been an attempt to *limit*, rather than encourage, the phenomenon. Of these many episodes, one stands out for its theological audacity. It was recorded by the Jewish historian Shlomo ibn Verga (fifteenth to sixteenth centuries) and concerns the Spanish expulsion:

> I heard from some of the elders who came out of Spain that one of

---

11. Josephus *Antiquities of the Jews*, bk. 18, chap. 8. Cited in Milton Konvitz, "Conscience and Civil Disobedience in the Jewish Tradition," in *Contemporary Jewish Ethics*, ed. Menachem Kellner (New York: Sanhedrin Press, 1978), 242–43.
12. *Sanhedrin* 74a. The three sins were murder, idolatry and incest. Martyrdom was a complex problem at various points in Jewish history. Jews found themselves torn between two conflicting ideals. On the one hand, self-sacrifice was the highest form of *kiddush Hashem*, sanctification of God's name. On the other, Judaism has a marked preference for life and its preservation. The rabbinic literature does not mention the martyrs of Masada who killed themselves rather than be taken captive by the Romans. The medieval halakhic authorities were ambivalent about the collective suicide of groups of North European Jews during the Crusades.

the boats was infested with the plague, and the captain of the boat put the passengers ashore at some uninhabited place. And there most of them died of starvation, while some of them gathered up all their strength to set out on foot in search of some settlement.

There was one Jew among them who struggled on afoot together with his wife and two children. The wife grew faint and died, because she was not accustomed to so much difficult walking. The husband carried his children along until both he and they fainted from hunger. When he regained consciousness, he found that his two children had died.

In great grief he rose to his feet and said: "O Lord of all the universe, You are doing a great deal that I might even desert my faith. But know You of a certainty that – even against the will of heaven – a Jew I am and a Jew I shall remain. And neither that which You have brought upon me nor that which You may yet bring upon me will be of any avail."

Thereupon he gathered some earth and some grass, and covered the boys, and went forth in search of a settlement.[13]

One is awestruck by such faith – such obstinate faith.

Almost certainly it was this idea that lies behind a famous Talmudic passage about the giving of the Torah at Mount Sinai:

And they stood under the mountain: R. Avdimi b. Ḥama b. Ḥasa said: This teaches that the Holy One blessed be He, overturned the mountain above them like a barrel and said, "If you accept the Torah, it will be well. If not, this will be your burial place." R. Akha b. Yaakov observed: This constitutes a strong protest against the Torah. Said Rava, Even so, they re-accepted it in the days of Ahasuerus, for it is written, the Jews confirmed and took upon them, meaning, "they confirmed what they had accepted before."[14]

13. In Nahum Glatzer, *A Jewish Reader* (New York: Schocken, 1975), 204–5. It was this passage that inspired Zvi Kolitz's famous Holocaust fiction about one man's defiance of God in the name of God, *Yossl Rakover Talks to God* (New York: Vintage, 2000).
14. *Shabbat* 88a. See essay "Mount Sinai and the Birth of Freedom," p. 149.

The meaning of this strange text seems to be this: at Sinai (according to R. Avdimi) the Jewish people had no choice but to accept the covenant. They had just been rescued from Egypt. God had divided the sea for them; He had sent them manna from heaven and water from the rock. Acceptance of a covenant under such conditions cannot be called free.

The real test of faith came when God was hidden. Rava's quotation from the Book of Esther is pointed and precise. The book is one of only two in Tanakh which does not contain the name of God. The rabbis suggested that the name Esther is an allusion to the phrase *haster astir et panai*, "I will surely hide My face." The book relates the first warrant for genocide against the Jewish people. That Jews remained Jews under such conditions was proof positive that they did indeed reaffirm the covenant. Obstinate in their disbelief during much of the biblical era, they became obstinate in their belief ever afterwards. Faced with God's presence, they disobeyed Him. Confronted with His absence, they stayed faithful to Him. That is the paradox of the stiff-necked people.

Not by accident does the main narrative of the Book of Esther begin with the words "And Mordechai would not bow down" (Esther 3:1). His refusal to make obeisance to Haman sets the story in motion. Mordechai too is obstinate – for there is one thing that is hard to do if you have a stiff neck, namely, bow down. At times, Jews found it hard to bow down to God – but they were certainly never willing to bow down to anything less. That is why, alone of all the many peoples who have entered the arena of history, Jews – even in exile, dispersed, and everywhere a minority – neither assimilated to the dominant culture nor converted to the majority faith.

"Forgive them *because* they are a stiff-necked people," said Moses, because the time will come when that stubbornness will be not a tragic failing but a noble and defiant loyalty. And so it came to be.

Shabbat and the Golden Calf: Reflections on the Great Crash of 2008

I n the introduction to *Covenant and Conversation, Genesis,* I quoted the saying of the sixth Lubavitcher Rebbe that "We must live with the times – this means we must live with *parashat hashavua,* the weekly Torah portion."[1] It is that interface between the timeless and the timely that generates new understandings, both of the Torah, and the times in which we live. Sometimes the connection is so striking that it becomes a kind of epiphany, as we sense the word of God leaping across the millennia to address us in the existential present, in all its pristine power. So it was during the financial collapse that will surely come to be known as the Great Crash of 2008.

Less than a week before the collapse at the beginning of August 2008, the British artist Damien Hirst put a sculpture up for sale at Sotheby's. It was sold for £10.5 million, one of the highest prices ever paid for the work of a living artist. In light of all that happened subsequently, it

---

1. Jonathan Sacks, *Covenant and Conversation: Genesis, the Book of Beginnings* (Jerusalem: Maggid Books and Orthodox Union, 2009), 1.

was as if heaven had sent a signal of what was going wrong in the contemporary West. The symbolic nature of the event lay in the name of the sculpture. Hirst called it The Golden Calf.[2]

The connection with the biblical precedent went deep. Like the Golden Calf in the days of Moses (Exodus 32:1–6), Hirst's sculpture was a symbol of what can happen when people turn gold, a medium of exchange, into an object of worship. The result, both times, was collective folly, irrational exuberance; what Charles Mackay – one of the first to analyze the phenomenon, in 1841 – called "the madness of crowds."[3]

Adam bahul al mamono, said the sages, meaning, the pursuit of wealth can make us do self-destructive things.[4] It happened in the tulip craze in Holland at the end of the sixteenth century, the South Sea Bubble of 1720, and the Florida Real Estate boom in the 1920s that led to the Great Crash of 1929. Exaggerated expectation leads to waves of investment, reinforced by rising prices, until the boom can no longer be sustained. Like Jonah's gourd, it flourishes overnight and dies the next day.[5] The losers are often those least able to afford it.

Gold, like money, is a means, not an end. When it becomes an end in itself, that is a prelude to disaster. In the case of the early twenty-first century boom, people were becoming obsessed with money: salaries, bonuses, borrowings, expenditures and expensive luxuries they could live without. *When money rules, we remember the price of things and forget the value of things.* In 2008 this applied especially to house prices.

The value of a house is that it is a home. Hebrew combines both ideas in a single word, *bayit*, which means both house and home. A home is a haven in a heartless world.[6] It's where we belong and where, if we are lucky, we raise a family. Home is where we learn the poetry of everyday

---

2. *The Guardian*, July 29 2008: http://www.guardian.co.uk/artanddesign/2008/jul/29/art.
3. Charles Mackay, *Extraordinary Popular Delusions and the Madness of Crowds* (Wordsworth Reference, 1995: originally published 1841).
4. *Shabbat* 117b.
5. Jonah 4:6–9.
6. The phrase is taken from Christopher Lasch, *Haven in a Heartless World* (New York: Basic Books, 1977).

life, the choreography of *ḥesed*, the countless daily acts of reciprocity and kindness that constitute the language of love.

At a certain point, though, some began to think of a house less as a home than as a capital investment. Value began to take second place to price. The market responded accordingly. House prices began to rise. Even people who had no thought of capital gain were forced to join the race. They sought to borrow more, and banks and building societies duly obliged, devising ways, most notoriously subprime mortgages, to leverage loans ever higher.

Borrowings lost all proportion to average earnings, and prices rose higher still. It was unsustainable. The more perceptive investment bankers – Warren Buffett, George Soros – had said so years before, but no one was listening. People, contemplating what they would get if they put their house on the market, thought they were getting richer, but in real terms they weren't. Prices rose, but the value of a house remained unchanged. It could not but end in tears.

What is fascinating is the remedy the Torah proposes for the Golden Calf syndrome. Immediately before and after the event (Exodus 31:12–17; 35:1–3), Moses gives the Israelites a command: in both cases the *same* command, namely Shabbat. Why this command then?

Shabbat is the antidote to the Golden Calf because it is the day when we stop thinking of the *price* of things and focus instead on the *value* of things. On Shabbat we can't sell or buy. We can't work or pay others to work for us. It's the day dedicated to the celebration of the things that have value but no price. Husbands sing a song of praise to their wives. Parents bless their children. We take time to have a meal together with family and friends. In the synagogue we renew our sense of community. People share their joys – a new child, a bar or bat mitzva, an engagement, a forthcoming wedding – with others. Those saying Kaddish find comfort for their grief. We listen to Torah together, reminding ourselves of the story of which we are a part. We pray together, thanking God for our blessings.

Shabbat is our refuge from what has become, in the late capitalist economies, a consumer culture. Consumerism has become the new religion. Its cathedrals are shopping centres, its most heinous sin is *not having this year's model*, and it promises "retail therapy," salvation by shopping, and remission of sins by credit card. Shabbat is precisely the opposite: the one day in seven on which we live the truth of Ben Zoma's aphorism, "Who is rich? One who rejoices in what he has."[7]

Consumer societies are based on stimulating demand to generate expenditure to produce economic growth. Advertising offers us a thousand blandishments to focus our minds on what we don't yet have. Buy this, wear that, shop here, holiday there, and you will find happiness – until next month when you discover all the other things you still don't have. The financial collapse happened because people borrowed money they didn't have, to buy things they didn't need, to achieve a happiness that wouldn't last.

Through constant creation of dissatisfaction, the consumer society is in fact a highly sophisticated mechanism for the production and distribution of unhappiness. That is why an age of unprecedented affluence has also become an age of ever-increasing drug and alcohol abuse, eating disorders, stress-related syndromes and depressive illness.[8] No enslavement was ever more gentle and seductive than consumerism, yet enslavement it is, for despite automation, computerisation and the many time- and labour-saving devices we have at our disposal, people work harder today than they did fifty years ago, with little if any self-reported rise in happiness. That is the contemporary version of the Golden Calf syndrome.

It is unsustainable, economically, environmentally and psychologically. The most important contribution of Shabbat to the late capitalist societies of the twenty-first century is that it reintroduces into thought and life the idea of limits. There are limits to our striving, our labours, our consumption of the earth's finite resources, and what Thomas Hobbes called the "perpetual and restless desire of power after power, that ceaseth only in death."[9] Any culture that loses its sense of limits eventually self-destructs. The liberal democratic West will be no exception.

It goes without saying that this is not what the Golden Calf epi-

7. Mishna, *Avot* 4:1.
8. See, for example, Oliver James, *Britain on the Couch: Why We're Unhappier Compared with 1950 Despite Being Richer* (London: Century, 1997).
9. Thomas Hobbes, *Leviathan*, part 1, chap. 11, "Of the difference of manners."

sode, or the command of Shabbat, were originally about. Yet there is a serious point at stake. The Torah continues to be relevant and incisive in our time – and this is part of what Torah *min hashamayim*, "Torah from heaven,"[10] actually means. If Torah is, as we believe, the word of God, then we cannot interpret it as we would a human document. Just as God is eternal, so is His word. Hence the primacy in Judaism of *midrash* (the applied sense) as against *peshat* (the "plain" sense).[11] I would define the difference between them thus: *peshat* is what the text meant then; *midrash* is what the text means now. The susceptibility of Torah to new interpretation in every generation derives from our belief that, through its words, God is communicating with us, here, now.

Shabbat has meant many things over the course of time. During the biblical era it was a sustained protest against slavery. For one day in seven even a slave was free. In later ages it was a defence against poverty and oppression, a moment in which a much-afflicted people found serenity and breathed a more spacious air. Judah Halevi said that on Shabbat even the poorest Jew was freer than the most powerful king.[12] In modern times it has become a counterforce to stress and the ever more intrusive presence of emails, mobile phones and the pressures of work. In the foreseeable future it will become a major force in the battle against overexploitation of the environment.

There is a larger point at stake. In his remarkable 1977 book on the economy, *The Reigning Error*, William Rees-Mogg (then editor of *The Times*) began with a paean of praise for Jewish law. His argument was that inflation – like the boom-crash cycle – is a "disease of inordinacy," that is, a lack of moderation and restraint. "Every generation, every movement, which has tried to reject the limitations of humanity,

10. The phrase comes from Mishna, *Sanhedrin* 10:1.
11. See on this the important methodological note by Rashbam in his commentary to Genesis 37:2. The sages, he says, were preoccupied by midrash; he dedicates his commentary to "the deep plain sense of Scripture" (*omek peshuto shel mikra*). There is a large literature on the subject, but see especially Raphael Loewe, "The 'Plain' Meaning of Scripture in Early Jewish Exegesis," *Papers of the Institute of Jewish Studies*, vol. 1 (London:, 1964); David Weiss Halivni, *Peshat and Derash: Plain and Applied Meaning in Rabbinic Exegesis* (New York: Oxford University Press, 1991).
12. *The Kuzari*, book III, 10.

has been involved in the same delusion and has suffered similar and similarly inevitable consequences."[13]

Jews acquired an immune system against this disease because they were schooled in suffering. "The wisdom of suffering is the wisdom of humility. It is prosperity that tempts men to forget the limits of human nature and the limits of human power. Suffering educates men to accept their own limited natures in the same way that the discipline of a parent, however gentle, educates a child to accept ordinacy as an individual."[14]

Jewish law turned this into an ongoing discipline of self-restraint, a "boundary for the energy of human nature." Rees-Mogg compares it to the cladding needed to contain nuclear energy. "In the same way, the energy of the Jewish people has been enclosed in a different kind of container, the law. That has acted as a bottle inside which this spiritual and intellectual energy could be held; only because it could be held has it been possible to make use of it. It has not merely exploded or being dispersed; it has been harnessed as a continuous power."[15] Halakha, Jewish law, sets limits and establishes boundaries. That is why Jewish energies survived undiminished through time. Though Rees-Mogg does not refer to it specifically, Shabbat is a, even the, supreme example.

Shabbat, one of the first commands Moses gave the Jewish people, remains as relevant now as it was then. It tells us that happiness lies not in what we buy but in what we are; that true contentment is to be found not by seeking what we lack but by giving thanks for what we have; and that we should never allow ourselves to be so busy making a living that we have all too little time to live. Above all, we should never be led by the crowd when it stampedes in pursuit of gain, for that is how gold becomes a Golden Calf.

13. William Rees-Mogg, *The Reigning Error: The Crisis of World Inflation* (London: Hamilton, 1974), 9–11.
14. Ibid., 10.
15. Ibid., 12.

Counting Jews

This week's *parasha* begins with God's command to Moses to take a census of the people. But it is phrased in a most curious manner. Moses is told not to count the people directly, but obliquely. Each was to give half a shekel, and only thus was their number to be calculated. This is the verse in which the command is given:

> When you take a census [literally, "when you lift the head"] of the Israelites to determine their number, each one is to give to the Lord an atonement offering for his life when they are counted, so that they will not be stricken by plague when they are counted. (Exodus 30:12)

Evidently, it is dangerous to count Jews. This is confirmed by a later episode in Jewish history, recounted in II Samuel 24. On one occasion, King David decided to take a census of the people. His chief of staff, Joab, strongly advised against it:

> But Joab replied to the king, "May the Lord your God multiply the troops a hundred times over, and may the eyes of my lord

the king see it. But why does my lord the king want to do such a thing?" (II Samuel 24:3)

David overruled him, however. Once the census was taken, he began to realize that he had done a great wrong; he was conscience-stricken after he counted the fighting men, and said to the Lord, "I have sinned greatly in what I have done. Now, O Lord, I beg you, take away the guilt of your servant. I have done a very foolish thing" (24:10). The result, despite David's repentance, was tragedy. A plague struck the people, taking many lives.

There is a tantalizing mystery here. Why is it dangerous to count Jews? The commentators on *Ki Tissa* offer many suggestions. Rashi says that counting is fraught with the danger of "the evil eye."[1] Rabbenu Bachya suggests that when people are being counted, they are numbered one by one rather than all together. For a moment they are individuals, separated from the community. Hence there is a danger that an individual's merit may not be sufficiently great to save him from adverse judgement.[2] Sforno says that a census reminds us of change; it draws attention both to those who have died and those who are still alive. This too is dangerous, since it raises the question: by what right am I here and others not?[3] To avert this we must give, by way of ransom, a gift to the Temple and its divine service.

If only by way of midrash, and with no suggestion that this is the plain sense of the verse, I offer another interpretation. Why do nations normally take a census of their population? To establish their strength: military (the number of people who can be conscripted into an army), economic (the number from whom taxes can be raised) or simply demographic (the numerical growth or decline of the nation). The assumption beneath every census is: there is strength in numbers. The more numerous a people, the stronger it is.

That is why it is dangerous to count Jews. We are a tiny people. The late Milton Himmelfarb once wrote that the total population of

---

1. Rashi, commentary to Exodus 30:12.
2. Rabbenu Bachya, commentary to Exodus 30:12.
3. Sforno, commentary to Exodus 30:12.

Jews throughout the world is smaller than a small statistical error in the Chinese census.[4] We are a fifth of a percent of the population of the world: by any normal standards too small to be significant. Nor is this true only now. It was then. In one of his concluding addresses in Deuteronomy, Moses said:

> The Lord did not set His affection on you and choose you because you were more numerous than other peoples, for you are the fewest of all peoples. (Deuteronomy 7:7).

The danger in counting Jews is that if they believed, even for a moment, that there is strength in numbers, the Jewish people would long ago have given way to despair.

How then do you estimate the strength of the Jewish people? To this, I suggest, the Torah gives an answer of surpassing beauty. *Ask Jews to give, and then count their contributions.* Numerically we are small, but in terms of our contributions to civilization and humankind, we are vast.

Think only of the makers of modern thought: in physics, Einstein; in philosophy, Wittgenstein; in sociology, Durkheim; in anthropology, Levi-Strauss; in psychiatry, Freud; in economics, a whole string of great thinkers from David Ricardo to Milton Friedman to Alan Greenspan to Joe Stiglitz (including forty percent of the winners of the Nobel Prize for economics). In literature, there were writers from Proust to Kafka to Agnon to Isaac Bashevis Singer; in music, classical composers like Mahler and Schoenberg and popular composers like Irving Berlin and George Gershwin, as well as some of the world's greatest soloists and conductors.

Jews have won forty-eight Nobel prizes in medicine. They have made an outstanding contribution to law (in Britain, where they are one-half of a percent of the population, they contributed two of the last three Lord Chief Justices, the highest judicial office in the land: Lords Peter Taylor and Harry Woolf). And all this without mentioning the Jewish contribution to industry, finance, academic life, the media, and politics (under the British Prime Minister John Major, at one time both

---

4. Milton Himmelfarb, *Jews and Gentiles*: (New York: Encounter Books, 2007), 141–42.

the Home Secretary and Foreign Secretary were Jews: Michael Howard and Malcolm Rifkind). At the time of writing – early 2010 – the speakers of both Houses of Parliament, Lords and Commons, are Jewish (John Bercow and Baroness Hayman).

In America too, Jews were among its most distinguished jurists: Louis Brandeis, Benjamin Cardozo, Felix Frankfurter and Ruth Bader Ginsburg. Psychotherapy – a Jewish invention – continues to be dominated by Jewish practitioners, among them Aaron T. Beck, creator of cognitive therapy, and Martin Seligman, pioneer of positive psychology. Hollywood was virtually a Jewish creation, and American Jews have made disproportionate contributions to the arts, music, medicine, and academic life.[5]

But it is, of course, the Jewish contribution to the life of the spirit that is not only unique but has shaped the entire course of Western civilization.[6] Somehow this tiny people produced an unceasing flow of patriarchs, priests, poets and prophets, masters of halakha and *aggada*, codifiers and commentators, philosophers and mystics, sages and saints, in a way that almost defies comprehension. It was not once that the Jewish imagination caught fire, but in century after century, sometimes under the worst persecution known to any nation on earth. Time and again, in the wake of tragedy, the Jewish people renewed itself in a burst of creativity. The destruction of the First Temple gave rise to systematic Torah study in Babylon. The destruction of the Second Temple precipitated the great literature of the Oral tradition: Midrash, Mishna and Talmud. Encounters with Karaites, and later, Christians, produced the great Torah commentaries. The challenge of Islamic neo-Platonism and neo-Aristotelianism provoked one of the great ages of Jewish philosophy, in Spain between the twelfth and fourteenth centuries.

If you want to know the strength of the Jewish people, ask them to give, and then count the contributions. That is the majestic idea at the opening of this week's *parasha*.

---

5. For two interesting studies, see Andrew R. Heinze, *Jews and the American Soul* (Princeton University Press, 2004), and Yuri Slezkine, *The Jewish Century* (Princeton University Press, 2004).
6. See Thomas Cahill, *The Gifts of the Jews* (New York: Nan Talese, 1998).

Nor is this mere conjecture. At least one biblical episode seems to hint at this truth. It occurs in the sixth and seventh chapters of the Book of Judges. The Israelites had suffered a devastating series of attacks from the Midianites. God called on a warrior, Gideon, and told him to wage war against them. Gideon duly assembled an army of thirty-two thousand men. God responded with what must surely be one of the strangest lines in history: "You have too many men for Me to deliver Midian into their hands" (Judges 7:2). God tells Gideon to announce that anyone who wishes to go home should go home. Twenty-two thousand men did so; a mere ten thousand remained. God said: There are still too many men.

He told Gideon to take the men to a place of water and observe how they drank. Nine thousand seven hundred kneeled down to the water to drink it directly. A mere three hundred cupped the water in their hands and stayed standing. God told Gideon to dismiss the vast majority of the troops, leaving only the three hundred, an absurdly small number for any military engagement, let alone a war against a powerful enemy. Only then did God say to Gideon: "With the three hundred men that lapped I will save you and give the Midianites into your hands" (7:7). Mounting a surprise attack at night, and using ingenious tactics to suggest the presence of a large army, Gideon struck and won.

Clearly this is not just a story about war. Tanakh is a religious text, not a military one. What God was saying to Gideon – what He has been saying to us and our ancestors tacitly for forty centuries – is that to win the Jewish battle, the battle of the spirit, the victory of heart, mind and soul, you do not need numbers. You need dedication, commitment, study, prayer, vision, courage, ideals, hope. You need a people who are instinctively inclined to give, to contribute. Give, then count the contributions: the finest way ever devised to measure the strength of a people.

Awakening from Above, Awakening from Below

Framing the epic events of this week's *parasha* are two objects – the two sets of tablets, the first given before, the second after, the sin of the Golden Calf. Of the first, we read:

> The tablets were the work of God; the writing was the writing of God, engraved on the tablets. (Exodus 32:16)

These were perhaps the holiest objects in history: from beginning to end, the work of God. Yet within hours they lay shattered, broken by Moses when he saw the calf and the Israelites dancing around it.

The second tablets, brought down by Moses on the tenth day of Tishri, were the result of his prolonged plea to God to forgive the people. This is the historic event that lies behind Yom Kippur, the Day of Atonement, the day marked in perpetuity as a time of favour, forgiveness and reconciliation between God and the Jewish people. The second tablets were different in one respect. They were not wholly the work of God:

Carve out two stone tablets like the first ones, and I will write on them the words that were on the first tablets, which you broke. (Exodus 34:1)

Hence the paradox: the first tablets, made by God, did not remain intact. The second tablets, the joint work of God and Moses, did. Surely the opposite should have been true: the greater the holiness, the more eternal. Why was the more holy object broken while the less holy stayed whole? This is not, as it might seem, a question specific to the tablets. It is, in fact, a powerful example of a fundamental principle in Jewish spirituality.

The Jewish mystics distinguished between two types of divine-human encounter. They called them *itaruta de'l'eylah* and *itaruta de'letata*, respectively "an awakening from above" and "an awakening from below."[1] The first is initiated by God, the second by mankind. An "awakening from above" is spectacular, supernatural, an event that bursts through the chains of causality that at other times bind the natural world. An "awakening from below" has no such grandeur. It is a gesture that is human, all too human.

Yet there is another difference between them, in the opposite direction. An "awakening from above" may change nature, but it does not, in and of itself, change human nature. In it, no human effort has been expended. Those to whom it happens are passive. While it lasts, it is overwhelming; but only while it lasts. Thereafter, people revert to what they were. An "awakening from below," by contrast, leaves a permanent mark.[2]

Because human beings have taken the initiative, something in them changes. Their horizons of possibility have been expanded. They now know they are capable of great things, and because they did so once, they are aware that they can do so again. An awakening from above temporarily transforms the external world; an awakening from below per-

---

1. The concepts are present in the Zohar. See Byron Sherwin, *Kabbalah: An Introduction to Jewish Mysticism* (Lanham, Rowman and Littlefield, 2006), 165.
2. See essay "A Portable Home," p. 189.

manently transforms our internal world. The first changes the universe; the second changes us.

There are two examples from within the book of Exodus that illustrate this concept beautifully.

The first concerns the Israelites in their encounters with their enemies. Both before and after the division of the Reed Sea, the Israelites were confronted by enemies: before, by the Egyptians, after, by the Amalekites. The difference in these encounters is total.

Before the Reed Sea, the Israelites were commanded to do nothing: "Stand still and you will see the deliverance God will bring you today...God will fight for you; you need only be still." (14:13–14). Facing the Amalekites, however, the Israelites themselves had to fight: "Moses said to Joshua, 'Choose men and go out and fight the Amalekites...'" (17:9). The first encounter resulted in an "awakening from above," the second, an "awakening from below."

The difference was palpable. At the first conflict, the Israelites complained bitterly: "Was it because there were no graves in Egypt that you brought us to the desert to die? What have you done to us by bringing us out of Egypt? Didn't we say to you in Egypt, 'Leave us alone; let us serve the Egyptians'? It would have been better for us to serve the Egyptians than to die in the desert!" (14:11–12). But during the war against the Amalekites, there were no complaints. The Israelites simply fought, under Joshua's leadership, drawing inspiration from Moses' upstretched hands (17:11). It was as if they had become a different people. The battles fought for us do not change us; the battles we fight, do.

The second example is Mount Sinai and the Tabernacle. The Torah speaks about these two revelations of "God's glory" in almost identical terms:

> Mount Sinai: "The glory of God settled on Mount Sinai. For six days the cloud covered the mountain, and on the seventh day God called to Moses from within the cloud." (Exodus 24:16)

> The Tabernacle: "Then the cloud covered the Tent of Meeting, and the glory of God filled the Tabernacle." (Exodus 40:34)

The difference between them was that the sanctity of Mount Sinai was momentary, while that of the Tabernacle was permanent (at least, until the Temple was built, centuries later). The revelation at Sinai was an "awakening from above." It was initiated by God. So overwhelming was it that the people said to Moses, "Let God not speak to us any more, for if He does, we will die" (20:16). By contrast, the Tabernacle involved human labour. The Israelites made it; they prepared the structured space the Divine Presence would eventually fill. Forty days after the revelation at Sinai, the Israelites made a Golden Calf. But after constructing the Sanctuary they made no more idols – at least until they entered the land forty years later – and that generation, not at all. That is the difference between the things that are done for us and the things we have a share in doing ourselves. The former change us for a moment, the latter for a lifetime.

There was one other difference between the first tablets and the second. According to tradition, when Moses was given the first tablets, he was given only *Torah she-bikhtav*, the "written Torah." At the time of the second tablets, he was given *Torah she-be'al peh*, the Oral Torah as well:

> "R. Yochanan said: God made a covenant with Israel only for the sake of the Oral Law, as it says [in the context of the second tablets]: "For by the mouth [*al pi*] of these words I have made a covenant with you and with Israel." (Exodus 34:27)[3]

The difference between the Written and Oral Torah is profound. The first is the word of God, with no human contribution. The second is a partnership – the word of God as interpreted by the mind of man. The following are two of several remarkable passages that express this idea:

> R. Yehuda said in the name of Shmuel: Three thousand traditional laws [halakhot, rules belonging to the Oral Law] were forgotten during the period of mourning for Moses. They [the Israelites] said to Joshua: "Ask" [through *ruah hakodesh*, the holy spirit]. Joshua replied, "It is not in heaven." They said to Samuel, "Ask."

3. *Gittin* 60a.

He replied, "These are the commandments – implying that no prophet has the right to introduce anything new."[4]

"If a thousand prophets of the stature of Elijah and Elisha were to give one interpretation of a verse, and one thousand and one sages were to offer a different interpretation, we follow the majority: the law is in accordance with the thousand and one sages and not in accordance with the thousand prophets."[5]

Any attempt to reduce the Oral Torah to the Written – by relying on prophecy or divine communication – mistakes its essential nature as the collaborative partnership between God and man, where revelation meets interpretation. Thus, the difference between the two precisely mirrors that between the first and second tablets. The first were divine, the second the result of divine-human collaboration. This helps us understand a glorious ambiguity. The Torah says that at Sinai the Israelites heard a "great voice *velo yasaf*" (Deuteronomy 5:18). Two contradictory interpretations of this phrase are given. One reads it as "a great voice that was never heard again,"[6] the other as "a great voice that did not cease,"[7] – i.e., a voice that was always heard again. The reason for this ambiguity is that both are true. The first refers to the Written Torah, given once and never to be repeated. The second applies to the Oral Torah, whose study has never ceased.

It also helps us understand why it was only after the second tablets, not the first, that "When Moses came down from Mount Sinai with the two tablets of Testimony in his hands, he was unaware that his face was radiant because he had spoken with God" (34:29). Receiving the first tablets, Moses was passive. Therefore, nothing in him changed. For the second, he was active. He had a share in the making. He carved the stone on which the words were to be engraved. That is why he became a different person. His face shone.

In Judaism, the natural is greater than the supernatural in the

4. *Temura* 16a.
5. Rambam, commentary to the Mishna, introduction.
6. Saadia Gaon, Rashbam, and Ibn Ezra, to Deuteronomy 5:18.
7. Rashi, commentary to Deuteronomy 5:18, on the basis of Targum Onkelos.

sense that an "awakening from below" is more powerful in transforming us, and longer-lasting in its effects, than is an "awakening from above." That was why the second tablets survived intact while the first did not. Divine intervention changes nature, but it is human initiative – our approach to God – that changes us.

Vayak-hel
ויקהל

Immediately after his return from the mountain top, having secured forgiveness for the people after the sin of the Golden Calf, Moses assembles them and commands them, first, about the Sabbath, and then about the making of the Tabernacle. The *parasha* repeats much of what was said earlier in *parashat Teruma*, with this difference: that there we read the instructions, here, their execution. The people give willingly, and Betzalel and Oholiab, the craftsmen, fashion the various structures.

The first of the following essays looks at the different placements of the command about Shabbat, here and in the earlier account. Here it precedes the commands about the Tabernacle, there it followed them. Why the difference? The second looks at the word that gives the *parasha* its name, *Vayak-hel*, a word with the same root as *kehilla*, community. There are three forms of community in Judaism. What are their differences? The third asks why the long account of the Tabernacle appears in Exodus, a book about nation-building. The answer to this question has a surprising relevance to the problems of today's multicultural societies. The fourth, taking its cue from Betzalel's artistry, explores the place of aesthetics in Judaism.

The Sabbath: First Day or the Last?

In the immensely lengthy and detailed account of the making of the Tabernacle, the Torah tells the story twice: first as divine instruction (Exodus 25:1–31:17), then as human implementation (chapters 35–40). In both cases, the construction of the building is juxtaposed with the command of keeping the Sabbath (31:12–17; 35:1–2).

There are halakhic and theological implications to this. First, according to Jewish tradition, the juxtaposition was intended to establish the rule that the Sabbath overrides the making of the Tabernacle.[1] Not only is the seventh day a time when secular work comes to an end. It also brings rest from the holiest of labours: making a house for God. Indeed, the oral tradition defined *melakha*, "creative work, craft," – that which is prohibited on the Sabbath – in terms of the thirty-nine activities involved in making the Sanctuary.

At a more metaphysical level, the Sanctuary mirrors – is the human counterpart to – the divine creation of the universe.[2] Just as

---

1. *Shabbat* 49b; see Rashi, commentary to Exodus 3:13, 35:2.
2. See essay "The Home We Make for God," p. 199.

divine creation culminates in the Sabbath, so too does human creation. The sanctity of place takes second place to the holiness of time.[3]

However, there is one marked difference between the account of God's instruction to Moses to build the Sanctuary, and Moses' instruction to the people. In the first case, in the *parasha* of *Ki Tissa*, the command of the Sabbath appears at the end, after the details of the construction. In the second, in *Vayak-hel*, it appears at the beginning, before the details. Why so?

The Talmud raises the following question: what happens if you are far away from human habitation and you forget what day it is? How do you observe the Sabbath? Two answers are offered:

> R. Huna said: "If one is travelling on a road or in the wilderness and does not know when it is the Sabbath, he must count six days [from the day he realises he has forgotten] and observe one." R. Ḥiyya b. Rav said: "He must observe one, and then count six [week] days." On what do they differ? One master holds that it is like the world's creation. The other holds that it is like [the case of] Adam.[4]

From God's point of view, the Sabbath was the seventh day. From the point of view of the first human beings – created on the sixth day – the Sabbath was the first. The debate is about which perspective we should adopt. Thus, at the simplest level, we understand why the Sabbath comes last when God is speaking about the Tabernacle, and why it comes first when Moses, a human being, is doing so. For God, the Sabbath was the last day of creation; for human beings it was the first.

However there is something more fundamental at stake. When it comes to divine creation, there is no gap between intention and execution. God spoke, and the world came into being.[5] In relation to God, Isaiah says: "I make known the end from the beginning, from ancient times,

3. For more on this, see A.J. Heschel's *The Sabbath* (Farrar, Straus and Giroux, 1983).
4. *Shabbat* 69b.
5. The phrase comes from the prayer *Barukh She'amar*, in the morning service.

what is still to come. I say: My purpose will stand, and I will do all that I please" (Isaiah 46:10). God knows in advance how things will turn out.

With human beings, it is otherwise. Often, we cannot see the end at the beginning, the outcome at the outset. A great novelist may not know how the story will turn out until he has written it, nor a composer, a symphony, nor an artist, a painting. Creativity is fraught with risk. All the more is it so with human history. The "law of unintended consequences" tells us that revolutions rarely turn out as planned. Policies designed to help the poor may have the opposite effect.[6] Hayek coined the phrase "the fatal conceit" for what he saw as the almost inevitable failure of social engineering – the idea that you can plan human behaviour in advance.[7] You can't. Therefore large-scale social engineering is bound to fail.[8]

One alternative is simply to let things happen as they will. This kind of resignation, however, is wholly out of keeping with the Judaic view of history. The sages said: "Wherever you find the word *vayehi* ['and it came to pass'] it is always a prelude to tragedy."[9] When things merely come to pass, they rarely have a happy ending.

The other solution – unique, as far as I know, to Judaism – is to reveal the end at the beginning. That is the meaning of the Sabbath. The Sabbath is not simply a day of rest. It is an anticipation of "the end of history," the messianic age. On it, we recover the lost harmonies of the Garden of Eden. We do not strive to do; we are content to be. We are not permitted to manipulate the world; instead, we celebrate it as God's supreme work of art. We are not allowed to exercise power or dominance over other human beings, nor even domestic animals. Rich and poor inhabit the Sabbath alike, with equal dignity and freedom.

No utopia has ever been realized (the word "utopia" itself means "no place") – with one exception: "the world to come." The reason is that

---

6. One classic example is the failure of the welfare policies of the 1960s in America and Britain to reduce poverty. By the 1980s it was higher than before. See Charles Murray, *Losing Ground* (Basic Books, 1984).
7. Friedrich Hayek, *The Fatal Conceit* (London: Routledge, 1988).
8. This was also the view of Karl Popper, *The Poverty of Historicism* (Routledge and Kegan Paul, 1961).
9. *Megilla* 10b; *Vayikra Raba* 11:7.

we rehearse it every week, one day in seven. The Sabbath is a full dress rehearsal for an ideal society that has not yet come to pass, but will do, because we know what we are aiming for – because we experienced it at the beginning.

We now begin to sense the full symbolic drama of the making of the Tabernacle. In the wilderness, long before they crossed the Jordan and entered the promised land, God told the Israelites to build a miniature universe. It would be a place of carefully calibrated order – as the universe is a place of carefully calibrated order. Nowadays, scientists call this the "anthropic principle" – the finding that the laws of physics and chemistry are finely tuned for the emergence of life.[10] Just so, did the Tabernacle have to be exact in its construction and dimensions.

The building of the Tabernacle was a symbolic prototype of the building of a society. Just as it was an earthly home for the Divine Presence, so would society become if the Israelites honoured God's laws. The ultimate end of such a society is the harmony of existence that we have not yet experienced, living as we do in a world of work and striving, conflict and competition.

God, however, wanted us to know what we were aiming for, so that we would not lose our way in the wilderness of time. That is why, when it came to the human execution of the building, the Sabbath came first, even though in global terms, the messianic age, the "Sabbath of history," will come last. God "made known the end at the beginning" (Isaiah 46:10) – the fulfilled rest that follows creative labour; the peace that will one day take the place of strife – so that we would catch a glimpse of the destination before beginning the journey.

Only those who know where they are travelling to will get there, however fast or slow they go.

---

10. See John Barrow, *The Anthropic Cosmological Principle* (Oxford University Press, 1988); Paul Davies, *The Goldilocks Enigma* (Allen Lane, 2006); Martin Rees, *Just Six Numbers: The Deep Forces That Shape the Universe* (Phoenix, 2000).

Three Kinds of Community

A long drama had taken place. Moses had led the people from slavery to the beginning of the road to freedom. The people themselves had witnessed God at Mount Sinai, the only time in all history when an entire people became the recipients of revelation. Then came the disappearance of Moses for his long sojourn at the top of the mountain, an absence which led to the Israelites' greatest collective sin, the making of the Golden Calf. Moses returned to the mountain to plead for forgiveness, which was granted.

Its symbol was the second set of tablets. Now life must begin again. A shattered people must be rebuilt. How does Moses proceed? The verse with which the *parasha* begins contains the clue:

> Moses assembled (*vayak-hel*) the whole Israelite community and said to them: "These are the things God has commanded you to do." (Exodus 35:1)

The verb *vayak-hel*, which gives the *parasha* its name, is crucial to an understanding of the task in which Moses is engaged. For it is the use of this word that reminds us of an earlier occasion on which it appeared:[1]

> When the people saw that Moses was so long in coming down from the mountain, they assembled (*vayikahel*) around Aaron and said, "Come, make us gods who will go before us." (32:1)

Moses' act is what the kabbalists called a *tikkun*: a restoration, a making-good-again, the redemption of a past misdemeanour. Just as the sin was committed by the people acting as a community, a *kahal* or *kehilla*, so atonement was to be achieved by their again acting as a *kehilla*, this time by making a home [*Mishkan*] for the Divine Presence as they earlier sought to make a substitute for it. Moses orchestrates the people for good, as they had once been assembled for bad.

However, to understand the profound significance of the opening verse of the *parasha*, we need to reflect more deeply on the nature of community in Judaism.

In classical Hebrew there are three different words for community: *edah*, *tzibbur* and *kehilla*, and they signify different kinds of association.

Edah comes from the word *ed*, meaning "witness." The verb *ya'ad*, from which *ed* comes, carries the meaning of "to appoint, fix, assign, destine, set apart, designate or determine." The modern Hebrew noun *te'uda* means "certificate, document, attestation, aim, object, purpose or mission." The people who constitute an *edah* have a strong sense of collective identity. They have witnessed the same things. They are bent on the same purpose. The Jewish people became an *edah* – a community of shared faith – only on receiving the first command:

> "Tell the whole community of Israel [*adat Yisrael*] that on the

---

1. This type of verbal allusion from one text to another was a standard principle of rabbinic interpretation, known as *gezera shaveh*. Franz Rosenzweig and Martin Buber developed the wider literary concept of a *motif-word*, while in the 1960s Julia Kristeva coined the term "intertextuality" to describe the yet broader way in which two or more texts can stand as commentaries to one another. The current example is a key instance of intertextuality.

tenth day of this month each man is to take a lamb for his family, one for each household." (Exodus 12:3)

An *edah* can be a gathering for bad as well as good. The Israelites, on hearing the report of the spies, lose heart and say they want to return to Egypt. Throughout, they are referred to as the *edah*, as in "How long will this wicked community (*la'edah hara'a*) grumble against Me?" (Numbers 14:27). The people agitated by Korach in his rebellion against Moses and Aaron's authority is likewise called an *edah*: "If one man sins, will You be angry with the whole community (*kol ha'edah*)?" (Numbers 16:22). Nowadays the word is generally used for an ethnic or religious subgroup. An *edah* is a community of the like-minded. The word emphasises strong identity. It is a group whose members have much in common.

By contrast the word *tzibbur*, belonging to Mishnaic rather than biblical Hebrew, comes from the root tz-b-r meaning "to heap" or "pile up." To understand the concept of *tzibbur*, think of a group of people praying at the Kotel, the Western Wall in Jerusalem. They may not know each other. They may never meet again. But for the moment, they happen to be ten people or more in the same place at the same time, and thus constitute a quorum for prayer. A *tzibbur* is a community in the minimalist sense, a mere aggregate, formed by numbers rather than any sense of identity. A *tzibbur* is a group whose members may have nothing in common except that, at a certain point, they find themselves together and thus constitute a "public" for prayer or any other command which requires a minyan (a quorum).

A *kehilla* is different from the other two kinds of community. Its members are different from one another; in that sense it is like a *tzibbur*. But they are orchestrated together for a collective undertaking – one that is involved in making a distinctive contribution. The danger of a *kehilla* is that it can become a mass, a rabble, a crowd.[2] That is what happened to the *kehilla* that made the Golden Calf. Moses, descending the mountain, sees the people dancing around it:

2. The classic study of mass behaviour is Elias Canetti, *Crowds and Power* (New York: Continuum, 1981).

Moses saw that the people were *broken loose* – for Aaron had let them *loose* for a derision among their enemies. (32:25)

The beauty of a *kehilla*, however, is that when it is driven by a constructive purpose, it gathers together the distinct and separate contributions of many individuals, so that each can say, "I helped to make this." That is why, assembling the people on this occasion, Moses emphasises that each has something different to give: "Take from what you have, an offering to God. Everyone who is willing to bring to God an offering of gold, silver and bronze... All you who are skilled among you are to come and make everything the Lord has commanded..." (Exodus 35:4–10).

Moses was able to turn the *kehilla* with its diversity into an *edah* with its singleness of purpose, while preserving the diversity of the gifts they brought to God:

> Then the whole Israelite community withdrew from Moses' presence, and everyone who was willing and whose heart moved him came and brought an offering to God for the work on the Tent of Meeting, for all its service, and for the sacred garments. All who were willing – men and women – came and brought gold jewellery of all kinds: brooches, earrings, rings and ornaments... Everyone who had blue, purple or scarlet yarn... Those presenting an offering of silver or bronze... Every skilled woman spun with her hands and brought what she had spun... The leaders brought onyx stones and other gems... All the Israelite men and women who were willing brought to God freewill offerings for all the work God, through Moses, had commanded them to do. (35:20–29)

The greatness of the Tabernacle was that it was a collective achievement – one in which not everyone did the same thing. Each gave a different thing. Each contribution was valued – and therefore each participant felt valued. *Vayak-hel* – Moses' ability to forge out of the dissolution of the people a new and genuine *kehilla* – was one of his greatest achievements.

According to Maimonides, this is the supreme challenge of leadership.[3] Homo sapiens is, he argued, unique in its diversity. "Such a variety among the individuals of a class does not exist in any other class of living beings. For the variety in any other species is limited. Only man forms an exception. Two persons may be so different from each other in every respect that they appear to belong to two different classes." This is why humans *need* society, because none of us has all the gifts necessary for survival. But it is also why humans find it hard to create society, because we are all so different.

That is why societies need leaders, and why they require such special gifts. "The well-being of society demands that there should be a leader able to regulate the actions of man. He must complete every shortcoming, remove every excess, and prescribe for the conduct of all, so that the natural variety should be counterbalanced by the uniformity of legislation, and the order of society be well established."[4] Leaders are society-builders.

Getting it right is difficult. Too much central control crushes individuality. Too little – as happened with Aaron during the episode of the Golden Calf – risks anarchy. Schopenhauer brilliantly described it as the problem of porcupines in winter. If they get too close, they injure one another with their spines. If they stay too far apart, they freeze.[5] Balance is all.

Many years later, Moses, according to the sages, returned to the theme. Knowing that his career as a leader was drawing to an end, he prayed to God to appoint a successor: "May God, Lord of the spirits of all flesh, appoint a man over the community" (Numbers 27:16). Rashi, following the sages, explains the unusual phrase "Lord of the spirits of all flesh" as follows:

> He said to Him: Lord of the universe, the character of each person is revealed and known to You – and You know that each is differ-

---

3. *The Guide for the Perplexed*, 2:40.
4. Ibid.
5. Schopenhauer, *Parerga and Paralipomena* (Oxford: Clarendon Press, 1974), II, 652.

ent. Therefore appoint for them [the Israelites] a leader who is able to bear with each person as his or her temperament requires.

To preserve the diversity of a *tzibbur* with the unity of purpose of an *edah* – that is the challenge of *kehilla*-formation, community-building, itself the greatest task of a great leader.

Nation-Building: Ancient Answer, Contemporary Problem

Sometimes the circumstances in which you arrive at a new understanding of Torah are as interesting as the understanding itself. This is the story of one such moment. Through it I came to learn something about the structure of the book of Exodus as a whole, and the place within it of the long narrative about the construction of the Sanctuary. I also discovered something no less important, namely that the Torah still has much to teach us – not only Jews but others also – as we strive to create a better, more inclusive society.

I came to know Tony Blair several years before he became prime minister of Britain. He was and is a deeply religious man who has an abiding love for the Bible. At that time, he told me, he read it nightly. Our first long conversation was, in fact, about Bible study. We were flying back, together with Prince Charles, from the funeral in Jerusalem of the late prime minister Yitzhak Rabin, on 6 November 1995.

During the flight I was studying the weekly *parasha*, using a standard *Mikraot Gedolot*, the classic edition of the biblical text printed together with the main commentaries: Rashi, Rashbam, Ibn Ezra,

Nahmanides and others. Tony Blair was intrigued by the layout of the book: a central text surrounded by commentaries. There is no English book set out in quite this way. He asked me what the book was, and why it was set out like that. I explained what each of the texts was, who the commentators were, their historical background and their distinctive approaches. I added that for us the biblical text always has to be understood against a background of commentary representing the way the Torah has been understood at different eras of Jewish life.

He was enthralled, and asked me to teach him the particular text I was studying. Prince Charles was listening intently from across the aisle. For the next hour I gave a *shiur*, a study session, to Britain's future king, and its next prime minister. At the end of the session I recalled the verse from Psalm 119:46 – "I will speak of Your statutes before kings and will not be ashamed" – and thanked God for the opportunity of fulfilling the verse. From then on, Tony Blair and I became friends, and when he became prime minister we continued this new tradition. During our meetings, once we had finished our agenda, we always ended with a brief study session about a biblical passage.

I never knew in advance what the topic would be: it was always the passage he had happened to read the night before. In this way we came to discuss the book of Job, the prophet Jeremiah, and various other texts. On our last session together, when he had already announced his resignation, we discussed the great sixth chapter of Micah, with its challenging summary of the religious life: "He has shown you, O man, what is good. And what does the Lord require of you? To act justly and to love mercy and to walk humbly with your God" (6:8). I reminded him that an American president, Jimmy Carter, had quoted this verse in his inaugural address.[1]

One day he said to me, "I've just come to the boring bit." "Which boring bit?" I asked. "You know," he said, "the passage about the Tabernacle at the end of Exodus. It does go on, doesn't it?"

I agreed, using the analogy of the way politicians judge the significance of a press item, by talking about "column inches" – the length of a newspaper article. I explained to him the linguistic parallels between

1. Available at http://www.bartleby.com/124/pres60.html.

the biblical account of the making of the Sanctuary and God's creation of the universe, and then quantified the difference. The narrative of creation takes a mere thirty-four verses, while the account of the making of the Tabernacle takes some five hundred verses.

I then offered the explanation given in a previous essay, "The Home We Make for God," (p. 199). I said that it is not difficult for an omniscient, omnipotent God to create a home for humankind. What is difficult is for finite, fallible human beings to create a home for God. This tells us that the Bible is not man's book of God, but God's book of humanity. What God is interested in is how *we* create, not how He creates. What the last third of the book of Exodus is telling us is that our primary task is to build a home for the Divine Presence. I then gave him the blessing Moses gave the builders of the Tabernacle: "May it be God's will that his presence rests in the work of your hands."

That might have been the end of the story but for one thing: I wasn't entirely satisfied with this answer. I remembered an occasion, described in a famous midrash, in which Rabban Yochanan ben Zakkai gives an explanation of the rite of the red heifer to a Roman, interpreting it as a form of exorcism. When the Roman departed, satisfied, the students turned to Rabban Yochanan and said, "Master, you have given him a shallow answer that satisfies him, but what will you answer us?"[2]

The answer may have been satisfactory as far as it went. But an obvious question remained: Why was this long narrative included within the book of Exodus, whose subject is *the making of a nation*? It belongs more naturally to the book of Leviticus, which deals with the service of the Tabernacle itself. What is it doing in the book dedicated to the liberation of the Israelites from slavery and their birth as a nation under the sovereignty of God? The question lingered in my mind, unresolved for several years.

In the meantime, a major social and political question arose in Britain and other European countries, most notably Holland. Having embraced multiculturalism – the idea that there should be no dominant culture in the ethnically diverse societies of contemporary Europe – these countries discovered that far from mitigating social conflict, the

2. *Bemidbar Raba* 19:8.

new doctrine exacerbated it. Far from promoting social integration, it was leading to segregation. It did not make societies more tolerant, but less so. The Dutch put it well. Tolerance, they said, ignores differences; multiculturalism makes an issue of them at every point.[3]

Was there – people began to ask – a way of moving beyond multiculturalism without sacrificing the idea of an inclusive society? It was then that my mind went back to the unanswered question about the place of the story of the Tabernacle within the book of Exodus. If the theme of Exodus is nation-building, then this is the book to which we should turn if we would seek biblical insight into the contemporary fragmentation of society.

Moses' challenge was precisely this: how to turn a group of escaping slaves into a cohesive nation. In chapter 1 of Exodus we find the first description of the Israelites as a nation. Pharaoh calls them an *am*, a people. But an *am*, as Rabbi Soloveitchik pointed out, is a community of fate, not yet a community of faith. For this latter the Torah uses the word *edah*.[4] An *am* shares a past; an *edah* shares a future, a set of ideals and aspirations. The path to nationhood in the book of Exodus might be described as the journey from *am* to *edah*.

Two things are striking about the people Moses leads. First, they are divided into twelve tribes or clans. The Torah emphasizes this at every point. They are not yet united into an overarching sense of identity. The second is that they include an unspecified "mixed multitude" (Exodus 12:38), a heterogeneous group who were not ethnically Israelites. Moses was faced, in other words, with a problem not unlike that of multi-ethnic and multicultural states.

What is equally striking as the narrative unfolds is that the Israelites lack the moral maturity to become a free nation. At every stage, they complain. They do so after Moses' initial intervention makes their burdens worse (5:21). They do so again as they come to the Reed Sea (14:11–12). After the crossing of the sea they twice complain about the

---

3. For this and the rest of this essay, see Jonathan Sacks, *The Home We Build Together* (Continuum, 2007).
4. See "*Kol Dodi Dofek*," in J. Soloveitchik, *Divrei Hagut Veha'arakhah* (Jerusalem, 1982), especially 41–43.

lack of water (15:23–24; 17:2), and again about the lack of food (16:2–3). The portrait the Torah draws is of a people with a slave mentality. This is not yet a people of faith, of trust in God, of responsibility and restraint. They cannot see beyond the present. And this, let us recall, is the people who had just witnessed the ten plagues and the division of the Reed Sea, the greatest miracles in history.

What happens next is the revelation at Mount Sinai, an unprecedented event when God appeared to an entire people. The Torah tells us that "When the people saw the thunder and lightning and heard the trumpet and saw the mountain in smoke, they trembled with fear" (20:18). Yet a mere forty-one days later, when Moses "delayed in coming down the mountain" (32:1), they made a Golden Calf. The Torah says that after the making of the calf: "Moses saw that the people were *broken loose* – for Aaron had let them *loose* for a derision among their enemies" (32:25). They had become a rabble. What more needs to happen to such a people before they are transformed into a cohesive group with a sense of identity and mission? There can be no greater miracles than the division of the sea and the revelation at Sinai. If they do not suffice, what will?

It is at this point, at the beginning of *Vayak-hel*, that Moses commands the people to construct the Tabernacle – and this is the stroke of genius. It is as if God had said to Moses: if you want to create a group with a sense of collective identity, get them to build something together. *It is not what happens to us, but what we do, that gives us identity and responsibility.* What transformed the Israelites is not what God did for them but what they did for God.

Until the making of the Tabernacle, the story of the Israelites is a sequence of events in which God acted for the people. He liberated them, divided the sea for them, gave them water from a rock and food from heaven. During all that time, they quarrelled and complained. Yet throughout the construction of the Tabernacle, there were no quarrels, no complaints. The people gave of their wealth, their time and their skills. They gave so much that Moses had to issue an order that they should stop (36:5–7). This is behaviour we have not seen before. The Israelites were indeed transformed – not by a miracle, but by their own efforts. What we do, not what is done for us, changes us.

It was now clear to me precisely why the story of the Tabernacle belongs in Exodus, not Leviticus – because it is a story about nation-building. The most effective way of transforming individuals into a group is by setting them a task they can only achieve as a group. This cuts across all other divisions, tribal, social and cultural. A nation does not depend on shared ethnicity. It can arise simply from the sense of collective responsibility that emerges from the performance of a shared task.

The Torah, in other words, offers a striking way out of the dilemmas of multiculturalism. It suggests that the citizens of a nation see themselves as co-creators of society seen as *the home we build together*. This then became the book I published, under that title, in 2007.[5] It is a radical alternative to most other contemporary political philosophies – those based on ethnicity, for example, or on citizenship as a set of rights, or on society as the embodiment of a moral consensus. It attaches positive value to ethnic and religious difference while giving equal weight to social cohesion. It invites us to bring our different heritages as contributions to the common good. It says in effect: *by being what I uniquely am, I give what I alone can give*. It makes a strong connection between building and belonging. I call this *integrated diversity*, and its source is the biblical narrative of the Tabernacle, whose length and detail so puzzled Tony Blair.

I tell this story not simply to show how a biblical passage can help solve a contemporary political and social problem but also to make a point fundamental to the study of Torah. Torah is not merely learned. It cries out to be lived. Nor is the Torah merely a private code of conduct. It is about the way we construct a society. By establishing a dialogue between Torah and contemporary society, we will find ourselves enlightened by new facets of its insight into the human condition.

I end with one further corollary of the argument developed here. Rabbi Norman Lamm, past president of Yeshiva University, once remarked that he knew of only one joke in the Mishna, namely the statement that "the disciples of the sages increase peace in the world."[6] Surely,

---

5. See note 3 above.
6. *Berakhot* 64a.

he said, this cannot be meant seriously, because rabbis are known for the number of arguments to which they give rise.

I replied: the statement is not a joke, but to understand it you have to read to the end of the passage. It quotes a verse from Isaiah (54:13), "All your children shall be taught of the Lord and great shall be the peace of your children" and continues, "Read not *banayikh*, your children, but *bonayikh*, your builders." When leaders become builders, they create peace; otherwise they merely create dissent. The proof is the Tabernacle. So long as the Israelites were builders there was peace among them. As John Ruskin wrote, "The highest reward for a man's toil is not what he gets for it but what he becomes by it." More simple still was the slogan of the early Zionist settlers who said that they came to the land *livnot u'lehibanot*, "to build and to be built."[7] We are made by what we make.

---

7. See Eric Zakim, *To Build and be Built: Landscape, Literature, and the Construction of Zionist Identity* (University of Pennsylvania Press, 2006).

The Beauty of Holiness or the Holiness of Beauty

> *Then Moses said to the Israelites, "See, the Lord has chosen Betzalel son of Uri, the son of Hur, of the tribe of Judah, and He has filled him with the spirit of God, with wisdom, understanding and knowledge in all kinds of crafts – to make artistic designs for work in gold, silver and bronze, to cut and set stones, to work in wood and to engage in all kinds of artistic craftsmanship." (Exodus 35:30–33)*

I n *Ki Tissa* and in *Vayak-hel* we encounter the figure of Betzalel, a rare type in the Hebrew Bible – the artist, the craftsman, the shaper of beauty in the service of God, the man who, together with Oholiab, fashioned the articles associated with the Tabernacle. Judaism – in sharp contrast to ancient Greece – did not cherish the visual arts. The reason is clear. The biblical prohibition against graven images associates them with idolatry. Historically, images, fetishes, icons and statues were linked in the ancient world with pagan religious practices. The idea that one might worship "the work of men's hands" was anathema to biblical faith.

More generally, Judaism is a culture of the ear, not the eye.[1] As a religion of the invisible God, it attaches sanctity to words heard, rather than objects seen. Hence there is a generally negative attitude within Judaism towards representational art.

There are some famous illustrated manuscripts (such as the *Bird's Head Haggada*, Bavaria, circa 1300) in which human figures are given bird's heads to avoid representing the full human form. Art is not forbidden as such; there is a difference between three-dimensional and two-dimensional representation. As Rabbi Meir of Rothenburg (c. 1215–1293) made clear in a responsum, "There is no trespass [in illustrated books] against the biblical prohibition ... [illustrations] are merely flat patches of colour lacking sufficient materiality [to constitute a graven image]."[2] Indeed several ancient synagogues in Israel had quite elaborate mosaics. In general, however, art was less emphasised in Judaism than in Christian cultures in which the Hellenistic influence was strong.

Positive references to art in the rabbinic literature are rare. One exception is Maimonides, who says the following:

> If one is afflicted with melancholy, he should cure it by listening to songs and various kinds of melodies, by walking in gardens and fine buildings, by sitting before beautiful forms, and by things like this which delight the soul and make the disturbance of melancholy disappear from it. In all this he should aim at making his body healthy, the goal of his body's health being that he attain knowledge.[3]

The very terms in which Maimonides describes the aesthetic experience make it clear, however, that he sees art in strictly instrumental terms, as

1. For a more nuanced view, however, see Kalman Bland, *The Artless Jew: Medieval and Modern Affirmations and Denials of the Visual* (Princeton University Press, 2001).
2. See Tosafot, commentary to *Yoma* 54a–b, s.v. *Keruvim*; *Responsa Rabbi Meir Mi'Rothenberg* (Venice: 1515), 14–16.
3. Rambam, introduction to commentary on Mishna *Avot, Eight Chapters on Ethics*, chap. 5.

a way of relieving depression. There is no suggestion that it has value in its own right.

The strongest positive statement on art of which I am aware was made by Rabbi Abraham ha-Cohen Kook, the first Ashkenazi Chief Rabbi of (pre-State) Israel, describing his time in London during the First World War:

> When I lived in London, I would visit the National Gallery, and the paintings that I loved the most were those of Rembrandt. In my opinion Rembrandt was a saint. When I first saw Rembrandt's paintings, they reminded me of the rabbinic statement about the creation of light. When God created the light [on the first day], it was so strong and luminous that it was possible to see from one end of the world to the other. And God feared that the wicked would make use of it. What did He do? He secreted it for the righteous in the world to come. But from time to time there are great men whom God blesses with a vision of that hidden light. I believe that Rembrandt was one of them, and the light in his paintings is that light which God created on Genesis day.[4]

Rembrandt is known to have had a special affection for Jews.[5] He visited them in his home town of Amsterdam, and painted them, as well as many scenes from the Hebrew Bible. I suspect that what Rabbi Kook saw in his paintings, though, was Rembrandt's ability to convey the beauty of ordinary people. He makes no attempt (most notably in his self-portraits) to beautify or idealise his subjects. The light that shines from them is, simply, their humanity.

It was Samson Raphael Hirsch who distinguished ancient Greece from ancient Israel in terms of the contrast between aesthetics and ethics. In his comment on the verse "May God enlarge Japheth and let him dwell in the tents of Shem" (Genesis 9:27), he observes:

---

4. *Jewish Chronicle*, September 9, 1935.
5. See Michael Zell, *Reframing Rembrandt: Jews and the Christian Image in Seventeenth-Century Amsterdam* (University of California Press, 2002), and Steven Nadler, *Rembrandt's Jews* (University of Chicago Press, 2003).

The stem of Japheth reached its fullest blossoming in the Greeks; that of Shem in the Hebrews, Israel, who bore and bear the name (Shem) of God through the world of nations...Japheth has ennobled the world aesthetically. Shem has enlightened it spiritually and morally.[6]

Yet as we see from the case of Betzalel, Judaism is not indifferent to aesthetics. The concept of *hiddur mitzva*, "beautifying the command-ment," meant, for the sages, that we should strive to fulfil the commands in the most aesthetically pleasing way. The priestly garments were meant to be "for honour and adornment" (Exodus 28:2). The very terms applied to Betzalel – wisdom, understanding and knowledge – are applied by the book of Proverbs to God Himself as creator of the universe:

The law and the Lord founded the earth by wisdom;
He established the heavens by understanding;
By His knowledge the depths burst apart,
And the skies distilled dew. (Proverbs: 3:19–20)

The key to Betzalel lies in his name. It means "In the shadow of God." Betzalel's gift lay in his ability to communicate, through his work, that art is the shadow cast by God. Religious art is never "art for art's sake."[7] Unlike secular art, it points to something beyond itself. The Tab-ernacle itself was a kind of microcosm of the universe, with one overrid-ing particularity: that in it you felt the presence of something beyond – what the Torah calls "the glory of God" which "filled the Tabernacle" (Exodus 40:35).

The Greeks, and many in the Western world who inherited their tradition, believed in the holiness of beauty (Keats' "Beauty is truth, truth beauty, that is all / Ye know on earth, and all ye need to know").[8] Jews believed in the opposite: *hadrat kodesh*, the beauty of holiness:

6. The Pentateuch, translated with commentary by Samson Raphael Hirsch (Gates-head: Judaica Press, 1982), 1:191.
7. The phrase is usually attributed to Benjamin Constant (1804).
8. The last lines of Keats' famous poem, "Ode on a Grecian Urn."

"Give to the Lord the glory due to His name; worship the Lord in the beauty of holiness" (Psalms 29:2). Art in Judaism always has a spiritual purpose: to make us aware of the universe as a work of art, testifying to the supreme Artist, God Himself.

Pekudei
פְּקוּדֵי

With *Pekudei*, the book of Exodus reaches its end, if not its closure. Moses orders an account to be made of all the donations given for the making of the Tabernacle and how they were used. The priestly garments are made. Moses finally erects the Tabernacle, and it becomes filled with the glory of the Lord.

In the essays that follow, the first looks at the principle of accountability for the use of public funds, as exemplified by Moses. The second looks at the Tabernacle as a symbol of the sacred order that lies at the foundation of a social order. The third analyzes a textual difficulty in the last two words of the book of Exodus. As interpreted by Rashi, they provide an insight into Jewish history and identity as a whole. The fourth looks at the narrative structure of the book of Exodus, the pattern beneath the surface, showing how tightly it, together with Genesis, form a literary unit of immense coherence and power.

Above Suspicion: Integrity in Public Life

*P*ekudei derives its name from the detailed account, or reckoning, of the contributions made towards the construction of the Tabernacle:

> These are the amounts of the materials used for the Tabernacle, the Tabernacle of the Testimony, which were recorded at Moses' command by the Levites under the direction of Ithamar son of Aaron, the priest. (Exodus 38:21)

The passage goes on to list the exact amounts of gold, silver and bronze collected, and the purposes to which it was put.

Why did Moses do this? And why was it recorded in the Torah, signalling that it contains a message for future generations? A midrash suggests an answer:

> "They gazed after Moses" (Exodus 33:8) – People criticized Moses. They used to say to one another, "Look at that neck. Look at those legs. Moses is eating and drinking what belongs to us. All that he has belongs to us." The other would reply: "A man who is in charge of the work of the Sanctuary – what do you expect? That

he should not get rich?" As soon as he heard this, Moses replied, "By your life, as soon as the Sanctuary is complete, I will make a full reckoning with you."[1]

Moses issued a detailed reckoning to avoid coming under suspicion that he had personally appropriated some of the donated money. Note the emphasis that the accounting was undertaken not by Moses himself but "by the Levites under the direction of Ithamar," in other words, by independent auditors.

There is no hint of these accusations in the text itself, and it may be that the midrash is based on two other moments, one in the life of Moses, the other relating to Samuel. During the Korach rebellion Moses says, "Do not accept their offering. I have not taken so much as a donkey from them, nor have I wronged any of them" (Numbers 16:15). Samuel, having appointed Saul as king, says to the people, "Testify against me in the presence of the Lord and His anointed. Whose ox have I taken? Whose donkey have I taken? Whom have I cheated? Whom have I oppressed? From whose hand have I accepted a bribe to make me shut my eyes? If I have done any of these, I will make it right" (1 Samuel 12:3).

It seems from these passages that accusations of corruption and personal enrichment were standard fare in the lifetimes of Moses and Samuel. "Power tends to corrupt," said Lord Acton, and much of Tanakh is dedicated to this theme. We might have thought that since God sees all we do, this is enough to safeguard against wrongdoing. Yet Judaism never says this. The Talmud records a scene at the deathbed of Rabban Yoḥanan ben Zakkai, as the master lies surrounded by his disciples:

> They said to him, "Our master, bless us." He said to them, "May it be God's will that the fear of heaven shall be as much upon you as the fear of flesh and blood." His disciples asked, "Is that all?" He replied, "Would that you obtained no less than such fear! You can see for yourselves the truth of what I say: when a man is about to commit a transgression, he says, I hope no man will see me."[2]

1. Solomon Buber, comp., *Tanḥuma, Pekudei*, 4.
2. *Berakhot* 28b.

No one is beyond temptation, and no one above suspicion.

Interestingly, though, there is a later passage in Tanakh that seems to indicate that Moses' account was not strictly necessary. The Book of Kings relates an episode in which, during the reign of King Yehoash, money was raised for the restoration of the Temple. "They did not require an accounting from those to whom they gave the money to pay the workers, because they acted with complete honesty" (II Kings 12:16). Moses may thus have acted "beyond the strict requirement of the law."[3]

It is precisely this – that Moses did not need to do what he did, and that there is, in the text, no explicit challenge to his probity – that gives the passage its force. There must be transparency and accountability when it comes to public funds, the Torah is telling us. Those who administer them must be above suspicion. In general, leaders must be, and be seen to be, people of moral integrity. Jethro, Moses' father-in-law, had already said this when he told Moses to appoint subordinates to help him in the task of leading the people. They should be, he said, "Men who fear God, trustworthy men who hate dishonest gain" (Exodus 18:21). Without a reputation for honesty and incorruptibility, judges cannot ensure that justice is seen to be done.

The general principle that we should act so as to be above suspicion was derived by the sages from a later statement by Moses. It arose in the context of the wish of the Reubenites and Gadites to settle on the far side of the Jordan where the land provided good grazing ground for their cattle (Numbers 32:1–33). Moses told them angrily that to do so would demoralise the rest of the nation: they would give the impression that they were unwilling to cross the Jordan and fight with their brothers in their battles to conquer the land.

The Reubenites and Gaddites made it clear that they were willing to fight, indeed to be in the front line of the troops, and would not return to the far side of the Jordan until the land had been fully conquered. Moses accepted the proposal, saying that if they kept their word, they would be "clear [*veheyitem neki'im*] before the Lord and before Israel" (Numbers 32:22). This phrase entered Jewish law and ethics as

---

3. A key concept in Jewish law (see e.g., *Berakhot* 7a, 45b; *Bava Kama* 99b), meaning supererogation, doing more, in a positive sense, than the law requires.

the principle that "one must acquit oneself before one's fellow human beings as well as before God."[4] It is not enough to do right. We must be *seen* to do right, especially when there is room for rumour and scope for suspicion.

There are several instances in the early rabbinic literature of applications of this rule. So, for example, when people came to take coins for sacrifices from the Shekel Chamber in the Temple, where the money was kept:

> They did not enter the chamber wearing either a bordered cloak or shoes or sandals or tefillin or an amulet, lest if he became poor people might say that he became poor because of an iniquity committed in the chamber, or if he became rich people might say that he became rich from the appropriation in the chamber. For it is a person's duty to be free of blame before men as before God, as it is said: "and be clear before the Lord and before Israel," (Numbers 32:22), and it also says: "So shall thou find favour and good understanding in the sight of God and man" (Proverbs 3:4).[5]

Those who entered the chamber were forbidden to wear any item of clothing within which they could hide and steal coins. Similarly, when charity overseers had funds left over, they were not permitted to change copper for silver coins of their own money: they had to make the exchange with a third party. Overseers in charge of a soup kitchen were not allowed to purchase surplus food when there were no poor people to whom to distribute it. Surpluses had to be sold to others so as not to arouse suspicion that the charity overseers were profiting from public funds.[6]

For the same reason, children of the family of Garmu, who prepared the showbread for the Temple, were never seen with fine bread. Brides from the family of Abtimas, the Temple's incense manufacturers,

4. Mishna, *Shekalim* 3:2.
5. Ibid.
6. *Pesaḥim* 13a.

never wore perfume.[7] In both cases this was to avoid suspicion that they had made personal use of Temple property.

The *Shulkhan Arukh* rules that charity collection must always be done by a minimum of two individuals so that each can see what the other is doing.[8] There is a difference of opinion between R. Joseph Karo and R. Moshe Isserles on the need to provide detailed accounts. R. Joseph Karo rules on the basis of the passage in II Kings – "They did not require an accounting from those to whom they gave the money to pay the workers, because they acted with complete honesty" (12:15) – that no formal accounting is required from people of unimpeachable honesty. R. Moshe Isserles however says that it is right to do so because of the principle, "Be clear before the Lord and before Israel."[9]

Are there limits to how far one is obliged to go in taking account of public perception? What if the general public is so cynical or sceptical of those in positions of leadership that it levels unwarranted charges? A midrash speaks of a generation when "people judged their judges."[10] The sages said about Moses' contemporaries that they were capable of imputing almost anything to him: when he left his house early they claimed his marriage was failing; when he left late they said that he was plotting schemes against the people.[11] Hence Moses' exasperated remark, "How can I bear alone your problems, your burdens and your disputes?" (Deuteronomy 1:12).

R. Shlomo Alkabetz writes that: "Even though we hold that we should be blameless not only in the eyes of God but also in the eyes of people, this is to be understood as referring to people whom God has given knowledge and discernment. One is not responsible for [the perceptions] of everyone; it is not necessary to be blameless in the eyes of mistaken or foolish people."[12] So there is a limit. A leader is not

---

7. *Yoma* 38a.
8. *Shulkhan Arukh*, Yoreh Deah 257:1.
9. Ibid., 257:2.
10. *Bereishit Raba* 41; the reference is to the beginning of the book of Ruth. The midrash reads, "And it came to pass when the judges judged," as "when the judges themselves were judged," i.e., when the judges no longer carried public respect.
11. Rashi, commentary to Deuteronomy 1:12.
12. Cited in *Melekhet Shlomo*, commentary to *Shekalim* 3:2.

answerable to wild or malicious criticism. But in every case where there is a reasonable doubt – where there is both temptation and opportunity – there must be transparency and accountability, and it begins with Moses' decision to give a public account of the moneys raised for the construction of the Sanctuary.

In 2009, a former prime minister and a former president of Israel faced trial on accusations of misconduct. Two other former ministers were found guilty, one of embezzlement, the other of bribery. In June 2008 an opinion poll taken by the Israel Democracy Institute showed that ninety per cent of Israelis believe that public leadership in Israel is rife with corruption.[13] Meanwhile, in Britain in 2009, parliamentarians suffered a blow to their reputation after a prolonged scandal about unwarranted expense claims.

Trust is of the essence in public life. A nation that cannot trust its leaders cannot function effectively as a free, just and open society. It is a mark of a free society that public leadership is seen as a form of service rather than a means to power, which is all too easily abused. Tanakh holds an honourable place in the history of the morality of public life. The prophets were the world's first social critics, mandated by God to speak truth to power and to challenge corrupt leaders. Elijah's challenge to King Ahab, and the protests of Amos, Hosea, Isaiah and Jeremiah against the unethical practices of their day, are classic texts in this tradition, establishing for all time the ideals of equity, justice, honesty and integrity as values in public life. Without them, a society quickly becomes demoralized.

Moses' personal example, in giving an accounting of the funds that had been collected for the first collective project of the Jewish people, does indeed contain a message for all time.

13. "Ninety per cent say Israel is tainted by corruption," *Jerusalem Post*, June 10, 2008.

God at the Centre

The *parasha* of *Pekudei*, and with it the book of Exodus as a whole, draws to a conclusion with an extraordinary litany of obedience. Seven times in chapter 39, describing how the Israelites constructed the Tabernacle, we hear the phrase "as the Lord commanded Moses."[1] Seven times in chapter 40, narrating how Moses set up the Tabernacle, we hear the phrase "as the Lord commanded him."[2] Where have we heard this language before?

The answer takes us back to another construction project, the first in the Torah: Noah's ark. Three times we hear virtually the same phrase:

> Noah did everything just *as God commanded him.* (Genesis 6:22)

> And Noah did *all that the Lord commanded him.* (7:5)
> The animals going in were male and female of every living thing, *as God had commanded Noah.* (7:16)

---

1. Exodus 39:1, 5, 7, 21, 26, 29, 31.
2. Exodus 40:16, 19, 21, 23, 25, 27, 29.

Is there any connection between these two passages? Do they, taken together, tell us something larger about the biblical vision? If so, what is it? I want in this essay to take a large speculative leap, which will lead to strong conclusions about the place of the Tabernacle – and later the Temple – within Israelite society, the connection between the Divine Presence and the pursuit of justice, and the relationship more generally between the holy and the good.

Let us begin by tracing some of the parallels between the book of Exodus as a whole and the earlier narrative of humanity from Adam to Abraham, contained in the first eleven chapters of Genesis.

Both tell the story of transgressions against the moral order. In Genesis this appears in several variations. There is Adam and Eve's sin in Eden (Genesis 3), Cain's murder of his brother Abel (4), and the culminating state of affairs before the Flood: "Now the earth was corrupt in God's sight and was full of violence" (6:11). In Exodus it takes the form of one nation, the Egyptians, enslaving another, the Israelites, together with the slow genocide implicit in Pharaoh's command to kill all male Hebrew children (Exodus 1:22).

In both cases, an offence against the moral order leads to what one might call retribution by the natural order. Nature turns against humanity. It does so in the case of Adam: "To Adam [God] said, 'Because you listened to your wife and ate from the tree about which I commanded you, you must not eat of it, cursed will be the ground because of you" (3:17). It does so more spectacularly in the form of the Flood that wipes out all life. Nature takes its revenge against the Egyptians in the form of the plagues.

In both cases, water is an agent of retribution: in Genesis in the Flood; in Exodus in the drowning of the Egyptian army at the Reed Sea (14:26–30). In both cases there is a new beginning that takes the form of a covenant: in Genesis 9 with Noah, in Exodus 20 with the Israelites at Mount Sinai.

In both cases, the covenant alone is not enough to secure obedience. After Noah, humanity sets about building the Tower of Babel (11:1–9). After Sinai the Israelites make the Golden Calf (32:1–6). Both cases are instances of human beings worshipping the work of their hands.

In both cases human beings are commanded to create a physical structure. Noah makes the ark. The Israelites make the Tabernacle. In both cases, the Torah goes into detail about the precise dimensions of the structure. In both, as we have seen, there is an emphasis on absolute obedience, "as the Lord commanded."

The major difference is, of course, that Noah's ark was temporary. It was needed only as long as the waters prevailed. The Tabernacle was permanent – at least until the temple was built in Jerusalem almost five centuries later.

There is deep symbolism here, if we can decode it. It seems to be this. God creates order. Human beings create chaos. It is only when human beings create their own symbolic order – the ark, the Tabernacle – by precise and exacting obedience to God's command, that there is a chance for humanity to survive.

This whole way of seeing things is diametrically opposed to myth. In myth, chaos is built into the structure of the universe. Gods fight. Elements clash. Tragedies happen, and not all the virtue in the world will save us from them. At best, we can try to placate or entice the gods. Conflict and chaos are "out there," in the capriciousness of nature and its fundamental indifference to humankind.

In Judaism the problem of chaos is not out there, but "in here," in the human heart. As Genesis puts it, "The Lord saw how great man's wickedness on the earth had become, and that every inclination of the thoughts of his heart was only evil all the time" (6:5). Or as Jeremiah (17:9) phrases it, "The heart is deceitful above all things, and beyond cure. Who can understand it?" God cannot cure the human heart. That is the self-limiting ordinance by which God gives us freedom. As we noted, even in the case of Pharaoh,[3] his hard-heartedness was of his own choosing, despite the fact that in the later phases it is described as the work of God. God cannot make us moral. Only we can do so when we freely obey the will of God.

With this we reach perhaps the deepest and most controversial thesis implicit in the book of Exodus, and central to Tanakh as a whole. *Without God, human beings will fail to create a just society.* Without the Divine Presence symbolised in the Tabernacle at the heart of the camp,

---

3. See essay "The Hardened Heart," p. 47.

human beings will do what they have always done: oppress one another, fight with one another, and exploit one another. There can be no just society without some form of *yirat shamayim*, some "reverence for heaven." As Abraham says to Abimelech, king of Gerar: "I said to myself, There is surely no fear of God in this place, and they will kill me because of my wife" (Genesis 20:11).

That is why Exodus culminates in the construction and placement of the Tabernacle at the centre of the camp. Without the visible presence of God, there is no justice. Without justice, there is no human equality and dignity. Without reverence for heaven, society becomes the rule of the strong over the weak. As Thucydides said: "Right, as the world goes, is only in question between equals in power: the strong do what they can and the weak suffer what they must."[4]

This is a large claim. Is it true? Let us be clear what question we are asking. It is not the simple one: do we need God, or the religious sense, to be moral? Individuals can be moral without being conventionally religious. You do not need to believe in God to rescue a drowning child, give food to the hungry or shelter to the homeless. We have, as Adam Smith argued, and science has recently demonstrated, a moral sense.[5] We have natural feelings of empathy and sympathy. Without these, humanity would not have been able to form groups, or even survive. The Torah describes the courage, for example, of Pharaoh's daughter, without implying that she was in receipt of a divine revelation. The Torah seems to use the phrase "fear of God" in roughly the same way as we speak about the moral sense.[6] Rav Nissim Gaon (990–1062) in his introduction to the Talmud[7] says that humans have been bound by the com-

---

4. Thucydides *History of the Peloponnesian War* 5:89.
5. Adam Smith, *The Theory of Moral Sentiments* [1790] (Oxford: Clarendon Press, 1976). See also James Q. Wilson, *The Moral Sense* (New York: Free Press, 1993). On recent science see Frans de Waal, *The Age of Empathy* (New York: Harmony Books, 2009); Dacher Keltner, *Born to Be Good* (New York: W.W. Norton, 2009); Michael Tomasello, *Why We Cooperate* (Boston: MIT Press, 2009).
6. See, e.g., Exodus 1:17.
7. Printed at the beginning of standard editions of Talmud tractate *Berakhot*. He writes: "All commands accessible to reason and the human heart have been obligatory for all since the day God created man on earth."

mands of morality since man first walked on earth. Individually, we can and should be moral, regardless of our specific religious commitments.

But man is a social animal. We form societies. And societies beat to a different pulse than do individuals. Reinhold Niebuhr made this distinction famous in the title of his book, *Moral Man and Immoral Society*.[8] We do not act *en masse* the way we do alone. That is why societies of people not themselves wicked can perform collective acts of great evil. The Holocaust is the supreme example.[9]

If this is so, then the placement of the *Mishkan* at the heart of the camp suggests that societies need, in the public domain, a constant reminder of the presence of God. That, after all, is why the *Mishkan* appears in Exodus, not Genesis. Genesis is about individuals, Exodus about societies.

Significant thinkers believed likewise. John Locke, the pioneer of toleration, thought so. He considered that atheists were ineligible for English citizenship since membership was gained by swearing an oath of allegiance, and an oath, being a vow to God, could not be sworn by an atheist.[10] In his farewell address, George Washington said:

> Of all the dispositions and habits which lead to political prosperity, religion and morality are indispensable supports ... let us with caution indulge the supposition that morality can be maintained without religion. Whatever may be conceded to the influence of refined education on minds of peculiar structure, reason and experience both forbid us to expect that national morality can prevail in exclusion of religious principle.[11]

Why should this be so? A fascinating answer is suggested by the American sociologist and cultural critic, Philip Rieff (1922–2006). At the end of his life he published a book, *My Life among the Deathworks*.[12] It is

---

8. Reinhold Niebuhr, *Moral Man and Immoral Society* (New York: Scribner, 1932).
9. See Jonah Goldhagen, *Hitler's Willing Executioners* (New York: Knopf, 1996).
10. John Locke, *A Letter Concerning Toleration* [1689] (Indianapolis: Hackett, 1983), 51.
11. Available at: http://avalon.law.yale.edu/18th_century/washing.asp.
12. Philip Rieff, *My Life among the Deathworks*, (University of Virginia Press, 2006).

a strange work, quirky, idiosyncratic and not always easy to follow (it is, incidentally, an explicitly Jewish work). In it, he proposed a fascinating, schematic history of human culture.

Rieff discerned three stages in the human story. In the first – the pagan era – people see the world in terms of primordial powers indifferent or hostile to humanity. Its elites are magicians who seek to control these powers, but ultimately humanity is helpless against their overwhelming force. The keyword of such cultures is *fate* – the destiny we seek to avoid but cannot.

The second age – initiated by Judaism and followed by Christianity and Islam – sees the world as governed by a single transcendental power who discloses his will for humanity in the form of revelation. Human action is not about controlling the forces of nature but about keeping, or breaking, the divine command. This is the age of *faith*.

The third age, our own, has lost belief in both fate and faith. There is no overarching meaning to life. There is no ultimate truth; there are only the stories we tell ourselves, and these have no authority other than the fact that we chose them. There is, in fact, no moral authority beyond the self. Nothing is forbidden in and of itself. All that matters is what we decide. The creative artist replaces the prophet; the psychotherapist replaces the priest. All that is left by way of meaning is the stories we fantasize for ourselves. Rieff called this the age of *fiction*. Hence human history is the move from fate to faith to fiction.

Rieff believed that the third age is unsustainable. He called it an anti-culture. The reason is that neither meaning nor morality make sense without what he calls a *sacred order*. That for him is the very essence of a culture. Cultures, he says, can only exist when the social order is seen as in some way mirroring the sacred order. Without that, there is no morality, because there is no commanding truth. All that remain are "values," and values are always interchangeable with other values. There is no authority, other than power. There is no truth, merely our private imaginings:

> Culture and sacred order are inseparable…No culture has ever preserved itself where it is not a registration of sacred order…The

third culture notion of a culture that persists independent of all sacred orders is unprecedented in human history.[13]

In the end there will be no democracy, since "Democracy depends upon the perpetual rediscovery that the world is not ourselves, that there is a not-I who is master of limits, both imaginatively and in social action."[14]

If Rieff was right, he provided a striking explanation for the *Mishkan*. For what it represents, as I have argued throughout these essays, is *the sacred order*, the human creation that mirrors the divine creation of the universe as a whole. Hence the precision and detail; hence the insistence that the Israelites made it exactly as God commanded. Hence, too, its role at the heart of the Israelite camp. It was a potent, living symbol of the fact that *the social order must mirror the sacred order if society is to exist at all on the basis of justice rather than the rule of power.*

This was Rashi's explanation for the fact that the civil laws of *Mishpatim* (Exodus 21–23) immediately follow the laws of the altar (20:24–26): "Why are the civil laws placed in juxtaposition to the laws concerning the altar? To tell you to place the Sanhedrin [the Supreme Court] near to the Temple."[15] The social order, embodied in civil law, must never lose its connection with the sacred order, represented by the Sanctuary.

More than a century ago, Lord Acton came to a strikingly similar judgment about Athens, the birthplace of democracy. The Athenians were "the only people of antiquity that grew great by democratic institutions." But they did not last long. "The possession of unlimited power, which corrodes the conscience, hardens the heart, and confounds the understanding of monarchs, exercised its demoralising influence on the illustrious democracy of Athens." Because the Athenians recognised no sacred order, they could conceive of no law superior to that of the state.

13. Ibid., 13.
14. Ibid., 175.
15. Rashi, commentary to Exodus 21:1.

It followed that the sovereign people have a right to do whatever was within its power, and was bound by no rule of right or wrong but its own judgement of expediency... In this way the emancipated people of Athens became a tyrant; and their government, the pioneer of European freedom, stands condemned with a terrible unanimity by all the wisest of the ancients.[16]

In a recent, magisterial work on justice, Yale professor Nicholas Wolterstorff has argued the same proposition on philosophical grounds.[17] Our whole Western concept of justice, founded on the idea of human rights, is built on religious foundations and cannot survive without them. If we become a secular society, there is no long-term future for either rights or justice. This is his conclusion:

> Our Judaic and Christian heritage neither denies nor overlooks the flaws of humankind; some strands in the heritage appear even to revel in them. But in the face of all the empirical evidence, it nonetheless declares that all of us have great and equal worth; the worth of being made in the image of God and of being loved redemptively by God. It adds that God holds us accountable for how we treat each other – and for how we treat God. It is this framework of conviction that gave rise to our moral subculture of rights. If this framework erodes, I think we must expect that our moral subculture of rights will also eventually erode and that we will slide back into our tribalisms.[18]

Let us now return to where we began. The first eleven chapters of Genesis and the book of Exodus as a whole tell a story of human failure – a failure to observe the moral order by which life, liberty and human dignity are sacred. The result in both cases was catastrophe: in the first, a world ruined by the Flood, in the second, an Egypt devastated

---

16. Lord Acton, *Essays in the History of Liberty* [1877] (Indianapolis: Liberty Press, 1985), 13–14.
17. Nicholas Wolterstorff, *Justice: Rights and Wrongs* (Princeton University Press, 2008).
18. Ibid., 393.

by the plagues. Both stories involve a physical construction, an ark and a Tabernacle, and in both, the Torah's emphasis is on precise dimensions ordained by God and faithfully carried out by human beings.

These were symbols of order in a disordered world. There is, to be sure, a great difference between them. Noah needed the ark only until the flood waters subsided. The Israelites needed the Tabernacle, or some equivalent of it (the Temple, later the synagogue), forever. It was the symbolic focus of their collective life. It told them that they were a nation at whose centre was the Divine Presence. It bore witness to the sovereignty of right over might, the rule of justice over the rule of power. If Lord Acton, Philip Rieff and Nicholas Wolterstorff are right, there is no other way. The good and the holy belong together. Without sacred order there is no social order. Without the Tabernacle through which the Israelites served God, they could not hope to create the new kind of society that would stand as the perennial alternative to Egypt, where rulers turned human beings into slaves.

William Safire, at the end of a book about the Bible and contemporary politics, wrote a sentence that eloquently expresses the idea advanced in this essay:

> Man's God leans toward order, God's Man leans toward chaos, and the tension in that eternal tug-of-war generates the energy of freedom.[19]

19. William Safire, *The First Dissident: The Book of Job in Today's Politics* (New York: Random House, 1992), 226.

Encampments and Journeys

A t the very end of the book of Exodus there is a textual difficulty so slight and subtle that it is easy to miss, yet – as interpreted by Rashi – it contains one of the great clues as to the nature of Jewish identity: moving testimony to the unique challenge of being a Jew.

The setting is this: the Tabernacle is finally complete. Its construction has taken many chapters to relate. No other event in the wilderness years is portrayed in such detail. Now, on the first day of the month of Nisan, exactly a year after Moses told the people to begin their preparations for the exodus, he assembles the beams and hangings of the Tabernacle, and puts the furniture and vessels in place. No sooner has he done so than there is an epiphany, a majestic disclosure of the Divine Presence:

> Then the cloud covered the Tent of Meeting, and the glory of the Lord filled the Tabernacle. (Exodus 40:34)

There is the "sense of an ending."[1] The story has reached closure. After a tangled tale full of setbacks, the Israelites have made a home for God and His presence is now constantly in their midst. However, in the Torah, nothing is as simple as it at first seems. The text tacks on the following brief paragraph:

> When the cloud lifted from above the Tabernacle, the Israelites went onwards *in all their journeys*, but if the cloud did not lift, they did not set out until the day it lifted. So the cloud of the Lord was over the Tabernacle by day, and fire was in the cloud by night, in the sight of all the house of Israel *in all their journeys*. (Exodus 40:36–38)

The plain sense is clear. The Tabernacle was constructed in such a way as to be portable. It could quickly be dismantled and its parts carried as the Israelites made their way to the next stage of their journey. When the time came for the Israelites to move on, the cloud moved from its resting place above the Tent of Meeting to a position outside the camp, signalling the direction they must now take.

However, there is a small but significant difference between the two instances of the phrase "in all their journeys" (*bekhol mas'ehem*). In the first instance the words are to be taken literally. When the cloud lifted and moved on ahead, the Israelites knew they were about to travel. In the second instance, the words cannot be taken literally. The cloud was not "over the Tabernacle" in all their journeys. On the contrary: it was there only when they stopped travelling and instead pitched camp. During the journeys the cloud went on ahead.

Noting this, Rashi makes the following comment:

> A place where they encamped is also called *masa*, "a journey"... Because from the place of encampment they always set out again on a new journey, therefore they are all called "journeys."[2]

---

1. The phrase is taken from Frank Kermode, *The Sense of an Ending* (Oxford University Press, 1973).
2. Rashi, commentary to Exodus 40:38.

The point is linguistic, but the message is momentous. Rashi has encapsulated in a few brief words the existential truth at the heart of Judaism. In Jewish history, even an encampment is called a journey. So long as we have not yet reached our destination, even a place of rest is merely temporary. There is a way still to go. In the famous words of Robert Frost:

> The woods are lovely, dark and deep.
> But I have promises to keep,
> And miles to go before I sleep.[3]

To be a Jew is to travel, and to know that here where we are is a mere resting place, not yet a home. It is defined not by the fact that we are here, but by the knowledge that eventually – after a day, a week, a year, a century, sometimes even a millennium – we will have to move on. Thus, the portable Tabernacle, even more than the Temple in Jerusalem, became the symbol of Jewish life.

Why so? Because the gods of the ancient world were gods of a place: Sumeria, Memphis, Moab, Edom. They had a specific domain. Theology was linked to geography. Here, in this holy place, made magnificent by ziggurat or temple, the gods of the tribe or the state ruled and exercised power over the city or the empire. When Pharaoh says to Moses: "Who is the Lord that I should obey Him and let Israel go? I do not know the Lord and I will not let Israel go" (Exodus 5:2), he means – here, I am the sovereign power. Egypt has its own gods. Within its boundaries, they alone rule, and they have delegated that power to me, their earthly representative. There may indeed be a God of Israel, but his power and authority do not extend to Egypt. Divine sovereignty is like political sovereignty. It has borders. It has spatial location. It is bounded by a place on the map.

With Israel, an old-new idea (it goes back, according to the Torah, to Adam, Cain, Abraham and Jacob, all of whom suffered exile) is reborn: that God, being everywhere, can be found anywhere. He is what Morris

3. "Stopping by Woods on a Snowy Evening," in *The Poetry of Robert Frost* (London: Vintage, 2001), 224–25.

Berman calls the "wandering God."[4] Just as in the desert His cloud of glory accompanied the Israelites on their long and meandering journey, so, said the rabbis, "when Israel went into exile, the Divine Presence went with them."[5] God cannot be confined to a specific place. Even in Israel, His presence among the people depended on their obedience to His word. Hence there is no such thing as physical security, the certain knowledge that here-I-am-and-here-I-stay. As David said in Psalm 30:

> When I felt secure, I said,
> "I will never be shaken."
> … but when You hid Your face,
> I was dismayed.

Security belongs not to place but to person, not to a physical space on the surface of the earth but to a spiritual space in the human heart.

If anything is responsible for the unparalleled strength of Jewish identity during the long centuries in which Jews were scattered throughout the world, a minority everywhere, it is this – the concept to which Jews and Judaism gave the name *galut*, exile. Unique among nations in the ancient or modern world, with few exceptions they neither converted to the dominant faith nor assimilated to the prevailing culture. The sole reason was that they never mistook a particular place for home, a temporary location for ultimate destination. "Now we are here," they said at the beginning of the *seder* service, "but next year, in the land of Israel."

In Jewish law, one who rents a house outside Israel is obliged to affix a mezuza only after thirty days.[6] Until then it is not yet regarded as a dwelling place. Only after thirty days does it become, de facto, home. In Israel, however, one who rents a house is immediately obligated, *mishum yishuv eretz Yisrael*, "because of the command to settle Israel." Outside Israel, Jewish life is a way, a path, a route. Even an encampment, a place of rest, is still called a journey.

---

4. Morris Berman, *Wandering God: A Study in Nomadic Spirituality* (State University of New York Press, 2000).
5. *Megilla* 29a; *Sifrei*, Numbers, 161.
6. *Yoreh De'ah* 286:22.

In this context, one detail stands out in the long list of instructions about the Tabernacle. It concerns the ark, in which were kept the tablets of stone that Moses brought down the mountain, permanent reminders of God's covenant with Israel. On the side of the ark were gold rings, two on each side, within which poles or staves were fitted so that the ark could be carried when the time came for the Israelites to move on (Exodus 25:12–14). The Torah adds the following stipulation:

> The poles are to remain in the rings of this ark; they are not to be removed. (25:15)

Why so? Rabbi Samson Raphael Hirsch explained that the ark was to be permanently ready when the need arose for the Israelites to travel. Why was the same not true about the other objects in the Tabernacle, such as the altar and the menorah? To show supremely, said Hirsch, that the Torah was not limited to any one place.[7]

And so it was. The Torah became, in the famous phrase of Heinrich Heine, "the portable homeland of the Jew." Throughout history Jews found themselves scattered and dispersed among the nations, never knowing when they would be forced to leave and find a new home. In the fifteenth century alone, Jews were expelled from Vienna and Linz in 1421, from Cologne in 1424, Augsburg in 1439, Bavaria in 1442, Moravia in 1454, Perugia in 1485, Vicenza in 1486, Parma in 1488, Milan and Lucca in 1489, Spain in 1492 and Portugal 1497.[8]

How did they survive, their identity intact, their faith, though sorely challenged, still strong? Because they believed that God was with them, even in exile. Because they were sustained by the line from Psalms (23:4), "Though I walk through the valley of the shadow of death, I will fear no evil, for You are with me." Because they still had the Torah, God's unbreakable covenant, with its promise that "In spite of this, when they are in the land of their enemies, I will not reject them or abhor them so as to destroy them completely, breaking my covenant

---

7. The Pentateuch, translated with commentary by Samson Raphael Hirsch (Gateshead: Judaica Press, 1982), 2:434–35.
8. Paul Johnson, *A History of the Jews* (Weidenfeld and Nicolson, 1987), 230–31.

with them. I am the Lord their God" (Leviticus 26:44). Because they were a people used to travelling, knowing that even an encampment is only a temporary dwelling.

Emil Fackenheim, the distinguished theologian, was a Holocaust survivor. Born in Halle, Germany, in 1916, he was arrested on Kristallnacht and interned at the Sachsenhausen concentration camp, from which he eventually escaped. He recalled a picture hanging in his parents' house when he was a child:

> It was not our kind of picture ... because what it portrayed was not a German-Jewish experience: Jews fleeing from a pogrom. Even so it moved me deeply, and I remember it well. The fleeing Jews in the picture are bearded old men, terrified, but not so much as to leave behind what is most precious to them. In the view of antisemites these Jews would doubtless be clutching bags of gold. In fact, each of them carries a Torah scroll.[9]

There is nothing in history quite like this Jewish ability to travel, to move on, accompanied by no more than the divine word, the promise, the call, the faith in an ultimate destination. That is how Jewish history began, with God's call to Abraham to leave his land, his birthplace and his father's house (Genesis 12:1). That is how Jewish history has continued for most of four thousand years. Outside Israel, Jews' only security was faith itself and its eternal record in the Torah, God's love letter to the Jewish people, His unbreakable bond. And during all those centuries, though they were derided as "the wandering Jew,"[10] they became living testimony to the possibility of faith in the midst of uncertainty, and to the God who made this faith possible, the God of everywhere, symbolized by the Tabernacle, His portable home.

And when the time came for Jews to make one more journey, to the land first promised to Abraham and that Moses spent his life as a leader travelling towards, they did so without hesitation or demur.

---

9. Emil Fackenheim, *What Is Judaism?* (New York: Macmillan, 1987), 60.
10. See Galit Hasan-Rokem and Alan Dundes, *The Wandering Jew: Essays in the Interpretation of a Christian Legend* (Bloomington: Indiana University Press, 1986).

Scenes of leavetaking were repeated time and again during the years 1948–51, when one after another, the Jewish communities in Arab lands – the Maghreb, Iraq, Yemen – said goodbye to homes they had lived in for centuries and left for Israel. They too knew that those homes were mere encampments, stages on a journey whose ultimate destination lay elsewhere.

In 1990, the Dalai Lama, who had lived in exile from Tibet since 1951, invited a group of Jewish scholars to visit him in North India. Realising that he and his followers might have to spend many years in exile before they were allowed back, he had pondered the question, how does a way of life sustain itself far from home? He realised that one group above all others had faced and solved that problem: the Jews. So he turned to them for advice.[11]

Whether the Jewish answer – which has to do with faith in the God of history – is applicable to Buddhism is a moot point, but the encounter was fascinating nonetheless, because it showed that even the Dalai Lama, leader of a group far removed from Judaism, recognised that there is something unparalleled in the Jewish capacity to stay faithful to the terms of its existence despite dispersion, never losing faith that one day the exiles would return to their land.

How and why it happened is contained in those simple words of Rashi at the end of Exodus. Even when at rest, Jews knew that they would one day have to uproot their tents, dismantle the Tabernacle, and move on. "Even an encampment is called a journey." A people that never stops travelling is one that never grows old or stale or complacent. It may live in the here-and-now, but it is always conscious of the distant past and the still-beckoning future. "But I have promises to keep / and miles to go before I sleep."

11. The full story of the encounter is told in Roger Kamenetz's book, *The Jew in the Lotus* (HarperOne, 2007).

Exodus: The Narrative Structure

The time has come for us to survey the structure of the book of Exodus as a whole. On the surface it looks like a historical narrative, punctuated by various laws and dominated, for the last third, with an account of the Sanctuary that does not sit easily with what has gone before. Read sequentially it seems to say: that and that happened, in a certain chronological order, and this is a report of those events.

Specifically, it reads like a story of divine intervention into the course of human history, changing it forever. The Israelites were enslaved; God set them free. The miracles of Exodus are on a scale unparalleled in any other book of the Bible, any other age of Jewish history, any other religious literature. The ten plagues, the division of the Reed Sea, the revelation at Mount Sinai, manna from heaven, water from a rock: these are supernatural events that have left their mark on Jewish consciousness ever since. And not only Jewish consciousness: the book of Exodus inspired the English revolution in the seventeenth century, the American revolution in the eighteenth, and twentieth-century liberation movements from South America to South Africa. The exodus is the West's meta-narrative of hope, its inextinguishable tale of freedom.

Yet the Torah never records *mere* history. Exodus represents history with a purpose, an underlying theme, a moral structure, a starting point and destination. It is history made not just by the human decisions of human protagonists. For God too is an essential part of the story, both as its director and as a key actor. Nor is this accidental. Egypt, the "house of bondage" where an entire people is enslaved and threatened with destruction, is what happens when human beings – pharaohs, rulers, tyrants – think of themselves as gods: when the lawmaker is above the law. It still happens. We have only to think of Nazi Germany, Stalinist Russia, and the many murderous regimes in power today, to understand why the story of the exodus is not mere history, something of interest only because it happened long ago. The Torah's themes are eternal and will not cease to be relevant as long as human beings seek to dominate others by the use of power.

Nor is Exodus – read carefully, with an attentiveness to nuance and structure – simply a divine drama in which all the important acts belong to God. There is a subtext, a counter-narrative running through the book, that tells a very different story indeed. This second story is about the repeated handing back of responsibility from God to human beings. It is less about divine power than about divine empowerment. It is as if God had said to the Israelites: I will save you, but then I will teach you how to save yourselves. I will deliver you into freedom, but then I want you to learn how to create a free society. God the educator is as much in evidence in Exodus as God the liberator, and the same is true of the central human figure in this drama, Moses. There is much that is supernatural in Exodus, but much that is natural too. God shows us the way, but then expects us to follow it and to learn how to read the map of redemption and navigate our way through the wilderness of time and the dangers that constantly threaten the pursuit of liberty.

Surveying the book in its entirety, we see that the narrative is divided into two massive arcs, each with a chiastic, or mirror-image, structure. The first, from chapter 1 to chapter 24, is the story we might entitle, "From slavery to freedom." It goes as follows:

> Unjust society (chapters 1–6)
>> Liberation: ten plagues (chapters 7–13)
>>> Division of the Red Sea (chapters 14–18)

Liberty: ten commandments (chapters 19–20)
Just society (chapters 21–24)

The story begins with slavery in Egypt. It ends with a law code
that includes the liberation of slaves in the seventh year and a number
of laws specifically referring back to the experience of the Israelites in
Egypt. "Do not hurt the feelings of a stranger or oppress him, for you
were strangers in Egypt" (22:20). "Do not oppress a stranger. You know
how it feels to be a stranger, for you were strangers in Egypt" (23:9). The
society the Israelites were commanded to construct would have none of
the imperial grandeur of Egypt. It would be an anti- or counter-Egypt,
predicated not on power but on respect for human freedom and dignity.

The Torah does not abolish slavery, but it mitigates and restricts
it in such a way as to steer the nation towards its eventual abolition. We
tend to forget how long this took, even in the most advanced societies. Slavery was not abolished in Britain and the United States until the
nineteenth century, and even then, in America, not without civil war.
The most powerful force tending in this direction was the Sabbath: "Six
days shall you labour and do all your work. But the seventh day is the
Sabbath to God your Lord. Do not do any work: not you, your son, your
daughter, your slave, your maid, your animal, nor the stranger within your
gates" (20:9–10). One day in seven a slave breathed the expansive air of
liberty. Nothing was more revolutionary than this: the turning of slavery from a fact and fate of birth to a temporary and revocable condition.

That is the first, highly structured narrative, with the division of
the Reed Sea as the turning point, when the people crossed over from
Egypt, the domain of Pharaoh, to the desert – no-man's-land – in which
nothing intervened between the Israelites and God. Two similar scenes
occur at the beginning and end. In the first we see Moses at "Horeb, the
mountain of God" (3:1) alone with God at the burning bush. In the second we see Moses, on the same mountain (Horeb = Sinai), alone with
God, while "the appearance of God's glory on the mountain top was
like a devouring flame" (24:17). Between these two events, everything
has changed. Moses has become a leader. The people have been set free.
Miracles have been wrought. A tyrant has been defeated. But, as if to
emphasize the mirror-image symmetry of the narrative, the story ends

as it began, with God addressing Moses on the mountain in the midst of fire. The cast of the drama has been huge – the Egyptian nation and the by-now numerous children of Israel – but in the framing scenes there is only one man, Moses, and the divine voice, as if to say that this is how history is changed, by the inner dialogue between a single soul and the God of freedom and dignity.

The second arc is less about politics than about spirituality, and the place of God in society. Its symbol is the Sanctuary, and its structure is as follows:

> Tabernacle: instruction (25–31:11)
>   Sabbath (31:12–18)
>   Golden Calf (32–34)
>   Sabbath (35:1–3)
> Tabernacle: construction (35:4–40)

Here the structure turns on the episode of the Golden Calf, and the problem it addresses is what Max Weber called the "routinization of charisma."[1] How do you turn epic events into daily routines? How do you sustain inspiration when the charismatic leader is no longer there? The Golden Calf episode happened when the effect of the revelation at Sinai began to fade and Moses was absent, perhaps feared to be gone forever. It is this fear of absence, rather than idolatry, that lies behind the making of the Calf.

It was Sigmund Freud who, in a quite different context, provided an insight that takes us to the heart of the problem. For Freud, the central human drama was the tension between fathers and sons. Children resent the presence of the father, who detracts from the attention of the mother towards the child. But when the father is absent, they feel a mixture of guilt and fear and they construct a kind of substitute father.[2]

---

1. Max Weber, *Theory of Social and Economic Organization*, trans. A.R. Anderson and Talcott Parsons (New York: Oxford University Press, 1947).
2. Freud developed this argument in *Totem and Taboo* (1913); *The Future of an Illusion* (1927); *Civilization and Its Discontents* (1930); and *Moses and Monotheism* (1939).

That is what the Golden Calf is: a substitute for an invisible God and the missing leader and father figure, Moses.

We are, thought Freud, children who long for, even as we resent, a father figure, and this has consequences for nations. It explains the craving for strong leaders – a Napoleon, a Hitler – who make us feel secure even as they rob us of our liberty. So, in a sense, the Golden Calf has a political dimension as well. When a nation disintegrates in the absence of a strong leader, it shows itself not yet ready for freedom.

Hence the Sanctuary has two quite different significances. The first was the Sanctuary itself, a visible symbol of the presence of God in the midst of the people. This was to reassure them that God was there among them, and they need not fear His absence or abandonment.

The second, no less consequential, was the *making* of the Sanctuary. Until that point, everything had been done *for,* and almost nothing *by,* the people themselves. As I argued in an earlier chapter, it is what we do, not what is done for us, that changes us. For once the Israelites were charged with a constructive task, one to which they could each contribute, the response was remarkable. Though contributions were voluntary, the people gave willingly, so much so that Moses had to call a halt to the collection. Too much had already been donated. The making of the Sanctuary was the first chance the Israelites had to act like free and creative human beings. It was part of their apprenticeship in liberty.

The Sanctuary, with its daily order of worship, was the routinization of charisma. It was a kind of portable Sinai, and it meant that the fire of God was with them not just once, at the moment of revelation, but every day, wherever they were. It also involved a new kind of leadership: that of the priest as opposed to the prophet. Prophets deliver the word of God for a specific time and place. Priests live the word of God at all times and places. Prophets are charismatic, priests are not. The priestly task is not spontaneity but continuity.

On the face of it, the first and second parts of the book of Exodus are unrelated, but I have argued otherwise. The radical thesis of Exodus, and of Judaism as a whole, is that a society needs the presence of God in its midst if it is to avoid repression and corruption, tyranny and injustice. The essence of the covenant at Sinai, unique in the annals of religion, is that Israel is *a nation under the sovereignty of God.* It may have human leaders: Moses was one type, the judges another, kings a third, and in the contemporary state of Israel, we have a democratically elected Knesset. But in Judaism, all human power is circumscribed by the overarching authority of God. Might is secondary to right. A prophet may criticize a king. No ruler is above the law. There are moral limits to power. These are the very foundations of a free society then and now.

When people forget to worship God they begin to worship human beings, and from there it is but a short distance to tyranny. Hence the social legislation of Exodus (chapters 21–23) is intimately related to the construction of the Sanctuary, symbol of the Divine Presence at the centre of the camp, the heart of a free society.

There is a further narrative arc that remains hidden until the very end of the book. As we have seen in an earlier essay, "The Home We Make for God," it is precisely at the end of the long account of the Sanctuary that we hear words that take us back to the beginning of the Torah and the creation of the universe:

Creation of the universe	Construction of the Sanctuary
And God **saw all** that He had **made**, and **behold**, it was very good … By the seventh day God had **finished** the **work** he had been doing; so on the seventh day he rested from all his work. And God **blessed** the seventh day and made it holy, because on it he rested from all the work of creating that he had done. (Genesis 1:31, 2:2–3)	When Moses **saw all** the work – and **behold**, they had **made** it as the Lord had commanded – Moses **blessed** them. (Exodus 39:43) So Moses **finished** the **work**. Then the cloud covered the Tent of Meeting, and the glory of the Lord filled the Tabernacle. (Exodus 40:33–34)

The verbal resonances are unmistakable. "Saw," "all," "made," "behold," "finished," "work," "blessed" – these seven words occur in both passages. As we saw, the number seven plays a key role in the last chapters of Exodus. The phrase "as God commanded Moses" occurs seven times during the account of the making of the priestly robes (39:1–31), and seven times in the account of Moses setting up the Tabernacle (40:17–33). The consecration of the priests and the altar took seven days (29:35–37). These parallel the seven days of creation and the seven times it says, "God saw that it was good."

The Israelites' construction of the Tabernacle mirrors God's creation of the universe. Indeed the *date* of the completion of the Tabernacle – the first day of the first month (40:17) – is the anniversary of creation, as well as the day on which dry land appeared after the Flood (Genesis 8:13), the start of the recreated universe after the great destruction. So human creation mirrors divine creation. The home God makes for humanity is counterbalanced by the home humanity makes for God. The end of Exodus brings us back to the beginning of Genesis.

This is a real literary surprise. Throughout the book of Exodus we have been a world away from the metaphysical themes of the opening chapters of Genesis. Exodus is about history; Genesis 1–2 are about cosmology. But this unexpected turn discloses something remarkable about the biblical story thus far: Genesis and Exodus are joined as a single mirror-image symmetry whose structure is this:

Creation of the universe (Genesis 1–3)
　Humanity and its failings (3–6)
　　Flood (7–10)
　　　Hubris: the tower of Babel (11)
　　　　The family of the covenant (12–50)
　　　　The people of the covenant (Exodus 1–4)
　　　Hubris: Pharaoh (5–6)
　　Plagues (7–11)
　The people and its failings (12–18; 32–33)
Creation of the Sanctuary (25–31, 34–40)

As we can see, the difference between Genesis and Exodus is that the family of the covenant has become the people of the covenant. But Pharaoh's hubris matches that of the builders of Babel who thought they could take the place of God. The plagues are to Egypt what the flood was to the world. The violence of humans that makes God regret that

He created them (Genesis 6:5–6) is matched by the waywardness of the Israelites that makes God regret He had chosen them (Exodus 32:9–10). Framing the narrative as a whole are two parallel scenes: the universe and the Tabernacle, macrocosm and microcosm, both precisely ordered into three domains (day/night, upper/lower waters, sea/dry land; outer enclosure, inner enclosure and holy of holies). Both are the result of God's commanding word, and both were filled with the Divine Presence.

At the heart of Genesis and Exodus are journeys: Abraham's from the East in Genesis, Moses from the West in Exodus. There is, the narrative implies, a way back from sin to harmony, exile to return. Seen from this perspective, the Sanctuary is more than an atonement for the sin of the Golden Calf. It is a kind of atonement for the sin of Adam and Eve in Eden. After the Flood, God accepts the fact of human sinfulness. After the Golden Calf, He accepts the fact of Israel's sinfulness. When people sacrifice – when they offer something of themselves to God – God grants atonement. The second tablets that rested in the Ark as a permanent sign of divine forgiveness are thus, for Israel, the counterpart of the rainbow in the days of Noah, with its promise that God would never again destroy all life. God is just, but God forgives. Human beings are sinful, but humans can be forgiven.

The overarching theme of both books is the tension between order and chaos. In this the Torah is not unique. Order and chaos have been the twin polarities of human thought since the birth of civilization, and they remain so today, whether in society or nature (modern science has yielded a new discipline called chaos theory). What makes the Torah unique is the way it conceptualizes the two.

In myth as in science, chaos is written into the structure of the universe. The gods fight; elements clash; tectonic plates shift. Entropy – the potential for disorder – increases over time. Order is therefore always fragile. Judaism, with its belief that the universe is the result of a single creative will, maintains to the contrary that order is natural, and it is threatened primarily by the waywardness of humankind. It is we who create chaos by sin, which leads to violence and the abuse of power, and eventually to murder or enslavement, robbing other humans of their lives or their liberty.

But *there is a moral order in the universe.* That is what Genesis 1 means when it repeatedly describes creation as "good." It is also what lies beneath the literary form of much of the Torah, namely the chiasmus or mirror image symmetry: A-B-C-B-A. It tells us that what happens to us is a mirror image of what we do. If we do good, good is done to us. If we do harm, harm is done to us. It is this on which Genesis-Exodus turns. Towards the end of Genesis, Joseph's brothers seek to kill him, and eventually sell him as a slave. At the beginning of Exodus, Pharaoh seeks to kill the Israelites, or at least their male children, and eventually turns them into slaves. The entire experience of slavery in Egypt is to teach the Israelites what it feels like to be enslaved so that they will not enslave others.

The ideal society, according to the Torah, is one of *ordered liberty*, brought about by the rule of law. So the presence of the Sanctuary with its precisely ordered spaces at the heart of the camp is not just a symbol of God's presence, but also of God's order, which characterizes both creation (natural order, science) and redemption (social order, justice). The ordered society the Israelites are commanded to create brings to a kind of closure the story with which the Torah began, God's creation of an ordered universe.

The beauty of the narrative is that, just as we have to labour to see its highly unified structure beneath the apparent chaos of events, so in life we have to labour to see the unity of God beneath the apparent randomness of history and circumstance. Genesis-Exodus is a single literary unit, in which the meaning of the universe and our place within it is explored through a series of dramas, some personal, others political, yet adding up to a momentous proposition: that just as God created order in the universe, so we are called on to create order in our personal lives and in society as a whole. We are God's image; we are God's children; we are God's partners. Within us is the breath of God. Around us is the presence of God. Near us is the home we build for God. Ahead of us is the task set by God: to be His agents of justice and compassion. Never has a nobler account been given of the human condition, and it challenges us still.

About the Author

An international religious leader, philosopher, award-winning author, and respected moral voice, Rabbi Lord Jonathan Sacks (1948–2020) was the laureate of the 2016 Templeton Prize in recognition of his "exceptional contributions to affirming life's spiritual dimension." Described by HRH The Prince of Wales as "a light unto this nation" and by former British Prime Minister Tony Blair as "an intellectual giant," Rabbi Sacks was a frequent and sought-after contributor to radio, television, and the press, both in Britain and around the world.

He served as chief rabbi of the United Hebrew Congregations of the Commonwealth for twenty-two years, between 1991 and 2013. He held seventeen honorary degrees, including a Doctor of Divinity conferred to mark his first ten years in office as chief rabbi, by the then-archbishop of Canterbury, Lord Carey.

In recognition of his work, Rabbi Sacks won several international awards, including the Jerusalem Prize in 1995 for his contribution to Diaspora Jewish life, the Ladislaus Laszt Ecumenical and Social Concern Award from Ben-Gurion University in Israel in 2011, the Guardian of Zion Award from the Ingeborg Rennert Center for Jerusalem Studies at Bar-Ilan University, and the Katz Award in recognition of his contribution to the practical analysis and application of halakha in modern life in Israel in 2014. He was knighted by Her Majesty the Queen in 2005 and made a Life Peer, taking his seat in the House of Lords in October 2009.

The author of more than thirty books, Rabbi Sacks published a new English translation and commentary for the *Koren Sacks Siddur,* the first new Orthodox siddur in a generation, as well as powerful commentaries for the *Rosh HaShana, Yom Kippur, Pesaḥ, Shavuot,* and *Sukkot Maḥzorim.* A number of his books have won literary awards. *Not in God's Name,* was awarded a 2015 National Jewish Book Award in America and was a top ten Sunday Times bestseller in the UK. Others include *The Dignity of Difference,* winner of the Grawemeyer Award in Religion in 2004 for its success in defining a framework for interfaith dialogue between people of all faiths and of none, and National Jewish Book Awards for *A Letter in the Scroll* in 2000, *Covenant & Conversation: Genesis* in 2009, and the *Koren Sacks Pesaḥ Maḥzor* in 2013. His Covenant & Conversation commentaries on the weekly Torah portion, which are translated into Hebrew, Spanish, Portuguese, and Turkish, are read in Jewish communities around the world.

After achieving first-class honours in philosophy at Gonville and Caius College, Cambridge, he pursued post-graduate studies in Oxford and London, gaining his doctorate in 1981 and receiving rabbinic ordination from Jews' College and Yeshivat Etz Chaim. He served as the rabbi for Golders Green Synagogue and Marble Arch Synagogue in London before becoming principal of Jews' College.

Rabbi Lord Sacks was married to Elaine for fifty years. They have three children and several grandchildren.

www.rabbisacks.org / @RabbiSacks

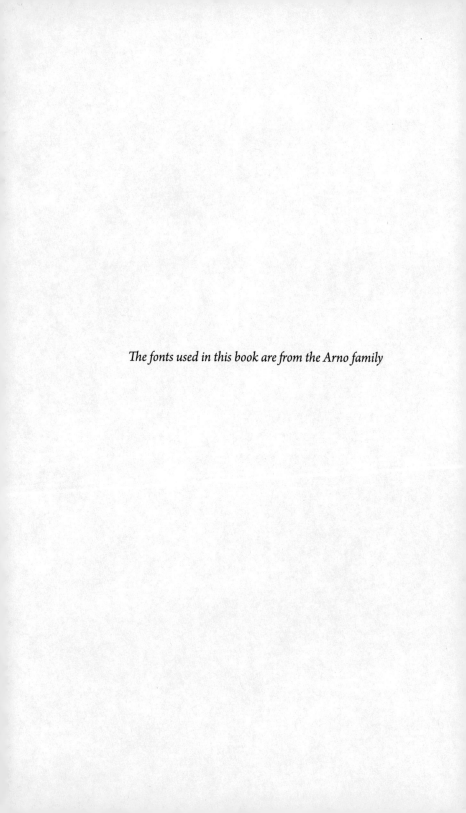

The fonts used in this book are from the Arno family

The Covenant & Conversation Series:

Genesis: The Book of Beginnings
Exodus: The Book of Redemption
Leviticus: The Book of Holiness
Numbers: The Wilderness Years
Deuteronomy: Renewal of the Sinai Covenant

Ceremony and Celebration
Essays on Ethics
Judaism's Life-Changing Ideas
Lessons in Leadership
Studies in Spirituality

Maggid Books
The best of contemporary Jewish thought from
Koren Publishers Jerusalem Ltd.